The Bush Rebels

Barbara Cornwall

THE
BUSH
REBELS
A PERSONAL ACCOUNT
OF BLACK REVOLT
IN AFRICA
/\/\/\/\/\/\/\

Holt, **R**inehart and **W**inston
New York   Chicago   San Francisco

For My Husband
and for
Those Inside "The Country"

Unless specifically noted, all photographs are
courtesy of Barbara Cornwall.

Published simultaneously in Canada by Holt,
Rinehart and Winston of Canada, Limited.

ISBN: 0-03-091346-2

Library of Congress Catalog Card Number:
77-181490

First Edition

Designer: Bob Antler

Printed in the United States of America

Prologue

AN AFRICAN GUERRILLA WAR, LIKE ANY OTHER, IS expensive, dangerous, and inconvenient. The glory is in retrospect, and the romance is for outsiders like me who come and go and remember only the good.

All of the essentials necessary to the newcomer's image of the guerrilla experience are there, certainly—the long marches across neck-high savanna, the armed band drifting through the forest villages by moonlight, the rough camaraderie after the sweaty ambush.

But the first casualty is always the glamour seemingly inherent in the revolutionary situation. The long marches, which are unavoidable because there are no other means of transport, can be carried out under heat so intense as to trigger a hysterical urge to shriek at the cadre ahead because he cannot possibly be so miserable as you; the enemy may well be lying in wait for the phantom rebel beyond the village waterhole; and a successful guerrilla operation needs skilled planning and the endurance of an Olympic runner should anything suddenly go wrong.

What emerges, therefore, is not the bearded band swing-

1

ing along to war, but a cautious, highly disciplined unit heavily dependent for survival upon its reconnaissance men and on each other. A well-conducted revolution in Africa is made up not only of guerrillas and, later, the army in the field, but of watchful accountants, logistics experts, political mobilizers, first-aiders, and rice-fed elders willing to haul heavy equipment on their backs and heads over dirt tracks for hundreds of miles through the bush.

It is made up of lonely women with children who spend long years in their straw villages waiting for brief visits from their rebel husbands while the task of childrearing falls solely upon themselves, another form of heroism and one barely marked.

"Above all," recalling the words of a cadre friend, "it is made up of ordinary people. We are not born revolutionaries, just people who could no longer support a situation. You get caught up in a revolution and then you see it through."

A revolution is a way of life and in time it is the only life that a seasoned rebel remembers. He is uneasy in another environment for his vision has changed and, with time, his priorities have subtly altered. He has no home and no belongings except what he carries in his pack. His only compensation for his rootlessness is the unique form of friendship and mutual aid within the guerrilla unit which springs from shared and seemingly endless hardship and which years of living across the street from one another in normal circumstances might never bring.

During short stays for briefing or reassignment at his organization's exterior base in a friendly country across the border—if there *is* a friendly country across the border—the African insurgent is a transient in his own billet. He sleeps with twenty others in a small rented house, eight to a room; the verandas pulsate with snoring bodies and the bathroom plumbing is faulty. Soon he longs for his return to the interior, to "the country" where the issues are sharp and the impact from his own masses tangible and instant. Better the war and discomfort of bush life than the crowded safety of the guerrilla *foyer*.

In the confines of a town one realizes how much like ordinary people these revolutionaries are—they quarrel over who broke the communal iron, hopefully hang wet laundry out in the tropical humidity, and guard small innocent possessions.

An almost visible transformation occurs when the rebel steps back into the bush—a new sureness, a restored balance, even gaiety. He is home. I was to share this home for three months while living with black guerrillas in Mozambique in East Africa, and in Portuguese Guinea in West Africa.

Both are colonies of Portugal and there, as in Angola, a vicious but little-known war is being fought daily between black insurgents and a combined force of 160,000 Portuguese troops who are charged with holding African territories that have been the property of the white motherland, in one form or another, for 500 years, down through the centuries of the slave trade, and long before the European "scramble" for Africa was begun.

Their black opponents, armed and numbering several thousand, are equally determined to winkle them out. Their object: independence.

This is no regular war and there are no front lines—only mile after mile of mountains, green valleys, swamp, savanna, and rivers, a vast and potentially fertile land which is known in Africa as "the bush." It is in this hostile wilderness that Portugal is fighting her African wars, for the insurgents do not yet hold any major ports or towns. Instead, in a combined politico-military operation against great odds and vastly superior arms, black mobile guerrilla units have wrested from the Portuguese sizable chunks of territory throughout the countryside where the majority of black civilians traditionally live.

3

These lands are referred to as "liberated zones" and as they have expanded with the war, the old Portuguese administrative system with its isolated *chefes do posto*, backwoods mission stations and trading centers dominated by walled forts and surrounding black settlements, has fallen away. The resulting vacuum is being filled with new administrative structures introduced by the liberation movements themselves; they have also inherited the hundreds of thousands of impoverished or displaced African civilians who were bombed out of their villages by rebel-hunting jets or flushed out by the hazards of war and famine.

The government in Lisbon refers to these disputed lands as "integral parts of the motherland," and her troops dispatched to fight the bush wars are told that their opponents are the Chinese, the Communists, the black bush rebels, or all three. In fact, they are black nationalists indigenous to the country.

The Portuguese have modern weapons, helicopters, jet fighters, and bomber support. The Africans, less well-armed and often shoeless, can strike hard and run fast. They have the added advantage of civilian support in the liberated zones and the detailed knowledge of their own terrain that comes from a lifetime of treading its length and breadth. They also have little to lose.

After 500 years of the Portuguese presence, the black population is 97 percent illiterate and the average life span is 35 years. Half of the black children are dead of disease by the age of five. In the interior, during one Portuguese administration, there were only a limited number of missionary schools, few doctors or nurses, no roads except dirt tracks linking one fort with another, no piped water, electricity, or telephones, and no shops except the small trading posts run generally by foreigners. The missionary schools still function in Portuguese-held areas, but not in those under guerrilla control.

In many areas, the Portuguese troops now being told literally to "hold the forts" are in fact sealed up within and can be supplied only by helicopter or by river craft with gunboat support. They are subject to lethal raids by guerrilla shock troops and venturing on foot beyond the boundaries of their forts can mean death on an ambush track.

In turn they mount punitive raids by helicopter and jet on civilian villages in rebel-held zones, burn the food plantations, and mortar the peasants in the cornfields. Their object is to force withdrawal of civilian support to the guerrillas, hunt for arms dumps, and pin down armed stragglers.

To check the rising desertion rate which has reached embarrassing proportions within the Portuguese army, the men are told that capture by the "bush bandits" in these jungles means death in the cooking pot, a notion that undoubtedly stiffens the fighting spirit of the less enthusiastic among them.

Who are these bush rebels? How do they think? What do they believe in? How do they live? What do they eat and say and value? Can they fight, and if so, by what rules and why? What of the civilians under their control in the liberated zones?

With these guerrillas in Mozambique and Portuguese Guinea I trekked through villages so impoverished and lost in time that their inhabitants don't know what a wooden plow looks like. I attended their political rallies, visited their military camps far inside the country, accompanied them on a raid against a Portuguese fort, and crawled gratefully into an African hut at sundown after a long day's march.

They are among the toughest guerrilla forces on earth, and they think nothing of trekking from dawn until dusk with 50-pound packs on their backs, often without food or water. How would they react to a white journalist who had suddenly been thrust among them, a woman, one who had

5

always driven the mile to the telegraph office or the grocery, whose athletic achievements had been limited to a rare game of tennis or a walk around the block?

This is a personal account of what I saw and heard and thought while living with these black partisans. Part was recorded in Dar es Salaam and Conakry, but most was written inside "the country" in African huts along the way while tired escorts shifted in their hammocks outside, or at makeshift plank tables before the heat rose and another long day's humidity settled around us. The story begins in Dar es Salaam, Tanzania, which is a center for African liberation movements and a key country in the black fight for independence. To the south lies the Ruvuma river and the Mozambique frontier.

Mozambique

1

MOST OF THE AFRICAN LIBERATION OFFICES LIE AT THE shabby end of Nkrumah Street where Dar es Salaam's busy main street trails off into scrub. They are narrow, cramped, and airless, and like the false fronts in a Western film set, their aging façades sag against each other for support.

They are rent-free, courtesy of the Tanzanian government. In a town where comfort costs money and accommodation is scarce, the rebels are grateful to have them.

Down the road along the cracking pavements is a walkup Chinese restaurant where customers eat with chopsticks from painted porcelain bowls and drink local Tusker beer under the ceiling fan every night except Monday.

Above the rotting two-story buildings live the poorer Indian and African families whose children lean out over the cacophony below through yellowing curtains limp in the heat. Heavy oil tankers take on fuel from a noisy gas station nearby, and the recently modernized "New Chox" cinema is advertising a censored Indian melodrama of unrequited love in Bombay (no kissing). Popcorn, sweets, and cigarettes are on sale in the lobby and there are special matinees for Indian ladies. Sepia posters at the entrance show a round-faced leading man, mouth slack in despair, and an aloof Brahmin in gossamer sari looking out indifferently in the foreground. In the inset cowers the girl who loves him all along.

The daily *Standard* headlines President Nyerere's latest speech stressing that "Our Freedom Is for All—Use It to Rid Us of Evil." The inside pages counsel tourists of the many luxurious hotels along the seafront, invite bids for contracts for ambitious development projects, and assure readers that the Tanzania Pest Control Company will deal ruthlessly with any problems concerning bats, rats, and woodborers.

Weary Indian tailors sit crosslegged and barefooted in their dank cubicle shops while at the fashionable end of the avenue the more affluent in their community manage much of the town's business and retail trade.

For Tanzania, it is a period of fast-moving transition, accompanied by all the incredible achievements and sad mistakes inherent in such a social and economic trauma. Caught up in the resulting confusion is the minority Indian community whose ancestors, mostly contract laborers, helped clear the malarial swamps upcountry and hack out roads. Like the dwindling European community, it is wary of its future because its comparative affluence has aroused a certain antagonism from the awakening African who feels that, given the opportunity, he could manage things in his own country just as well.

This antagonism springs from a vague discontent with his educational lot in life, a shortage of work, a suspicion that he is consistently overcharged in the shops, and the centuries of neglect that he must rapidly compensate for in the encroaching technological age. For the present, African frustration is channeled into a series of bitter debates in the government-controlled press over such issues as the wearing of European fashions, wigs, hair-straighteners, and tight trousers by a segment of the town Africans.

Letter columns have run to a full page for three weeks, with the opponents insisting that adoption of European dress is a subversion of the African heritage. In merciless rebuttal, the defenders point out that most tribesmen have been half-naked for centuries; therefore what relevance has clothing to anybody's background? At the core of the debate is the African search for an acceptable identity after centuries of cultural and colonial neglect.

Each community lives in its own quarter with an invisible line drawn sharply between them by bisecting thoroughfares. The Africans and the poorer Indians seem to inhabit the hottest apartments, the dimmest streets, and the noisiest neighborhoods ringing the downtown area. Beyond live the wealthier Indian merchant families with servants and private homes, while across the wide expanse of a handsome bridge lives the small foreign community on contract to the government or still in private business.

Although a few settlers still maintain graceful homes in breezy Oyster Bay along with top Tanzanian government and embassy staff, most dwell in modest frame homes which must still appear luxurious to the average African have-not.

Over at the sleek, Israeli-built Kilimanjaro Hotel, an Italian band blasts out "Bill Bailey, Won't You Please Come Home" in the softly lit Simba Nightclub. Down the road at the spacious New African Hotel—a relic of the German administration—an Indian pop group plays violent rock for its blissful brown and white audience as the fans whirr overhead and the walnut paneling groans.

Next door a more sedate crowd gathers for cocktails and dinner at the Agip Motel; the headwaiter is a meticulous Castilian and the cook an Austrian. It is reputed to have the best menu in town and the air conditioning in the busy dining room sweats from noon until midnight leaving little puddles on the verandas that black waiters in butterscotch jackets resignedly mop up.

The bar is the mecca for the old settler families in bush shorts and jodhpurs, Europeans on government contract, earnest businessmen from Nairobi and Lusaka, and prosperous Africans and Indians from Dar—"Visitors are kindly asked to wear national dress or business suits in the dining room after 7 P.M.," says a discreet plaque over the swinging door.

Down along the waterfront, across the well-kept Coconut Walk, and past the old German mission church lies Dar es Salaam port, once a supply stop for the steamers, and now a thriving harbor where giant cranes whine throughout the night unloading cargo . . . the Holland Afrika Line, Christensen, the *Hiroshima Maru,* the *Nicolay Pirogov,* the *Maas Lloyd* from San Francisco, Los Angeles, and Portland.

The rainy season begins next month and the evenings are sultry. "Where to Go" in Dar, reads the free brochure. There's Margot's Restaurant for Ethiopian specialties on Saturdays, a Congolese band at the New Palace Hotel, a French film festival downtown which features "the story of a doomed man who burns himself up in the Parisian night," and Sinda Island for picnics, shell collecting, family outings.

Hundreds of miles away in the bush, Swahili-speaking experts from mainland China have completed a seemingly endless survey and work has begun on a rail line linking landlocked Zambia (formerly Northern Rhodesia) with Tanzanian ports. When built, it will end expensive dependence on Hell Run, a notorious highway which periodically washes out in the monsoons and sends shrieking trucks spinning off into the bush. The drivers earn danger money and sometimes do two or three runs without rest.

To the north, myth-shrouded Mt. Kilimanjaro rises to over 19,500 feet above great valleys and game reserves, a favorite of European tourists from Nairobi who believe they are still in Kenya, much to the annoyance of the Tanzanian tourist offices.

Another attraction is legendary Zanzibar, once the biggest slave center on the East African coast and still a producer of cloves and brass-studded chests.

Only 25 miles from Dar es Salaam, Zanzibar was anchored politically to the Tanzanian mainland in 1964, a year after its sultan was deposed during a coup. A rumble from Zanzibar still brings instant military maneuvers from the mainland because its political importance is far disproportionate to its size. From Zanzibar seeps a steady trickle of Afro-Maoism which is snapped up in Dar es Salaam and funneled to the masses at one shilling a copy in all bookshops and kiosks.

At present, Tanzania is among the few African countries which openly support black rebel movements against apartheid South Africa, Southern Rhodesia, and the Portuguese colonies. The support takes many forms and varies in degree, depending upon domestic or external pressures and commitments.

At the least, she permits certain insurgent groups an office from which to operate on the continent and in comparative proximity to their battlegrounds. At most, she tacitly agrees to the import of arms, food, and clothing destined for rebel-held territory. In addition, small enclaves are given over for rebel training camps.

Dar es Salaam also houses the headquarters of the African Liberation Organization, the aid arm of the Organization of African Unity (OAU) whose 38 members, all African states, have pledged financial and political help to black guerrilla movements. Some are delinquent in back dues.

2

IN THE BUSY GLOOM OF THE ALMOST-SLUM DOWN NKRUMAH
Street is the general headquarters of the Mozambique Liberation Front (FRELIMO), a black politico-military revolutionary party which has pledged to liberate the homeland
across the border from the Portuguese and already holds a
fifth of the country.

Although physically present in Tanzania, it carefully
stays out of its host's political business, dutifully attends embassy sundowners at Karimjee Hall, and maintains a busy
network of departments at headquarters, each responsible
for an aspect of the revolution—internal affairs, security,
defense, foreign relations, rehabilitation—a government in
the wings, and at the head a Central Committee.

*"FRELIMO vencera, FRELIMO ganhara, AFRICA tri-
umfara"* say the banners in Portuguese: "We will win, we
will conquer, Africa will triumph." At headquarters, gentle
eyes and black faces appear in the dim brown doorway
while neighbor children screech on the steps . . . past what
looks like a pay-out window and along a narrow corridor to
the offices in the rear. The partisans wear civilian clothes—

12

shortsleeved white shirts or Tanzanian reds and greens with giant sunbursts exploding across the chest. The sun slides over the high backyard wall and through the barred windows, a precaution against theft, not sabotage.

Eduardo Mondlane, the president of FRELIMO, remonstrates on the telephone next door: "You have got to give us some leeway." His voice rises. Later, Eduardo was to be blown up in a friend's out-of-town villa on the Indian Ocean where he often went to write undisturbed. The murder is still unsolved; he left a white American wife and three children.

Across the hall is the Rev. Uria Simango, a quiet bespectacled ex-Presbyterian minister who resigned the cure of souls and joined the revolution: "Perhaps I could save hundreds of souls as a minister, but millions as a revolutionary." After Mondlane's death, Simango was to be suspended by FRELIMO's Central Committee for publicizing an alleged assassination plot against himself which implicated certain of his colleagues, a charge which they immediately denied and which led to his suspension. Simango's office is neat, the desk tidy, and a map of Mozambique's nine provinces hangs on the wall.

Next door sits Jorge Rebello, the party's public relations man. He is a bearded mulatto who works in perpetual clutter, his thin poet's face barely visible over stacks of FRELIMO publications. He also programs the rebel radio station beamed into the Mozambique wilds. "Can't you clean up this office?" somebody asks in Portuguese from the doorway. Rebello types on.

A windowless room opposite is the office of FRELIMO's secretary for foreign affairs, Marcelino Dos Santos. Also a poet and a mulatto, he is married to a white South African. Now 40, he has been a revolutionary from university days. Lisbon, Paris, poverty, poetry—"and vagabondage," he smiles, recalling the years in shabby rooms, or no rooms; a dark man's Paris.

Every Sunday morning he swims with his wife and daughter in a lagoon near the quiet house he shares with another FRELIMO couple in a Dar es Salaam suburb. They lunch on mangoes and bananas bought from a glum Chinese greengrocer who maintains a tiny, unexpected shop in a tangled forest enroute. The Dos Santos' have a water filter and screened windows, luxuries for a revolutionary.

"When will you be ready to cross the border?" Marcelino asks me. "Can you march? Sometimes there is no food. Can you speak French or Portuguese or Swahili or Makonde? You'll have a difficult time of it, and the marches are hard. We had to carry out one visitor. He was an ex-colonel and his legs swelled all the way up to his pelvis, like tree trunks. He thought he had elephantiasis, but it was just the walking. It's hot and you may have to sleep in the bush. Our food isn't the same as yours . . . you may not like it."

Marcelino handed me a mango. "Sometimes they booby-trap the mangoes," he said, his eyes amused.

Eduardo Mondlane, big and healthy and smiling and concerned, a Ph.D. in sociology from Northwestern, wore ankle-high safari boots and walked with a hitching lope. He was intellectually nimble, dynamic, and dominated the movement. He loved jokes, especially ridiculously childish ones, and rose at 6 A.M. daily to work out with springs and rope before the office opened.

Eduardo formulated an exercise plan for me which I was to follow without fail while waiting to cross the frontier. It entailed a ten-mile walk every afternoon to accustom me to both heat and distance. I was to start from the cast-iron Askari monument in Dar es Salaam's city center, then follow the coast road to the Oyster Bay Hotel. There I was to rest over tea for approximately fifteen minutes (I wasn't permitted an extension), then start back. They were obviously afraid that I might collapse inside rebel-held territory, like the colonel.

In the meantime, I was becoming accustomed to nasal

14

Portuguese and the mélange of black and white and mulatto faces at headquarters. Sometimes I visited the South Africans across the street—the African National Congress rebels in the little office with the apple-green pillars and giant photographs of imprisoned ANC heroes on the peeling walls. Or the Angola man with malaria who broke into a sweat every morning around eleven and ferried the children of his fellow exiles to school in the organization's only car. "He's in the crisis," said a voice on the telephone one afternoon when I called.

Sometimes I walked over to the backstreet office of ZAPU, the black insurgent group pledged to free Southern Rhodesia, which they call Zimbabwe. Their policy of "one man, one vote" was opposed by the white minority in the country and ZAPU was organizing guerrilla war. As I talked to their representative about Southern African problems, the cost of living, and the heat, three of his countrywomen in exile marched into the office, swathed in tattered white with their infants tied across their backs. There was a long conversation in a tribal dialect and no one was embarrassed when one of the visitors swung her infant expertly around to breast-feed it. "There are many problems," the ZAPU man told me after they had left. "There is never enough money, never enough food."

I was to cross into Mozambique with FRELIMO soon, but there were a few days left for final arrangements. In the meantime, would I like to see their country school at Bagamoyo, a farming hamlet along the Tanzanian coast which was once a major collection point for slaves? The name means Broken Heart.

For almost two hours we careered down a one-lane highway in a borrowed Peugeot, spewing up the red dust around the curves. "Everybody in Africa drives like this," said FRELIMO's head of education, just before he nodded off in the backseat. "You would never arrive otherwise." I kept a close watch on the rutted roads as we swept past the forests.

15

There was a glimpse of the tiny, green little village of Bagamoyo with its coconut palms and sprawling truck gardens, then another country road to the school.

Here FRELIMO brought its brightest youngsters after three years of primary instruction at bush schools inside Mozambique. Under guerrilla protection, they sometimes walk for a week to the border and are fed along the way at rebel-held villages. Trucks then bring them to Bagamoyo. They may be separated from their parents for several years, but the children are encouraged to leave. Education is their only hope, and they are their country's future when the revolution ends.

The clearing once housed a military camp, and the children sleep and attend classes in thatched barracks or wooden sheds that they have helped build themselves. Outside, I watched as three ten-year-olds who had been excused from lessons that morning prepared lunch for their classmates. They stood over a large cast-iron cooking pot, in patched trousers and canvas shoes, stirring the day's bean soup under a thatched lean-to.

Their diet is usually bread, corn, beans, and vegetables with a meat course twice a week which is made to stretch as far as possible. They once tried raising chickens but they died off because there weren't enough funds for pesticides. Water is hauled from a well down the hillside and the latrines stand off in the surrounding forest.

There are health problems sometimes—typhoid, malaria, skin diseases. A male nurse maintains a well-scrubbed first aid post in one of the sheds, but as usual there is never enough medicine, never enough clothing, never enough of the proper food.

Yet, for all their hardships, "they are better off here than in their own villages in the bush," one teacher told me. "They are learning, they have some clothing, however inadequate, and they are this side of malnutrition."

I attended a fourth-year history and geography class

16

which was being taught in Portuguese. A map of Southern Africa stood near the teacher's table and he was tracing boundaries with a wooden pointer. When I entered with Marcelino, the children rose and stood at attention. The eldest gave a welcoming speech and then the lesson went on. Twenty brown bodies in cast-off clothing and canvas shoes, thin brown legs and round innocent eyes, on their best behavior.

"No disciplinary problems?" I asked later. It seemed not. There were too many still inside Mozambique eager to attend the school, and too few places; a teacher shortage, not enough books and pencils or paper or food or clothing or accommodation. If you were reluctant to learn, there were hundreds to take your place. Bagamoyo was the first important step toward a higher education in a country roughly one and a half times the size of France, having still only a handful of university graduates among the Africans.

In the schoolyard outside, a black teacher who had degrees from Central Michigan and Pittsburgh was showing a class of twelve-year-olds how to lay out a field for planting. In Mozambique their parents were still scattering seed helter-skelter and yield was too low. The teacher dragged along behind him a homemade rake-harrow, made of three sticks and a bamboo crossbar. It produced three neat rows. "That way you don't choke the corn," he told them. "Our people must learn to work with what they find around them, with forest materials and bamboo and straw." He showed me a long bamboo stick marked off into meters, with smaller lengths notched into centimeters. There was only one master ruler in the school and the pupils used it as a guide in making their own.

They had also built their own beds out of logs and packing case boards. Blankets were folded double to serve as a mattress and over each lay a quilt donated from some charity abroad. They slept five to a room in barracks, and the girls' quarters had the added luxury of a corrugated iron roof to keep out the rain. During the monsoons the boys often awoke to find their bedding and dormitory floors inundated with water which had seeped through the thatched roofs above.

Over each bed hung a circular mosquito net suspended on a hoop from low rafters. Each child had a homemade bed table on which he kept his meager belongings, including a change of clothes. Some had cut photographs of their favorite revolutionary heroes out of magazines and pasted them over their beds—Mondlane, Che, Mao, Castro.

Most of their textbooks had been written by the teachers themselves and mimeographed at the party headquarters. Portuguese, the *lingua franca* of the country and the language of instruction, was a comparatively simple matter because there were grammars available from prerevolutionary days, although the insurgents still felt it necessary to modernize teaching methods. But subjects such as history and geography demanded entirely new books. "We want new ways of teaching, new approaches. We are a revolutionary country and this is a period of war; we must have books taking into consideration this aspect. We want to teach *our* history and *our* geography, not only that of Portugal. Before the war our black children didn't even know where their own rivers were."

3

THREE DAYS LATER I WAS AT A CAMOUFLAGED BORDER CAMP with a change of street clothes and a pile of new khaki shirts and trousers in my rucksack. I was already wearing a new pair of high boots which I had purchased before the journey and which gleamed like polished ebony in the late afternoon sun. They had also begun to hurt. As for the regulation uniform, I had had to content myself with khaki shirts and trousers from the Boy Scout department of a leading toy shop in my home city, a previous search through a World War II surplus store having yielded only British army shirts whose sleeves reached my kneecaps.

As the insurgents were clad in jungle-green from Cuba or Algeria and blended exactly with the vegetation, I felt very discernible in my mouse-brown gear, better suited, perhaps, to the desert terrain around Tobruk than the rich green of the tropics.

We were to cross at dawn and it was suggested that we all get some sleep in the meantime. I was billeted in a small room of concrete-block and as I lay on a cot I could hear the night noises of a camp settling down outside, then what sounded like heavy rainfall—actually the swaying and clacking of coconut palms along the forest's edge. It seemed that I had barely dozed off when it was 3 o'clock in the morning and a flashlight beam licked around the interior. *"Con licença,* we are going over now," said a gentle African voice. Then it disappeared. I fumbled through the mosquito net and into my Boy Scout shirt. Outside, waiting in the moonlight, were guerrillas from the platoon which would take me across the river and into the Northern Mozambican province of Cabo Delgado. There would be a short walk to the border, I was told, and someone slung my pack across his back. I was to learn from experience that a short walk to an African is one of approximately three hours' duration if he is not encumbered by knapsacks and heavy arms and ammunition cases. If so, it may take him a few minutes longer.

Fortunately we were met by a Land Rover along the route and were soon rolling to a halt at the edge of a clearing where long columns of barefooted Mozambican civilians had set down their loads for barter. They were Makondes from a tribe in Cabo Delgado, a purportedly fierce people who at puberty carve geometrical designs across their faces and then rub charcoal into the fresh wounds. The scarring is done during a ceremony for both boys and girls and the final result on their dark skins is quite impressive. More startling at first encounter are two additional operations, both optional, during which a metal peg is driven into the initiate's upper lip and secured on each side by an iron disc. Then the teeth are filed to points. The entire practice of maiming is a custom dating from the slave trade era when the Makondes hoped, often justifiably, that slavers would pass them over because of their grisly appearance. Their market price would not have covered the cost of their transport because few buyers would bid on a fanged slave when more presentable ones were available.

Their backs and legs streamed with sweat as they doubled their thin stork legs under them and sank to the ground beneath the shady umbrella of vast mahogany trees. They had carried their loads for fifteen miles and even at first light the humidity was becoming oppressive. Inside immense woven baskets were piles of smoked fish or cashew nuts which would be bartered for cloth or soap. This was a FRELIMO trading post and a jump-off point into Mozambique.

A handful of administration huts was barely visible only a few yards away, so well did the local material used in their building merge into the tangled landscape; they seemed to sprout from the ground like thatched mushrooms. The palm branches used as roofing had been lashed to a wooden frame with wet thongs which tightened into the taut firmness of rope when dried by sun and air.

It was cool under the giant trees, and green as far into the distance as I could see. The Makonde carriers, rested now, began to prepare their cooking fires and called to their children who had gathered in an interested circle around me. Strong white teeth smiled from tiny round faces as they reluctantly pulled themselves away. As they walked, the bottoms of their feet flashed up pink and calloused. They had no shoes and many wore only a rough sack from waist to knees, hitched into place by a rope.

Guerrillas who had just completed the fairly hazardous crossing from "inside"—the border had been bombed the day before—were hailed by fresh cadres on their way in. Some were led off by officers for debriefing; others flopped down against wide tree trunks or onto woven mats spread on the ground while they waited for transport. They seemed able to sleep anywhere, an art I was to learn later myself when exhaustion permitted me to sleep around the clock on concrete.

Orders were barked out in three languages, Portuguese, Swahili, or Makonde, and there was much loading and unloading of transport—large aluminum cooking pots, canned meat, packets of instant tea and coffee, stacks of packaged biscuits. They were taking these treats in for me from their precious stores to cushion the shock of bush life and had hauled them from headquarters. Piles of bulging rucksacks were flung in and out of jeeps and finally the metal doors slammed. This was the last outpost before the wilderness closed in around us, the last usable road.

It was here that I met the two partisans who would remain with me throughout the duration of the journey as others came and went from one sector to another on various missions. One was an intense young male interpreter called Cornelio Mboumila, a Mozambican who had been raised in Tanzania and hoped one day to study mechanical engineering. He was an expert in cannon but for the time being his mission was me. He had the exacting task of translating from English to Portuguese to Makonde and back through the three tongues again. On occasion, he also had to cope with French. He had finished only secondary school. An ardent fan of Congolese pop music and Kenyan *marenga,* Cornelio would willingly dance to them solo at the slightest encouragement, humming the tunes himself if they could not be raised on one of the transistors. Throughout the hottest days, he always wore a fur-lined jacket and leather cap with ear flaps.

The other constant companion was a woman guerrilla called Diolinda Simango. She was 24 and carried a German-made submachine-gun and a loaded military pack on her slender shoulders throughout our entire 200-mile march. The leather straps raised blue welts across her back, but I never heard her complain.

Diolinda had a model's figure, with long straight legs and a body almost perfect in its symmetry. Her skin was the color of burnt sugar and her face, even under her military casque, was sweetly feminine. To join the revolution she had left her home town in Manica e Sofala province farther south and lived for two months in the bush, making her way through Malawi, Tanzania, and finally to Dar es Salaam where she volunteered for military duty in FRELIMO. Altogether, she had traveled some 800 miles illegally, much of it on foot.

Diolinda produced tea and sugar from somewhere and we drank from tin cups as the platoon prepared to move off. The tension was mounting as guns were cleaned and ammunition cases counted and heaved into a waiting Land Rover. We were to ride as far as we could, then trek to the river. One of the men wrote my name on my rucksack and I saw it flash onto the top of the heap in the rear as Diolinda and I piled into the cab with the Makonde driver. Cornelio and the other cadres wedged into the back with their packs.

There was a quick, fanged smile and then, with a heavy sigh, the driver thrust the jeep into gear and we crashed off into the bush. His cap slid down over his ear and his arms flailed under checked shirtsleeves as he urged the car over steep banks and jarring ruts like a steeplechase jockey, hollering encouragement through the windshield at the roaring engine. Heat and evil fumes radiated from the dashboard and our legs were seared as they slammed against the trembling gearbox. I tried to keep my elbows out of his way as he screamed down to second or wrestled the gear into overdrive. Suddenly we shuddered to a halt. Felled trees and thick underbrush had brought the driver's surrender. "This is a pig of a road," he announced, and we all tumbled out, the men in the rear gray-faced and relieved.

It was only a short walk to the frontier and everyone scanned the sky for what they called Portuguese "birds." Before us lay the Ruvuma with the water line at its lowest just before the rainy season. The banks were teeming with Africans waiting to cross, and as they gathered their baskets for loading into the canoes, they paused frequently to listen for the sound of oncoming aircraft. Many were civilians whose wives and children had sought shade under the wide-branched trees nearby.

We groped our way down a steep embankment, slipping and reaching for handholds, then into a long, narrow boat hollowed out from a tree trunk. It held six passengers in a jackknifed position and the oval bottom swished with muddy water. Its pilot was a Charon-like figure in a shadowy cloak and as he adjusted the folds around himself he ordered everybody to "sit down flat." He made the crossing several times a day and besides the possibility of getting caught in a rocket attack there was the more immediate danger of the wobbly craft turning over. With a grunt he shoved a long pole into the sandy riverbed and we were skimming across the shallows toward Free Mozambique. Gratefully I plunged a sweaty palm into the water. "I wouldn't do that if I were you," said the watchful Cornelio, adjusting his ear flaps. "The hippo have been shot out of here but we never know when they may return from upriver."

I quickly withdrew my hand, peering into the murk for hippo bulk. Panting, the pilot let out a great grunt as we slurped toward the bank. In an instant he was out in the choppy water and the bow scraped dry land. I scanned the riverbanks for dozing crocs and hippo nostrils and was relieved to see that there was no reedy vegetation or slime where they might be lying in wait. My knowledge of African game came from books and zoos exclusively, and I hoped that I could identify a suspect nostril if I saw one.

There was a noticeable change in tempo and atmosphere as we waited for the next canoeload of guerrillas and carriers. The military were taking over. Orders were snapped out and the boatmen were bellowed at to paddle faster. There were answering shouts from the waiting figures dotting the shoreline across the water.

Armed men appeared behind me out of nowhere, their guns slung, hurrying to form the long columns for the march into the interior. There was no effective cover for miles around here and if caught in the open you had no alternative but to bury yourself in the sand if you could dig quickly enough, quicker than napalm, fire bombs, shrapnel.

Finally, when the last canoe had been pulled ashore and we were all lined up to the leader's satisfaction, we began a quickmarch that soon caused me to regret my somewhat indulgent attitude toward exercise programs back at headquarters. We had miles to cover before reaching a safe shelter in this favored bomb run and the sun blazed onto our heads and necks, sneering and merciless. Before us lay an endless sandy waste.

Guerrillas and carriers alike tightened the straps on their packs and baskets, hoisted them to shoulders or heads, snapped magazines onto machine-guns and rifles and took off like they were on springs. Some carried heavy ammunition cases on their heads, but they loped along manfully nevertheless. I carried nothing except an empty bright red water bottle which smelled of plastic. It was empty because I had forgotten to fill it.

The heat built up into the nineties and the humidity hung like a wet mantle around our heaving bodies. After we had covered the first mile, my new leather boots took on a life of their own. They had been handmade and there had been several fittings, but somehow they had turned out too long and too wide and too hard, despite a pair of thick woolen socks the salesman had suggested I wear to compensate for it all. They were always a fraction of a second ahead of me as I wallowed around inside them. At every step they sank to the ankles in the deep sand with a rasping sigh, then cunningly sought out the protruding noses of sharp little rocks lying just beneath the surface. They twisted and squeaked and tore protestingly at the flesh underneath. Stubbornly they clung to their beds in the sand and had to be jerked out with a loud "squonch." The unusual sucking sound attracted polite but puzzled glances from the marching cadres ahead and at one point the leader spun out of line and waited for the column to pass, his head cocked attentively.

25

After I had creaked by, he wordlessly sprinted back to the head of the column. I was filled with malice toward my boots and had begun to feel very sorry for myself.

The barefooted carriers, whose toes made a trail of tiny indents in the sand, were already a half-mile ahead with another section of guerrillas. The rest of the armed escort had been obliged to drop back as I hobbled across the wastes. The sun seemed to thrust itself into the eyeballs and explode like grenades, sending shrapnels of blinding pain from ear to ear. I longed for a green bush to wrap my drenched body around, never to be pried loose again. I was obviously not the stuff of which revolutionaries are made.

I recalled the words of a well-known revolutionary theorist: "If a single combatant lags behind a marching column, it affects the speed and security of the entire column. In the rear is the enemy; impossible to leave the comrade behind or send him home. It is up to everyone, then, to share the burden, lighten his knapsack or cartridge-case, and help him all the way."

Since they were already carrying everything short of myself and my empty water bottle, there wasn't much left in this direction that they could do. My breath was coming in shallow rasps and my head pounded to the rhythm of a heartbeat. The knuckles on my swollen hands were a mottled white and I thought of heat stroke and sudden death.

"You're responsible for me!" I wanted to shout to all of those bobbing heads in front. *"You're revolutionaries and you're responsible for me!"*

Far in the distance, I could see the carriers skimming across the sand like dark brown corks, in one great chain. Cornelio bounced along cheerfully in front of me, humming some tune from the Brazzaville Top Twenty that he fancied at the moment. Diolinda had been placed strategically in line behind me, perhaps to catch the corpse as it flopped over. I thought despairingly of a lonely grave in this wasteland, marked only by a crude headstone in Makonde. They

26

would bury me with my legs up under my chin and in those wretched boots as well. They had never seen me before in their lives, this puffing, red-faced stranger with her bloated hands and ridiculous boots. Perhaps they wouldn't even bury me, just push on with a grunt and a whispered exchange about unpreparedness and lagging and "did our best."

I looked back toward Diolinda and was immediately ashamed. Dark veins stood out in her delicate face and she was bent forward with the weight of her rucksack and gun, her open mouth gulping for air and her eyes half-closed in misery. Her oversized canvas shoes splayed across the sand and sweat poured from her face and neck in great drops, spreading across her collar and shirt in a dark stain. She smiled sympathetically at my crimson face and starting eyes and I thought that I had better pull myself together.

We plodded on in silence for another hour, occupied only with the tremendous physical feat of putting one foot in front of the other. The mind shut off and the skins of the mulattos in the column had taken on a russet hue. The blacks had turned a deep gray, like the wood ash in a cooking fire.

To my great relief we plunged into a tangle of tall reeds which lent intermittent shade and bordered the narrow footpaths snaking through them. We veered and climbed and then the path dissolved into the rushes only a few yards ahead. Suddenly we were on a plateau and the vegetation changed abruptly. Here was the sprawling green of Africa and in the distance gentle hills sweeping up to great mountains. Northern Mozambique changed its physical aspects frequently and without warning.

Past banana and mango trees near valley streams, we followed the footpaths into drying savanna where lizards rustled in the underbrush and the loudest locusts that I had ever heard buzzed without cease. From a blazing, burnt-out wasteland we stepped into forests so ancient, dark, and enormous that it was sundown in their cool stillness. There were countless variations of green, all of them gentle. Nothing intruded upon you from this landscape, nothing cried out to be noticed. It was vast and endless and somehow friendly.

We halted in a clump of trees and I sank to the ground, hoping that we would never leave this happy shelter again. The platoon was already giving me worried looks because my face was vermilion and I did everything in slow motion. My throbbing legs refused to straighten out, my fingers wouldn't bend, and my hands were like fat, swollen slugs. Above all, I wanted to rid myself of the boots but this entailed rummaging into my bulging sack where I had placed, with great foresight, a pair of canvas shoes. I would have to untie the rope and undo the straps of the rucksack, then work my way through the laces of those boots. Gentle hands and sympathetic faces loomed over me as I fumbled with the openings. They moved me against a tree trunk and dragged my pack over. Somebody flipped the straps open and helped me sort out the contents as Diolinda, concerned and smiling, gave me tea from a plastic cup. When one is very dehydrated, they told me, never drink water. After a few biscuits—I could not remember when we had eaten last —I felt that the worst was over. Even the sun seemed kinder as I loped off toward my place in the column, comparatively lightfooted in my canvas shoes.

4

WE TREKKED THROUGH A VILLAGE THAT HAD BEEN NA-
palmed during the raid on the border the day before. Several
huts had been burnt out and the women were searching
through the ruins for any clay pots that might be salvaged.
There had been no casualties because the villagers had run
with their children to the surrounding forests at the sound of
approaching aircraft. But their rice store had been destroyed along with whatever extra clothing they possessed.

Part of FRELIMO's leadership was already in Cabo Delgado for meetings with area commissars and trade organizers, and they had hurried to the scene to assess the damage.
They included the Rev. Simango, who was the organization's vice president, Marcelino Dos Santos, whose column
we had liaisoned with after the crossing, and Mariano Matsinge, the stocky, overall chief of mobilization in Mozambique's interior.

There would be an hour's wait until we moved on, and
time to talk while the column slept against their packs along
the footpaths. This village had been bombed because its inhabitants supported a national liberation movement and as

29

we watched them poke mutely through the underbrush, I asked how they had been brought to join a revolution which produced such spectacular reprisals.

In general, their complaints against the Portuguese administration had been forced labor with little or no pay; severe beatings for minor offenses; imprisonment if protests were made; heavy taxes on what few possessions they had; the lack of schools, hospitals, and development programs; unrelieved hunger and poverty; flagrant neglect; and the attitude on the part of the local Portuguese administrators, with few exceptions, that the African villager should not be encouraged to better himself, was incapable of learning any skills except those connected with servile tasks, and that whatever livestock he did possess should be handed over on demand to the local fort with little or no remuneration under the guise of taxes.

In addition, villagers had no outlet for their crops except through government representatives who enforced a system of one-crop farming and then purchased the harvest at prices set by themselves.

But however hostile to the Portuguese they may have been, I also knew that as individual, unarmed tribes operating singly and without firm direction, they had been doomed to ineffectuality, and that local, disorganized revolts that had flared out of sheer rage and despair had been quickly put down in the past.

What I was now witnessing did not seem a local spontaneous uprising which might later fizzle out because of national apathy or Portuguese reprisal, however. There was every sign that it had been carefully planned and nurtured, that the guerrillas expected a protracted war, and that the presence in the North of guerrillas and mobilizers from all parts of Mozambique indicated support from as far south as Lourenço Marques, the country's capital.

The question was not only that of arming and supplying

a guerrilla force, but equally important, how an ignorant and intimidated peasant mass, which had already learned the hopelessness of earlier rebellions, had been persuaded to support at whatever personal sacrifice, the embryonic revolt then being organized by FRELIMO.

The answer was careful and prolonged mobilization of the peasants long before the first shot was fired in September, 1964, and long before the first arms or guerrilla bands were filtered across the border into Northern Mozambique, where the new, peasant-based revolution was to begin.

The guerrillas could not have survived without the bush peasants, for on them they were dependent during the first years for food supplies, shelter on the run, information about enemy movements, and volunteers to help haul in war material. And in many cases of this nature, they still rely upon them heavily.

This vital task of mobilizing was undertaken by Mozambicans after intensive training courses in revolutionary concepts and politicizing techniques which had originally been organized by the FRELIMO leadership in Tanzania as part of its blueprint for a revolution under these circumstances.

These potential mobilizers had been drawn from all backgrounds and tribes, and some were illiterate. Several were recruited from the well of black refugees who had already left the country, others were city Africans already in exile for their part in urban agitation. Some were dissidents from the North who had already slipped across the borders.

As far as possible, the mobilizers were sent back into regions in which they had been raised and where they would have some familiarity with the forest trails and the habits of the population. Because most of Mozambique's blacks cannot read or write, it meant that the mobilizers could not reach them through leaflets or underground newspapers or other similar channels. Nor could they reach them openly in public meetings, for the Portuguese were quick to snap up a

31

revolutionary stray. There would have to be personal, word-of-mouth contact from village to village, region to region, all of it in secret and all of it on foot.

And it was not enough to harness the sum of their discontent through rhetoric and weld them into a grassroots brigade ready to snatch up *panga* and bow in the name of a revolutionary organization that they had barely heard of.

Before these people would join or support an uprising, they had to be taught not only how they could be free but why they could be so. Their grievances were real, but to them insolvable.

In their extreme isolation and ignorance they had never been exposed to the concepts of nationalism or individualism or civil liberty which could be appealed to as legitimate grounds on which to launch a risky rebellion. The indignant cry, "I got my rights," would be almost unheard of in an African village linked to a colonial administration, for there were no rights except in the narrow, tribal context.

Their lack of communication and exchange of ideas with other people compounded their enfeeblement. Each village, each region, had its own beliefs and prejudices and idiosyncrasies which were clung to fiercely as proven means of survival in the tribal experience. There was no sense of the unity necessary to a mass uprising, no sense of the oneness that gives courage in case of attack and solace in defeat.

Men from neighboring tribes were strangers—foreigners really. Even their language was different. This stagnation had persisted through centuries of little change, no challenge, and few other standards of comparison. Their only glimpses of another way of life had been in occasional encounters with missionaries or traveling Levantine traders, and through representatives of the Portuguese administration at the local forts who, with few exceptions, treated them with withering contempt.

Through centuries there had been no marked change in either their physical or cultural environment but rather a reinforcement, through visiting army patrols sniffing out discontent, of the administration's attitude toward them.

These villagers had been told for centuries how stupid they were, how obscene, how black, how unfit they were for anything but cheap manual labor. Their own history, as they heard it, had consisted only of ignominy and surrender.

When the first secret network of FRELIMO mobilizers infiltrated Northern Mozambique, they found the black peasantry in a wallow of despair and incomprehension, occupied only with the eternal battle for physical survival in an essentially hostile environment.

Distrustful, wary, and fearful of Portuguese reprisal, the bush-dwellers had somehow to be persuaded that the guerrillas still waiting across the border could, with local peasant help, assuredly drive out a government entrenched for so many centuries.

The peasants had neither the time nor the background for theoretical argument and abstract thought. They were complete pragmatists and illiterate as well. Through this appalling blankness the mobilizer must penetrate, slowly building up a political consciousness in terms that the average villager could understand.

There were grave risks for villagers and mobilizers alike at this time, for agents had already carried news of potential unrest to the forts.

A show of interest in these new, disruptive ideas or the harboring of a mobilizer in the village compound could mean an army raid, destruction of the huts, and probable execution of the inhabitants involved. The pattern of future Portuguese retaliation was already being set—it would be the villagers who would bear the brunt of reprisal for guerrilla action, and unless the insurgents could protect them adequately or at least insure revenge should lives be lost and villages leveled, there was little hope of peasant cooperation.

Still too weak to meet this requisite, or protect even himself adequately, the mobilizer lived like a starving nomad in the forests, never daring to approach a village unless certain that it was clear of troops or informers.

There was also real danger from the very black villagers in whose name the mobilizers were organizing, for among this timid stratum were scores willing to turn them over to the authorities for a few dollars. This was a substantial sum by local standards and could represent a year's wages. And if the mobilizer were from another tribe or province he ran even greater risks. It was not like turning in one's own after all, and what did this stranger mean by talking insurrection and endangering the entire village.

Many of the mobilizers were caught by the troops and hung up by their heels and burned alive in those days. Those who escaped the patrols moved only by night and lived off bush rats and wild roots, a diet which was occasionally supplemented by a meal of rice smuggled into the bush by a clandestine sympathizer.

As the months went by, the persistence of these ragged and barefooted politicizers won them key converts, for their lectures around the cooking fires had been in terms that their listeners could understand: chronic hunger, half of their children dead of disease at the age of five, the lack of shoes and clothing, no education, forced labor. Then there were the other long-simmering grievances. Already living at bare subsistence level, the black peasants were obliged to pay taxes on dwelling huts that they had built themselves from materials at hand—bamboo, thatch, palm leaves, and boughs. Then there were the taxes on canoes because the trees from which they had been constructed were considered Portuguese trees. There was even a tax on tribal ceremonies, their only relief from the long monotony of their years. And this revenue was to come from the pittance they had earned from their crops or from the few dollars a month they received as contract or forced labor.

As grievances were talked over afresh among themselves or with the mobilizer, stories of new outrages began to spread throughout the countryside—of Portuguese reprisals on a mass scale which often involved the innocent. Ironically, the Portuguese had begun to fan the very revolution which they were attempting so desperately to suppress.

As Mariano tells it: "As the villagers watched and waited, still hesitant about us and our new ideas, and even still betraying our mobilizers, the stories of executions and disappearances of black men persisted. Then, when their own village was raided or their own relatives killed, it only served to reinforce everything that we had been telling them about the Portuguese administration.

"We began to mobilize more openly and to convert some of the local chiefs and others with moral influence in the villages. We used them to promote FRELIMO ideas. Because there is a traditional attachment and obedience among villagers to their local chiefs, the Portuguese had always used them to rule on that level. When they came over to us, it meant that they brought with them whole blocs of villagers.

"We also found that the length of time needed to mobilize a group of people differed according to the intensity of their colonial experience. For example, the people who had returned from forced labor contracts in the towns were the most receptive to us. Or those who had been used for bridge- or roadbuilding, or for work on plantations growing sugar, tea, rice, or coconut."

Mariano said that the Portuguese had originally recruited them in their own villages by sending in police patrols which, with the cooperation of the chiefs, rounded up a specified number of villagers and sent them off for six months to two years on these work projects. Some went freely and were paid a few dollars monthly for their work; those who refused could be subject to false arrest on some niggling charge and made to work out their time without pay.

"The Africans call this system 'shibalo'—forced labor.

35

The administration called it 'a contribution to the state.' If a chief protested against the system, he was replaced by the administration with a more cooperative one. This is why the villagers could tolerate the chiefs who had helped in rounding them up. But they expected him to show remorse for it, and they resented those who didn't."

Slowly, as FRELIMO gained the trust of the peasantry, they could ask them for more than their attention.

It was now that the help which was to prove so vital to the guerrillas was concretely organized—the network of volunteers to carry in supplies, peasant families in certain villages who promised to feed the fighters, an information system based on civilian tipsters, "safe" villages in which to hide, huts in which the guerrillas could sleep or recuperate after illnesses, volunteer guides to lead them through strange forests to other zones, and also important: a nucleus of new guerrilla recruits from the villages.

Slowly, FRELIMO moved in arms, the first trained fighters, and mounted the first ambushes—a reassuring sign that the movement meant business. More of the farmers hid them and fed them and finally threw in their lot with the rebels. Through it all the mobilizers and their aides talked and reinforced and persuaded and encouraged as the Portuguese fought back in that northern wilderness, razing the villages and executing FRELIMO suspects as examples. The boys from Portuguese cities and tiny farming towns, mostly draftees, stepped on mines and walked down forest trails into ambushes. In turn they raided the black villages and bayoneted anything that moved, watching in fear and fury as the revolution spread like fire in the African grass.

Thousands of black refugees from Northern Mozambique streamed across the borders into Tanzania, Malawi, and Zambia, and those who remained were by now convinced Frelimistas. As more villagers joined the rebel army or came into contact with rebels from other provinces, the idea of a nation as opposed to small tribal units began to take hold. They all had at least one thing in common.

"We have always been poor," said Mariano. "There are no rich Africans in Mozambique, only those less poor than the others. Our entire black middle class is about 5 percent of the entire population, including the mulattos.

"Every appeal to the government in the past for more freedom, more education, more opportunity for the African either went unanswered or was turned down. We finally realized—and it took us years to come to this conclusion— that the Africans could only go ahead through an armed struggle."

It is from this small, middle-class nucleus that much of FRELIMO's leadership was drawn, although local party administrators and commanders in the field are often semi-illiterate.

While the mobilizers had been busy in the interior, other FRELIMO men had been traveling abroad to ask for arms, training facilities, or financial backing for the approaching revolution. The young movement had always considered itself a front rather than a political party of specific orientation, right or left; and the only condition for membership was being a nationalist willing to go to war for Mozambican independence. The leadership, believing that political factionalism could eventually rupture rather than unite a national liberation movement made up of so many diverse backgrounds, was careful to stress this point. No one asked the new recruit whether he was right, left, or center, and no one cared particularly.

Abroad, both Western and Communist governments were approached for moral and material aid, the assumption being that the obvious misery of 7 million black Mozambicans would outweigh any political or economic considerations to the contrary. It could also be truthfully stated that the movement's aim was not the ejection of the Portuguese civilians, the 200,000 whites who considered Mozambique their home as much as the blacks did. But the system which had brought so much misery to the African would have to go, to be replaced by a black majority rule which would welcome foreign economic investment under terms beneficial to the entire nation.

In those days, FRELIMO leader Eduardo Mondlane, who held a Ph.D. from an American university and later worked for the UN trusteeship committee, had hoped that the Western governments could also be persuaded to support, at least morally, a liberation movement in Mozambique.

But the West had NATO commitments and Portugal was a NATO member. There was also substantial Western business investment in Portugal's African colonies and in apartheid South Africa, her southern neighbor and ally. With bitterness, the rebel leaders saw NATO aircraft and arms originally earmarked for Portugal's internal defense being channeled instead into her African colonies for use by Portuguese pilots and foot patrols against black villagers there. The revolutionaries were well aware that without outside help, the underdeveloped "motherland," her budget already overstrained, would have soon been propelled to the conference table.

As the West lost the initiative, it was mainly the Eastern Bloc countries, the Soviet Union, China, certain North African states, and members of the Organization of African Unity (OAU) which showed concrete support for the rebellion with arms and training for FRELIMO's shabby guerrilla recruits.

Whatever their reasons, the fact remained that nonaligned and left-wing pronouncements of "solidarity" with the underprivileged masses were clearly in evidence for all to see and the West, with few exceptions, either ignored rebel pleas for aid or deliberately backed Portugal in her African war.

The average black peasant, whose political ideas were barely formed and who could muster little sympathy for NATO commitments when his village was being napalmed and his legless friends wheeled around in carts, could feel only gratitude for the nations who enabled him to fight back.

Although certainly supported by socialist and nonaligned countries, the black revolution in Mozambique was not inspired by them, despite Portuguese charges to the contrary. A revolutionary does not question the source of his arms, only their volume.

Without outside help and internal mobilization, the Rev. Simango estimated that a well-run revolution in an African country the size of Mozambique would cost its perpetrators about $25 million a year, and black Mozambicans simply did not have that kind of money. He valued a shipload of cannons, bazookas, and mortars at $2.5 million, right down to carrying charges, and then there were the estimates for uniforms, food, clothing, education, and medical supplies for cadres and civilians. There were office expenses at headquarters and information centers abroad, fuel and vehicle maintenance costs, and hospital bills for wounded cadres and civilians who could not be treated inside the country. And suppose the carriers who lugged equipment through swamps and forests were to be paid?

"Fortunately," he said, "90 percent of our effort is voluntary; the cadres are, of course, unpaid, and the civilians able to are growing their own food and carrying out countless other tasks for the revolution which cannot even be estimated in terms of money.

"Portugal," he continued, "spends about $90 million a year to fight us in Mozambique, besides the tremendous amounts she is spending in the two other colonies of Angola and Portuguese Guinea. We are fighting this kind of force daily."

He made no secret of his disappointment with the West's

position regarding the black war of independence and its feeble stand over apartheid in South Africa. Perhaps as a former churchman, he had expected more.

"It is unfortunate that the Christian West, which claims to be the champions of freedom, has not proved to be so in our experience," he said. "It seems that there are differences in interpretation of the worth of man. What they call freedom is telling an ignorant and impoverished man that he is free to find work, to make his own way."

As a Protestant minister working among his own people, both in neighboring Southern Rhodesia and in Mozambique, he had found himself becoming increasingly enmeshed in politics and was conscious of the dichotomy between this and what he considered the role of a churchman. "The situation was becoming too explosive in my country and in my life, and I had to make the choice. I finally left the church and joined the revolution, but I continue as a Christian."

5

THAT NIGHT, AFTER A SEVEN-HOUR MARCH WHICH THE guerrillas could have covered in two without me, we were settled into a camp of thatched huts and cooking fires. All along the route, civilian militiamen had been guarding the paths. As I struggled to keep pace with the column they had stepped silently from the vine-choked forests or loomed up around curves, a mute reminder that a nation was going to war in rags.

They took their role very seriously and stared ahead at attention, barefooted, and armed with rifles or bows and arrows. Their shirts literally hung in strips from their backs for there were no seams left to sew them to, and long bony shins poked from worn trouser bottoms. There were buttons missing and stains embedded on their sleeves and fronts that hours of pounding on stones at the riverbanks could never get out. Their gaunt, sweating faces carried Makonde slashes and they kept their backs rigid, military.

"Mashala, mashala," said the guerrillas as we passed, and the militia whispered back the Makonde greeting, the metal disc on their upper lip twitching for the instant. These

41

wretched bush villagers who were born on a straw mat and died on a straw mat were the backbone of the revolution and both they and the cadres knew it. Sometimes we passed civilian families on the footpaths, their bareshouldered women balancing the inevitable baskets on their heads and towing their children along behind, the youngest nearest to their skirts. Sometimes they stared at the puffing figure in shapeless khaki and asked in Makonde if I were a Portuguese prisoner of war. They were interested but not hostile and stopped on the path to watch us move by. One group of civilians whom we encountered on the banks of a running stream were amazed at my inordinate interest in the water, for I wanted to submerge my flaming face in it and if not held back by some remnant of self-control would have rolled in fully clothed. Perhaps the consciousness of my role as "first white woman in Free Mozambique," as someone had reminded me, had checked the impulse and I had to satisfy myself with gulps of water from a tin cup that I had commandeered from Diolinda.

"You're going to be very sick," warned Marcelino, as he snatched the cup away, substituting for it three mouthfuls of hot tea and a cigarette from his packet of Sportsmen. Later I was allowed half a cupful of water and they watched me closely for signs of nausea.

We were to spend three days in the first camp, which would give me time to recover until the next march. I wanted to tour the countryside, visit the villagers and militia in their own surroundings, watch guerrilla training, and see the workings of FRELIMO's administrative machinery which was to function in a situation of total war.

Besides the bombardment and the miserable poverty, there was a grave shortage of the most basic tools such as hoes, shovels, axes, and bush knives which the farmers had traditionally used to clear land and till the valleys. They had no nails, no sewing machines, no needles or thread, no shoemaking equipment, no carpentry tools or benches, no spinning wheels, or weaving shuttles, or simple printing presses. Unlike Western pioneering societies they did not even have Old World skills to help them through the early days of setting up a new country in their own image. Their only traditions were tribal.

The material for their sleeping huts had been cut from the bush with a *panga* (a long, curved knife) and the structure was a study in geometric form and balance, with the stress evenly distributed throughout. Their beds were either rush mats laid on the sand floors and rolled up in the morning, or tightly woven hammocks of fiber lashed to log posts and anchored to the wall like a ledge. The women do their laundry in plastic buckets or at the streams, pounding their wraparound dress lengths on the rocks. Much of their time is spent in preparing mealie which is a basic foodstuff made of coarse corn grown in their *shambas,* then pounded by hand to a white pulp and boiled down in water. It has the consistency of malleable dough and is the staple diet of guerrillas and villagers alike. It is usually served in a large communal bowl and eaten with the fingers after being rolled on the fingertips into small balls. There is an acute shortage of eating utensils and I never saw a dinner knife.

Housekeeping is not a time-consuming process. Most huts are of one or two rooms and are swept out morning and afternoon with a palm branch. Little else needs dusting as these forest-dwellers have few possessions and life is lived outdoors. An occasional hut is equipped with clay oil lamps fueled with palm oil to give some illumination, however inadequate, in that total darkness of an African hut at night.

Laundry is draped over bushes to dry and sometimes pressed with a heavy, old-fashioned charcoal iron kept replenished from the campfires. If a village is bombed, it is reconstructed elsewhere but in smaller units of five to ten families to minimize any future casualties.

That night I had my first bath in the bush, one of many that the men were to prepare for me whenever we entered a village for a night stop. We usually arrived after dark, which meant that an armed detail would haul water, by flashlight, from a source sometimes two miles down a mountainside or across a valley, then heat it for me in the mess tent. It was then carried in a bucket to the bath hut and left standing on the ground next to three narrow logs. These had been placed side by side to keep the bather's feet off the sand. Most villages had built one of these huts, a three-sided bamboo structure open from one side and from the top. A ground sheet or blanket would sometimes hang across the entrance, which was usually sited away from the village. The guerrillas themselves went off to bathe in the rivers.

Being unused to the rigors of bush life and consumed with false modesty, my first bath was a study in feverish activity and towelgrabbing. The hut was sited dangerously close to the communal dining table which was already beginning to fill up with uniformed cadres and militiamen. Its bamboo sides were not as closely laced as they might have been and I waited until long after dark before venturing in with bath articles, a change of clothing, and a waning flashlight. Sensing my timidity, Diolinda busied herself around the perimeter of the hut, adjusting bushes, and throwing towels over the more noticeable gaps. I realized later that no one took the slightest notice of me but at the time the problem was acute.

One eventually learns the quickest and most efficient way to bathe in a forest hut, without running water or towel bars, and with the water supply limited to one bucket, also the feeling that anyone may dash in at any moment or that there will be an enemy alert. I was unpracticed, however, and the routine was exhausting from the start. My feet, already aching from the march, kept slipping off the wet logs and into the sandy pool beneath. It was like riding a tiny logjam stark naked. There were no hooks or bars on which to hang anything which meant that both used and fresh clothing must be draped over the sides. Both are difficult to sort out later in the darkness and one was likely to discover that he had put his limp, perspiration-soaked clothing back on again. Soap must be wedged somewhere behind a support beam between use, and where does one put the soapy washcloth? Both were continually dropping onto the sand, by this time a muddy wallow due to frantic splashings and rinsings. Half of the precious water had been used in vain attempts to clean up the gritty soap and cloth before the bath itself was hardly underway. Because the water came from wells, it was soft and created a formidable lather difficult to rinse from the body after squandering most of the contents of the bucket.

Later, I became more cunning and learned how to emerge feeling reasonably clean and fresh, and with enough water remaining for minor laundry chores. I also eventually learned to bathe in the forest at night during a violent tropical thunderstorm and wearing a raincoat, with dry clothes resting on a nearby stump ready to put on. (The idea is to drape the first raincoat over your naked shoulders while you soap and then rinse; keep fresh, dry clothing in the second borrowed raincoat; and always wear plastic sandals during this ordeal so that dry shoes and socks can be put on back in the hut. This last increases the possibility of snakebite on one's bare toes enroute, but also reduces the likelihood of bronchial pneumonia.)

But the first bush bath is always the hardest and I emerged to find that I had, of course, put my grubby khaki back on again and the second round of men were already sitting down for dinner. Marcelino and Simango made room for me between them on the log bench and I sat gazing at the row of strangers, almost imperceptible in the light of a single flashlight suspended over the worn planked table.

Besides the traditional mealie, there was roast wild pig, a freshly killed chicken, and a large bowl of unidentified meat

45

covered in a pungent sauce. Next to it stood a large platter of rice.

"God has been good to us," said Simango. "There is meat tonight."

FRELIMO maintains a special section of trained hunters who fish the rivers or roam the forests for birds and wild game and they are considered part of the guerrilla unit. One band had shot a hippo that morning and carried the carcass in sections into camp. It had been stewing most of the day, but it was still tough and gamy. I found the wild pig and chicken fragrant and well-prepared, but physical exhaustion had curtailed my appetite and the guerrillas were immediately worried that I disliked the food. All guerrillas learn to eat well when the opportunity arises, for days may elapse before the next filling meal.

One of the men sitting opposite me in the darkness changed my tin plate several times, hoping to find a combination to tempt me. He was Calisto Mijigo, the commander of Cabo Delgado province at that time, and whom I was to march with until he left to organize a military operation far to the south.

From that first night the pattern was set: there would be unrelenting attempts to stuff me with food so that I could survive the strenuous marches and other difficulties. If I were too tired to eat, Mijigo or Diolinda or Cornelio would fuss about until I had taken something from the tin bowl heaped with rice and meat that they had set before me. If there were a roast chicken, Mijigo would tear it into pieces with his hands and drop the meatiest portion onto my plate with the accompanying clang of a spoon. If I got through one mound of rice, another great dollop would immediately replace it. Sometimes an enormous omelette of fresh pullet eggs would appear on the table or a vegetable broth which the cook had concocted from the drippings. This was not the normal guerrilla fare and I was aware that they had gone to great lengths to search out and prepare the kind of food to which they thought a foreigner was accustomed.

They were one of the toughest guerrilla forces on earth, yet they were to treat me with startling gentleness, always reserving the best of what they had for me and seeing to it that I was made as comfortable as possible while sharing their hardships. I noticed that the men never snatched at the food set before us, although we were often to miss meals because of the marches. At night, they would sit outside the lighted circle of the dining table, rough dark shapes in the African night. They patiently awaited their turn, eating only rice or mealie if that were what remained, and never begrudging me the rare delicacies that they would have appreciated so much themselves.

One of them told me that under Portuguese rule, no African in the countryside was permitted to eat around a table or use knives and forks. "Their patrols would come and tell us that we were above ourselves if we did that."

If I stumbled on a treacherous footpath, sympathetic hands would instantly restore the balance with a "sorry." When we walked into a village clearing, tired and hungry after what seemed to me a Herculean march—and I carried no pack—the precious eggs that welcoming villagers presented to us in banana leaves would go to the *"senhora"* for an omelette. If they saw that I had been marched beyond endurance, the men would halt the column at the forest's edge, always with sentries placed at danger points. They helped me up rugged mountainsides and across fast-running streams, always with a joke or smile or drink of tea —small things when regarded against the background of town conveniences, but so important when grappling with the hardships of the bush.

Guerrilla camps come awake at six or seven in the morning with the rattle of breakfast preparations and the blare of martial music from the underground radio station over the communal transistor. Usually there are a few early risers up from first light who talk and drink coffee at the log tables with the night watch until the cook pokes up the fire. There is news and popular music, battle communiqués and feature programs beamed at towns and villages in the war zones.

Sound carries far in the bush and camps on the perimeter of disputed sectors keep radioplaying, talking, and unnecessary noise to a minimum. All camps, whatever their position, maintain 24-hour watches within a radius of several miles.

We were still in a comparatively safe zone, and the pennywhistle *kwelas* from Johannesburg and Lorenzo Marques played nonstop throughout the early morning chill as the men did their laundry, cleaned equipment, or talked while their leaders from headquarters met in an isolated hut up the hill.

There was a trade problem that had to be solved, and the meeting was to last another day before we could move off. Diolinda and I had shared a small hut the night before and I had slept well on an air mattress that she had inflated and laid over my bunk. From somewhere she had produced a narrow length of cotton which she had folded double and used as a sheet. There was a woolen blanket for me also, for nights could be cold. Diolinda, army-trained in FRELIMO, never left her belongings around the hut however long we might expect to remain in one place. All clothing was folded neatly and repacked in her knapsack along with her hair oil, soap, and other personal belongings. She had two khaki uniforms, a pullover, socks and underwear, and one pair of canvas shoes, and she would be ready instantly should the column suddenly have to move.

I was to have exhausting bouts with my rucksack for I had made the mistake of carrying articles that were not absolutely essential. It was tightly packed and bulging and once something slipped to the bottom the entire contents

48

had to be emptied out on the bunk before the object needed could be found.

Invariably the most urgent requirement of the moment had worked itself to the bottom and I found myself wrestling with the sack several times a day. It was further complicated by having deep and seemingly bottomless pockets on the outside in which I had put various unguents, pomades, pharmaceuticals, and sun cream which I could never get at. Tubes split down the middle and their contents oozed out. Plastic bottles cracked and caps worked themselves off, never to be found again.

I was to learn that if you wanted to lay your hands on anything quickly, the rucksack must be packed in exactly the same order every time. It can save precious minutes in the predawn blackness when an entire section is stomping around outside your hut waiting to move off, you are still in your nightdress, the batteries in your flashlight have just given out, and you have forgotten in which direction is the *"retrete."*

One of the biggest problems for me, and for the women guerrillas, was in finding a suitably private grove near any new camp or bivouac that would serve as a *"retrete,"* the Portuguese word for rest room which translates literally as "retreat." It had to be within calling distance in case one was bitten by a startled snake or other forest creature, yet remote enough to avoid being stumbled across by a passing column or wandering civilian. The tangled pathways must be quickly memorized so that one could find one's way at night, if necessary. Since each new camp looked much the same as the last, I would spend much time crashing around in the underbrush before locating my private bush, and at night Diolinda always accompanied me at a discreet distance to search out snakes with a flashlight. Gradually one became less self-conscious, for the men carefully avoided the *retrete* staked out by the women, and in time one automatically looked away, as everyone did, if a head suddenly bobbed in a heavy clump of bushes. I became conscious of a surprising degree of privacy in the camps due, perhaps, to the matter-of-fact attitude of their inhabitants, their absolute naturalness, and their disinclination to discuss each other's personal affairs.

A women's detachment arrived in camp that day, led by their seventeen-year-old commander in the province, Pauline Mateos. With her second-in-command, Eriketa Joao, age twenty, she controls 200 women guerrillas from the age of fifteen.

They were billeted in a clutch of huts vacated for them by the militia and had set up their own dining shack and field post in a mango grove. Pauline was plump and seemingly placid, yet she had a high reputation both as a commander and mobilizer.

Pauline told me that she had joined the revolution at the age of twelve after hearing FRELIMO men lecturing in her village. For the first months she worked in a guerrilla base as a cook and first-aider, then, after military training in Tanzania, went on reconnaissance patrols with the men. Although the women are trained to fight if ambushed, their use in actual combat was avoided whenever possible.

They were found to be very useful as political mobilizers and in recruiting hesitant males as guerrillas. They achieved this by first converting their wives who in turn pressured their husbands into joining. "Some men have no heart for fighting," said Pauline. "They are afraid or they don't want to leave their families and fields. But once a woman tells her man to go and fight, he feels more inclined."

Women guerrillas are also effective in efficient management of food production, militia work, and the transport of wounded fighters. But they are capable of carrying out almost any mission, political or military, and can march vast distances.

Their early guerrilla training is tough and merciless.

"We undergo the same program as the men because we will be doing men's work. We stay in the same camps often and we regard them as our brothers. We suffer hunger and thirst and heat as they do, and we learn to handle all kinds of arms. When we first begin our training we think that we will die of hunger and fatigue. With the men we are marched past water holes and rivers and not permitted by our trainer to drink although we might be near collapse with thirst. This is done to toughen us for the times when we might want to drink water from sources suspected of being poisoned by the enemy.

"Finally," said Pauline, "when we are strong enough to have overcome all of these trials, we find that we can suffer as much and march as long as any of the men, even with our packs and rifles. Sometimes we overpass men who have collapsed."

Having solved the endurance problem, what of sexual incidents which could arise from close proximity to so many men? There was a pause while Pauline and the girls thought over the question.

It seemed that there were occasional love affairs and if the woman became pregnant the couple were expected to marry. The hardships of guerrilla warfare, however, together with almost continual mobility left little time or energy for trysts in the bush, and when not on a mission the girls lived in a separate base camp.

Many of the men were already married and had wives in nearby villages or in other regions. The problem only became acute if the behavior of guerrillas and local girls violated whatever tribal customs prevailed in a particular area. And whether these tribes were predominantly Moslem, Catholic, or animist, all were relatively strict regarding sexual conduct.

Regarding the women guerrillas who had been recruited from several provinces, it was left to the individual to decide on her private life. I did notice, however, that although relations between guerrillas of both sexes were friendly, they nevertheless observed a certain military formality.

As a revolutionary organization, FRELIMO felt itself under continual obligation to set an example and was aware that the actions of the vanguard were under close scrutiny. Being dependent upon village good will and assistance in countless ways, it was incumbent upon the organization to observe local ethics and to urge its militants to restrain themselves whenever possible, even if given a certain encouragement by local girls who looked upon them as heroes.

Pauline told me that the attitude of the men toward guerrilla women was, in general, affectionate but brotherly and that their relationship was familial rather than sexual. Whether this was a result of female reluctance or male restraint, I could not conclude. But I did learn that in this particular province the man was considered as responsible as the woman for the violation of sexual taboos, especially if it resulted in a child. "After all," the girls told me, "he goes after *her*."

I talked most of the next day with guerrilla chiefs or cadres, with Cornelio interpreting almost nonstop. Because this was no regular war, there could be no clearly defined front lines and advance guerrilla forces often infiltrated far beyond the belt of defenses set up by the Portuguese either as patrolled areas or as manned forts. The rebels had cut a wide swath down the center of three provinces, Cabo Delgado and Niassa in the North, and Tete in the West, but being hit-and-run units could not hope to hold cities or coastlines for very long if captured. For the guerrillas, a zone controlled by FRELIMO meant that the front had effectively established an administrative machinery for all important matters including trade and justice, and that the Portuguese dared not enter except on lightning helicopter raids. These areas were always subject to heavy bombing, however.

52

A disputed zone, according to the men, was one in which the government still maintained fortified administrative points or forts, but were under continual harassment by rebel forces. Here, the Portuguese were often forced to supply their isolated forts by helicopter because normal land routes were under constant danger from mines or ambushes. Ultimately, when effective control was lost and administration broke down because of sheer inaccessibility to the population, the forts were abandoned altogether and the troops regrouped in another region.

This meant that FRELIMO could now mobilize openly in this abandoned zone, establish its own administrative infrastructure, and use it as a springboard to send advance men into neighboring regions, still in Portuguese hands, to start underground agitation there. Again, a fresh bloc of ignorant and impoverished civilians would be called upon to make the perplexing choice: should they inform the fort commandant a few miles down the river that unknown strangers were hinting at revolution? or should they attend their secret meetings as potential converts? Sometimes they did both, of course. The rude living conditions of the mobilizers could handicap the impact they had originally hoped to make, for when they first emerged ragged, dirty, and bearded after weeks in their forest hideouts the peasants sometimes fled in alarm, thinking they were deranged forest spirits.

Foreseeing these difficulties and thinking that a town-based uprising would hasten ultimate victory, Eduardo told me that early organizers had intended to spark the revolution from Mozambican cities. But reprisals such as that in one coastal town, when 600 people were gunned down one afternoon after being invited by the administration to air their grievances publicly, had brought home to the insurgents their inability to protect their own sympathizers. The Portuguese secret police, then called PIDE, had always been exceptionally alert in the cities and often paid blacks to infiltrate the underground organizations. There were further handicaps because of interruptions in the underground communications system.

Several years were lost in regrouping outside the country, but there was no other choice and it gave time to the leadership to examine past mistakes. The new plan—to infiltrate from the Mozambican countryside—contained certain positive points. The vast forests would protect civilians and guerrillas alike, throw the Portuguese on the defensive, and insure that new recruits would not be bottled up in the cities. It would also mean that the uprising would be essentially peasant-based rather than being underpinned by the black town proletariat, a minority which could be easily harassed. Although the latter tactic might have considerably shortened the duration of the war if successful, the present method could prove more effective in the long run since any future system of government would embrace an already politicized majority, the African peasant. Normally more conservative and reluctant than the townsmen, they would in this case constitute the progressive element whose years of contact with the revolution would insure their allegiance.

For the fighters, however, it would also mean years of sacrifice. Guerrilla life, never particularly comfortable, is doubly arduous in the African bush because there is not the occasional relief of a comparatively well-stocked village, a comfortable bed, or the fleeting experience of well-being that a small, unexpected luxury can bring. The forest-dwellers upon whom they were to rely were themselves engaged in a sunrise to sunset struggle to feed themselves and their families, clear land, cut wood, and graze their animals. It was a long walk to market; one didn't simply run down to the neighborhood grocery. Under the Portuguese there were occasional traveling merchants who hauled essentials to the villages, but most transactions meant miles on foot to the nearest fort-town where staples could be bought or bartered

54

for. Even this dubious convenience was to disappear as the Portuguese withdrew and the guerrillas moved in. Simultaneous with the military operations, therefore, was the necessity for an efficient trading system—and with whom? The problems sometimes seemed insurmountable.

The average African peasant in Mozambique had been brought to abject poverty, used, and left there for centuries, an expendable workhorse whose demise from malaria, sleeping sickness, or typhoid was only a temporary inconvenience to the administration; he could easily be replaced from the well of black labor in the countryside.

But the revolutionaries had promised him something better, had provided an unexpected outlet for the redress of grievances, had harnessed his inarticulate desire for things that he had only imagined but never seen. Part of FRELIMO's task was to explain that revolutions are not made overnight and that improvements would come steadily, but slowly. The war would be a long one.

Most were willing to wait and those who were not defected to the Portuguese. But the majority continued to support FRELIMO through the merciless early years of resettlement, bombardment, near-starvation, and bloody reprisal, one last demand on a patience that had endured through centuries.

When reprisals only stiffened resistance, the Portuguese began to flood the forests with leaflets dropped by aircraft, calling on the peasants to give up the fight, turn in their arms for money, and live in prosperity with their Portuguese brothers. Crude colored drawings showed kindly troops receiving submachine-guns from apprehensive black families in the bush while well-dressed Africans, obviously recent defectors, watched smiling in the background. Most villagers knew better and turned in the leaflets to FRELIMO men.

Although ignorant, their memories were vivid. The first political organizer in Northern Mozambique was 37-year-old Ali Thomas Chidudu, who readily recalled his life as a Makonde tribesman under Portuguese administration and later as a hunted outlaw following his decision to join FRELIMO.

He spoke matter-of-factly and referred to the fearful sufferings of that earlier time as "difficulties" or "problems."

"We were all under great difficulties during the Portuguese domination," he said. "They were beating us and there was no proper reason for it. They would come to our village and tell the people to cultivate for no money. If they made us work for them under contract, they sometimes paid us only $1.50 a month for six months and it was like working for nothing. The money was written on a card and at the end of each month half was cut for taxes. We had to stay in our own region and could not go into any other except as contract labor. We received a ration every month of corn flour, soya beans, or peas, but we had no clothing. Our families could not come with us and we worried always about how they would feed themselves while we were away.

"There were no government schools," Chidudu went on, "but the missionaries had some in the provinces. They left after the war started. The children of the *assimilados* (the small group of about 2 percent of the entire African population who were in the process of being absorbed into the Portuguese social and cultural system mainly as civil servants) could go to the government school in the towns where the whites went if they paid a certain amount. But most of us couldn't afford it.

"When the war started and the government knew that you might be involved, you would be found and tortured. Some of us died. By that time the people already hated the administration because of their past life. We finally took the decision to fight because the Portuguese were destroying us, killing us. It was the only thing to do.

"When I first began to organize, the people did not know

about politics. They only knew that they had been miserable all of their lives.

"I had many troubles in those days and I walked only during the night because the Portuguese knew my name and sometimes came looking for me. They called me a bandit.

"By day I remained hidden in the bush and my contact man in the village sometimes gave me food. Usually I lived on mealie and cassava and bush rats. I held meetings at night and the ones who joined us went to other villages to organize. I worked a year and a half like this before the war finally started in 1964, and always lived in the bush."

I had first become aware of Chidudu earlier, a still form who sat with folded hands at the end of a row as we ate, who always seemed to materialize from nowhere in whatever village we entered next. He seldom spoke and rarely smiled and I was told that he had not put so many sentences together since his mobilizing days. One could only imagine his life on the run in the spirit-filled bush of an African night, his dread of informers and capture, the triumph of snaring a rat for his supper, the utter misery without shelter in never-ending rain when clothes never dried, the overwhelming urge for human solace that never came and possibly never would, the small things that gnawed at the spirit —like eating and sleeping and running and thinking, all entirely alone.

He had rough, round farmer's hands, a straw hat, and glasses—the rimless ones that grandmothers wore—and he polished them frequently on his shirttail and inspected them for tiny cracks and other possible damage to the thin metal earpieces. Bush life was hard on glasses, for overhanging branches along the paths often reached down to snap them off the wearer. Once broken or lost in the underbrush they were impossible to replace for refinements like optical service did not exist in the wilderness.

Chidudu's face, usually expressionless behind the thick

layers of his old bifocals, was brown and leathery and his teeth were yellow. He ate delicately and unhurriedly, with his hands, and he was totally illiterate.

There was a detachment about him, as if he had survived some merciless test, and there were no expectations in his face. He ate his food and wore his clothes as if they didn't belong to him, and when he did speak he ran an index finger absently through the ridges on his scarred Makonde face, straining to put into words the appalling circumstances under which he had worked and which he seemed to think so commonplace.

6

WE LEFT CAMP BEFORE FIRST LIGHT THE NEXT MORNING
and almost immediately plunged into chill, dark wilderness,
feeling our way along the narrow footpaths by flashlight.
The column was sleepy, still warm from their billets, and the
men trekked mechanically past faint rustles and squeaks in
the thick undergrowth as tiny animals scurried for their
burrows.

It was too early for the transistors and the only audible
sound from the column was the faint whisper of khaki and
the pad of canvas shoes on the almost invisible path. There
was an occasional oath as someone wrenched an ankle on a
hidden creeper. There had been no time for breakfast but
the water bottles were full and there was tea in the thermos
which, with glucose tablets that I carried, would provide
temporary energy on the long march ahead. I did not want
to halt the column unnecessarily for this meant searching
out a safe place to rest while some 25 guerrillas and a chain
of carriers and civilians who invariably attached themselves
to us while on errands of their own were made to wait while
the *senhora* had her lifegiving tea.

I had noticed on the earlier march, and was to experience it again as an untoughened newcomer on subsequent ones, that after the first burst of energy following a period of rest, the next few hours produce an overwhelming fatigue as weak muscles are again overstrained and there never seems to be enough oxygen for the lungs. This is the period when hands swell and white faces redden, when flies bite with unnecessary viciousness and one recalls with sweet nostalgia that other world of iced drinks and cool gardens. Strangely there is no hunger although breakfast has been missed.

Then, a ten-minute rest seems to revive the ailing spirit and one can walk for several hours afterward with numb determination. The legs seem detached from the trunk and one foot appears in front of the other as if it were somebody else's.

Although the sun has in fact become hotter, the body tolerates it better, and one thinks of almost everything else except the trek. This is one reason, perhaps, why guerrillas are loathe to interrupt a column on the march; a rhythm has imposed itself and the unit moves as one, as if the energy of the mass has been parceled out.

Our final destination was military headquarters and a training camp far into the interior, but first they wanted me to see FRELIMO's food plantations. There we were to rejoin Marcelino and Mijigo who had taken another route to inspect a bush clinic.

Besides fighting, a guerrilla was also expected to help clear and cultivate land set aside for FRELIMO's own needs, a scheme intended to relieve the peasant whenever possible of feeding guerrillas on the move. However willing they may be, this was always a burden on the meager resources of the farmers.

We marched for six hours that morning and crossed charred, still smoking savanna that villagers had burnt out to enrich the soil for the next planting. This is a common practice in Africa and if done carefully, so that organic matter underneath is not destroyed in the fire, is thought to increase the soil's fertility.

As our column swung steadily toward the rivers and hills ahead, the smell of mangoes and jungle rot floated from forests and ravines. Mist hung over the valleys and one could almost hear the splash of fountains in the early morning. Then, as the sun climbed, the locusts signaled another hot and humid day.

We were a long column, headed by Mijigo's second-in-command. The escorts in the front and rear had begun to sweat under the weight of machine-guns. Heavily burdened civilians with pegged lips, the women swathed in their *khengas,* had appeared along the paths from invisible villages in the hinterland and swung in behind the column with cries of *"mashala,"* or the Swahili *"jambo."* This was market day and the civilians relied on guerrilla protection to cross a possible Portuguese ambush track not far ahead.

We marched steadily, bobbing through ravines as the sun tore through our shirts and made pools on our backs. The smell of preserved fish, which the civilians had packed between banana leaves in their raffia baskets, wafted forward and I wanted to gag. The flies plugged our noses and eyes and we snatched leafy branches from the bushes to use as fly swatters. We marched silently, in cadence, the sweat running into our eyes and mouths. It is an axiom that black bodies glisten. They do, for reserves of oil in the African skin act as a welcome lubricant in the punishing heat, a reason why blacks often look younger than they are. I deeply regretted the loss of my sun oil which had already distributed itself among my other belongings. My legs cramped and even my watch seemed a sticky burden. My uniform smelled of sweating khaki and mildew, though fresh only a few hours earlier. I fastened my watch around my belt and felt better but could not resist asking for a rest. We had trekked for over two hours and my legs had begun to tremble.

"Cansada!" cried out Diolinda in Portuguese, and the column moved toward a cool grove. We flopped against majestic trees with trunks like armchairs as sentries were posted in a wide circle within a quarter of a mile. When resting or stopping at water holes along the way, the guerrillas invariably post sentries against Portuguese foot patrols and never halt in open country. However secure the area may seem, their guns lay across their laps or at their sides, with automatic weapons on "safety" to prevent accidents. I noticed that they never played with their guns or snapped the magazines on and off or shot at game along the route.

In case of ambush I would be completely dependent upon them, for I was unarmed, hot and tired, and my reflexes would be slow. Mijigo had given them orders to "protect the *senhora* with your lives," which was a great deal to ask when the *senhora* was a red-faced blob wearing dirty khaki, munching glucose, and fanning the flies off her face.

There would be time for tea and some biscuits that Diolinda had hoarded for me, and a talk with Fernando Raoul, the 29-year-old administrative secretary of FRELIMO's department of defense (he later married Diolinda). His job took him frequently across Cabo Delgado and Niassa provinces and he always carried a Marcip submachine-gun and a transistor radio. His aide, a lanky youth in blue denim, dogged his footsteps carrying a leather briefcase on his head. This is a favorite method of transport among Africans, their hands usually being full of water buckets or *pangas* or children, and they were capable of carrying very heavy loads on their heads for miles without mishap.

Raoul told me from a military aspect how FRELIMO had studied in depth what he called the nature of the war and the tactics that would be necessary in the circumstances of Mozambique. "To begin a liberation movement of this kind," he said, "you must first decide whether it will consist of guerrilla or conventional warfare, offensive or defensive.

62

Is it likely to be prolonged or short, and how many phases are there likely to be?"

This phasing was important and it meant the levels of military and administrative accomplishment the movement was likely to reach in a given period and the coordination which this implied. There should be no vacuums left as the guerrillas pushed forward and the Portuguese withdrew, and obstacles had to be anticipated, not only in military situations but in other spheres involving the civilian population. Ultimately, the pattern would change from guerrilla to conventional warfare.

"We know that we must reconstruct the country as we progress," Raoul went on. "If we neglect this, we will have created chaos, not liberation, when it's all over.

"At each step, we must consider how to make the people understand the politics of the party, why we are doing what we are in a given situation, and why our war will be a long one.

"We know that every region has its own customs, and we must always take this into consideration. There is always a shortage of food and clothing, and our people are being bombed and shot by the enemy or forced to leave their villages. Many of these people have lost everything, even the little clothing that they had before the war. What remained to the rest is also being lost as the war improves from the military point of view. Each new region that we capture means that it has been a battleground in one form or another, with the resulting impoverishment of its people. They are now our responsibility and it is up to us to replace what they have lost. As an organization, this must be a main concern to us."

Raoul said that at present they get more from outside help than from their own production, despite large amounts of equipment, food, and clothing captured from government troops.

Then there was the question of military supplies for the

fighters. "Everything must be brought in from outside, on our heads, and we must plan these routes according to our geographical position. Most nearby countries are unfriendly to us, which means that our task is doubly difficult. Even now, it takes a month to carry a box of ammunition into Niassa province from the frontier, for example, because the distances are so enormous. Since we cannot ride, we must walk. And on the way, the guerrillas and carriers are contending with hunger, thirst, and sickness."

As early as 1964, war had broken out in two other provinces besides the three currently in revolt, he said. One was called Mozambique province, after the country itself, and the other was Zambezia. But the supply problem proved insurmountable at that time, and FRELIMO forces were withdrawn.

"We had to cross tremendous distances through Niassa to reach Mozambique province," Raoul said, "and then the attitude of the Malawi government brought a halt to activities in Zambezia."

He and other FRELIMO men were arrested in Malawi (formerly Nyasaland) that year as they carried ammunition across the country into Zambezia and Tete, another important province.

"They searched us and took our material and we spent two months in prison. We explained our purposes in crossing and Banda [the president of Malawi] finally freed us although the Portuguese had offered a large sum for handing us over. But his government kept our guns and ammunition and we knew that this route would remain closed to us."

Soon after, FRELIMO pulled out its remaining men and reinforced Cabo Delgado and Niassa, and later extended the war to Tete, the site of the controversial Cabora Bassa dam project.

The Cabora Bassa, which will cost $300 million to build, will be Africa's biggest hydroelectric project and the scope for agriculture and mining within its reach will be vast. According to South African newspaper accounts, the Portuguese hope to settle a million white immigrants from the motherland around the dam, which will generate enough power in its first phase to extend 800 miles into South Africa.

When completed, the dam will be 70 percent larger than Egypt's Aswan, and twice the size of the Kariba between Zambia and Southern Rhodesia. With that kind of power at her disposal, Portugal is determined to hold on in Mozambique, for it is expected to change the economic face of Tete province and the colony as a whole. She also expects the assistance of the expected farmer-immigrants from the motherland in beating off the guerrillas who have already made incursions.

For the Africans expect little change in their own living standards as a result of the dam, and already black farmers in the vicinity have been told to settle themselves elsewhere.

FRELIMO claims that Portugal's defense system in Tete has been stiffened by the addition of several South African battalions who have already clashed with its guerrillas near the dam, a development which the movement finds inevitable since South Africa will buy much of Cabora Bassa's power.

The guerrillas, along with certain African states, see the dam as a further attempt to reinforce white supremacy in Southern Africa, both directly and indirectly. New industries which spring up as a result of the project will almost certainly be controlled by whites or by the apartheid governments which they support, and the addition of another million Portuguese immigrants as civilian farmer-militia units will certainly mean more headaches for the liberation movement. They also question whether the future settlers, many from impoverished belts in their own country, have been told exactly what to expect as they pack up so hopefully for their new life abroad. They know what the settlers will be told by their government when attacked by the blacks, however—"It's the Chinese, the Communists, the bush bandits, or all three."

7

WE PUSHED ON WITHOUT INCIDENT AND BY NOON HAD
walked into FRELIMO's food-growing region after a punishing uphill climb that followed the drying course of rocky
mountain streams into a small village.

Even the guerrillas seemed tired as we sat nodding in a
thatched lean-to that served as the village school. There was
a small blackboard still covered with a recent Portuguese
language lesson, two wooden benches, and a small teacher's
table in the center. Hens scratched and clucked around the
clearing outside and the men filled their canteens from a
clay demijohn that local peasant women had brought. An
infant of about ten months was carried over for us to see,
the son of a guerrilla who had recently been killed in the
South. His mother, still in her teens, had dressed the child in
a long white pleated frock, freshly washed and pressed, and
he screamed in terror when he saw me, the first white face
that he had ever encountered. A young boy who had been
staring apprehensively through the gaps under the low roof
since our arrival suddenly blurted the question that had obviously been occupying his mind: was I a Portuguese sol-

dier and, if so, where had I been captured? The men laughed and the child was overcome with embarrassment; he hung about at a distance throughout our lunch of soup and rice, eyeing me with a puzzled incomprehension. He was apparently not satisfied with the story that I was a woman visiting the country and his village, for I did not resemble any woman that he had ever known. I was in all probability a Portuguese soldier, captured perhaps, but I would undoubtedly pounce upon him the moment that the guerrillas turned their backs. Eventually he trotted off toward his hut, and I did not see him again.

Marcelino and Mijigo arrived with an escort and a brilliantly colored flower that they had found on the way, saying that they had heard from the militia enroute that our group was already in camp and that it was my reward for a fast march with only one stop. I was pleased with the flower, an orange sunburst of great size, and kept it until the petals fell.

Several huts had been temporarily vacated for our use and we dozed through the long afternoon, the air heavy and still except for the flies and the locusts. It was late afternoon when we started for the plantations an hour's march away, and a light breeze blew gently through the forest. Mijigo was in the lead, with Marcelino just behind, then Diolinda, Cornelio, myself, and the rest of the column. Unlike most of the other guerrillas, Mijigo walked as if he had just come off the drilling field, in long strides at a steady gait and with his left arm swinging in an arc behind him. He could cover twenty miles at this pace, never tiring and without a pause. While many of the men carried their arms slung across their backs with their packs, the commander kept his late-model automatic rifle close to his side, with his arm lying flat along the stock and barrel. A wad of cotton was poked into the muzzle to keep the sand out. Mijigo was tall and slender, and his teeth had been filed to points.

When speaking in Makonde, Mijigo expressed superlatives or distances by drawing out a word and ending with a rising inflection, almost a falsetto. Thus: "Our fields come to an end way-y-y-y over there," and he would point out the boundaries that he meant. Or sometimes by repetition: "It's far far." The pitch of Mijigo's voice was totally different when speaking Portuguese, and I asked Cornelio if the commander was having a private joke. He told me that it was a common linguistic peculiarity with Makondes and some other tribes as well.

We crossed a high plateau just before sunset where it was cool and fresh and the locusts had stopped. Immense trees hundreds of years old darkened against an awesome sunset. "The sleep of the sun," said Cornelio. As the column marched single file along the edge of a plateau against the failing light, Mijigo pointed to a rolling valley beneath us.

"FRELIMO's plantation," he said, "the sweet rice of Mozambique." We scrambled down a steep path and onto the valley floor and sat on jagged fallen logs while he explained that both guerrillas and civilian volunteers had worked with *pangas* and hoes to reclaim this land from the jungle. He waved his hands toward the far distant boundaries. There was maize and cassava, and tiny green rice shoots poked up from the dark earth. Wisps of smoke rose in the distance where yet more forest was being burnt out to make way for new fields. It would begin to grow again next year unless the plantations were again fired.

"Before FRELIMO began the war," Mijigo said, "the people always got the short end of the bargain in any barter with the Portuguese. All shops belonged to the colonials and when the revolution started they stationed troops inside the posts where the shops were. After the Africans fled, they began to exchange their crops across the Ruvuma river at barter points operated by the movement. They are better off now and can produce more for trade unless their crops have been bombed in the meantime. But their food supplies to us

68

throw an additional burden on them which we want to alleviate as much as possible."

Mijigo and the other guerrillas were obviously proud of FRELIMO's fields and wanted me to see every seedling within a two-mile radius. It was a new venture and they took a personal interest in it. We clumped across the fields until nightfall, comparing one row of rice shoots with another, then made our way back to camp by flashlight. The cook had already heated water for baths and dinner was simmering in the calabashes.

I greatly admired the cook, who had been with us from the first day that we had entered Mozambique, hauling his equipment and cooking pots into every new camp. A string of carriers with bags of rice and mealie followed with the staples but after that the cook was on his own. He often had to organize his outdoor kitchen in complete darkness, first hauling in the three large stones that would contain the cooking fire, then poking through the bush for firewood.

The housewife's old lament, "What shall we have for dinner?" must have been particularly meaningful for him, for he was never quite certain what ingredients he would find at each new stop, and if he ran out of salt or sugar it meant a 50-mile hike back to a supply area. If the hunters had caught up with us in a new village, it meant fresh game for dinner from which he made thick soups and boiled the tough sinew until it was edible. But sometimes he had only his sack of rice to start with and somehow seemed able to give us adequate and appetizing food with admirable consistency. After dinner he scoured the pots and pans with sand, then washed each one with a bar of laundry soup in a bucket of water and rinsed it in a second. Dish towels were washed every night after dinner and hung over a bush to dry. We never had stomach trouble from meals in camp.

There were intestinal disorders from other sources, however, although many guerrillas along with the civilian population had apparently built up an immunity to some of the local microbes. I was certain that our unfiltered water supplies, especially from open wells, were polluted. The rainy season was yet to begin and the men climbed far down into ragged water holes along the route to fill our canteens from the muddy puddles that remained. The water was cloudy and dark but we drank it anyway for the risk of dehydration on the marches seemed greater at the time than the diseases lurking in these suspect pits. I was to learn that one's fastidiousness disappears quickly in the bush.

As we never had an opportunity to boil drinking water enroute, I dissolved Halazone tablets into mine to help counteract ill effects. While the men would drink from my canteen if offered, they refused the tablets for their own use because my supply was low. "We are accustomed," they would tell me, "but you are not." Anyway, the water would be fresher as we climbed toward the mountains.

Mijigo continued our conversation at dinner in the thatched lean-to where someone had suspended a flashlight from the rush ceiling. We peered at our tin plates and bowls of mealie under the pale white light, checking them for ants or flying insects that may have plopped in. There were not enough plates or forks to go around, and there was a flurry of dishwashing in a bucket nearby as new waves sat down. Diolinda hovered about with a torch and shone it into each pot as it was brought to the table. There were omelettes, too, a meat stew, and the contents of a can of corned beef which the cook had opened to vary the menu. He stood over us expectantly, watching for our reaction to this latest addition.

As usual, I could not consume the amounts that they thought I should and Mijigo, apparently suspecting that my dull appetite might have been due to the mounds of mealie being eaten with the hands, suddenly announced: "Food tastes better this way. It takes strength from the blood underneath." He watched for my reaction and I wanted to laugh.

I told him that people ate sandwiches with their hands abroad and therefore I was accustomed to the practice. But what I couldn't understand was how the blood transmitted its strength-making faculties through the skin and onto the mealie. He looked at me for a long moment and grinned, told me that I was complicating life unnecessarily, and ladled out another portion of meat stew onto my plate, next to which he wedged a generous mound of mealie. "Eat it," he said, "you're going mountain climbing tomorrow."

Mijigo had been commander in Cabo Delgado for four years after military training in Tanzania and, later, for tactics and strategy in Russia. He talked frankly about FRELIMO's problems, and a main concern to him was the third sector of Cabo Delgado which was still in Portuguese hands. The province was divided into three sectors for military purposes and the third lay farthest to the south. The Africans there were still under tight Portuguese control, were being herded into "strategic hamlets" next to the forts, and were still undergoing the mobilization process, he said.

"This year," Mijigo said, "we liberated more than 300 of our civilians from these hamlets who had been used for work inside the camps and on the surrounding roads.

"But sometimes," he went on, "our people run when they see our guerrillas because they look so wild. We don't have enough uniforms or clothing for our men and have to depend upon other countries or what we can capture from the forts. Sometimes our fighters are half-naked and if they storm a camp the civilian population living within the barbed wire truly think that we are bandits, as the Portuguese have told them. These villagers are very isolated and very ignorant."

Mijigo estimated that no more than half of FRELIMO's

insurgents had uniforms, but that this was being remedied through increasingly successful raids on Portuguese army camps.

The movement discourages volunteers from outside, he said, either as an International Brigade or as part of the guerrilla force itself. There was no lack of potential African recruits in the province—"the more we fight, the more people join us." What they lacked was uniforms and more arms.

"This is a war for the masses and we must fight it alone. A person from outside would be unable to overcome our difficulties and live as we do year after year. Would he understand why we were fighting? Could he make the sacrifices that we must make every day of our lives as guerrillas? One day, an outsider might be satisfied with a political compromise with the Portuguese—with partition or limited self-government. This would be a crime against the masses. We want complete independence and we cannot stop fighting until we reach Lourenço Marques.

"We lack many things," Mijigo went on, "but we have learned to survive. We can carry 90 tons of equipment into the country on our backs in one day. What we lack are the materials themselves."

He said that the shortage of medicine was sometimes acute, especially after fighting had been stepped up the previous year. First-aiders moving with the guerrillas had no supplies of antibiotics, antitetanus toxoid, or injections against gas gangrene or snakebite. Bandages and antiseptics were in low supply, there were no facilities for blood transfusions, and only very minor operations could be carried out in the bush.

If a badly wounded guerrilla was bleeding heavily, his comrades attempted to check the flow, then carried him in their arms, sometimes for 50 miles, to a bush clinic or first-aid station. Here there were dressers available, but no doctors or nurses. This shortage of medicine had cost scores of guerrillas their lives. "Some of us simply bleed to death," he said, "or lose our arms and legs because of gangrene."

Because these bush clinics are so often bombed, FRE-LIMO is building its main hospital across the border. But the transport of a casualty from far inside the country may take over a week—if he can survive the journey.

Despite the risks, just how confident are the "bandits" themselves? One of them, 29-year-old Augustino Cosme, is the political and military commissar of Cabo Delgado and has a wife and two children in the interior. For the past three years he has been operating almost entirely in the disputed third sector where he both mobilizes and fights. He described his life there, calling it a "good one."

"Because this part of the province is heavily patrolled," said Cosme, "I sleep anywhere at sunset. I arrange my sack and sleep in the bush. We don't have time to stay in houses. We eat whatever we meet, like cassava from the civilians, or roots or bananas and fruit that grow near the riverbanks. I am sufficient with that food and I become weak only if I am ill. If there is time, we catch fish or bush rats. If there are gazelle, the civilians hunt it for us with bows and arrows because the sound of gunshots would attract too much attention.

"There are six Portuguese forts in this sector, the largest being Macomia," he went on. "There is still much political work to do there because the civilians are under tight control and cannot easily hear our ideas. You cannot depend upon just any hut for shelter.

"I am continually moving on various missions, but I cannot estimate the distances that I walk in miles or kilometers because there is no way of measuring. We calculate by hours, on the basis of fifteen minutes to a mile if it is a very slow march. Usually we don't try to count the miles that we have done; we just walk until we reach our destination. My average is at least ten miles a day, but I remember one march which lasted for 48 hours and we did not stop for

73

food. We drank water from our canteens as we moved. We must have walked about 192 miles nonstop that time because we wanted to reach our headquarters without delay. Still, it was a slow march by our standards."

He described an attack on the fort of Nasupaku, in which he had taken part, and which he called a "typical attack." Six Portuguese soldiers had been killed, one wounded, and large quantities of arms and ammunition had been captured.

"We reached the fort at midnight and just lay in the dark outside and waited. There were about 180 of us, all guerrillas, and we knew the plan of the fort before going in. Normally, I don't feel very much fear during a raid, as I am too excited at the time. A person is frightened if his reconnaissance has been bad, but there is confidence if the attack has been well planned.

"We waited until 4:45 A.M. and then opened up with bazookas. We had no big guns, no cannons or mortars. At the first burst of the bazookas we rushed the fort and told them to surrender. They fled and later we found their casualties —six dead and one wounded. We took him prisoner, along with another Portuguese and an African soldier who was fighting on their side; a bazooka and mortar, a radio transmitter, fifteen Belgian FN rifles, ten Mausers, a light machine-gun, and uncountable quantities of food and clothing. We took the beds, too. They had put up no resistance and the whole operation, including preparation of the captives and the wounded man for transport, took only an hour. The fort was in our hands."

I asked if the insurgents preferred a particular type of gun.

"The best for an attack is an automatic rifle or submachine-gun," he replied. "But in a war all guns are good, especially for us who depend upon foreign countries for arms. You have to make do with what you are given. If you see a fighter who wants to choose his gun, you begin to think that he has no heart for fighting. We are taught to use all types and cannot always have the best. We all know this."

An almost equally important concern to fighters was the prevalence of malaria, said Cosme. "There is no proper place to stay to recuperate because we are always moving, sometimes without food if we are in a hurry."

A guerrilla down with malaria alternately shivers with cold or perspires profusely but cannot leave the marching column if on a mission far in the interior where Portuguese patrols are heavy. Only in areas where guerrilla activity is so intense that the enemy cannot leave the fort on foot will a stricken cadre stop in a village hut to recover. There is an acute shortage of antimalaria drugs in Mozambique and most guerrillas and civilians, including children, suffer from recurrent attacks which can neither be prevented consistently nor treated medically. If a villager feels out of sorts or feverish, the usual self-diagnosis is malaria and he resigns himself to the attack. His only protection, to some extent, would be a mosquito net which most cannot afford either to buy or to make.

I carried a supply of antimalaria tablets called Daraprim which I took faithfully each week and which proved effective; also a tube of mosquito repellent that I shared with Diolinda and some of the other cadres, for we had no nets and the cream enabled us to sleep before its effects wore off. Many of the men were bivouacked under the trees and I often heard them slapping at mosquitoes and groaning.

However, the absence of most other essentials complicates, but does not seriously disrupt, guerrilla life in the bush. Conveniences are quickly forgotten or not imagined at all, depending upon whether the cadre was raised in a town or village.

Cigarettes are a luxury. North Korea donates a brand called Deer which are distributed pack by pack to guerrillas who happen to be in the area when the occasional supplies

75

are dropped off. Beer or soft drinks are part of another life, and the sought-after refreshment is clear cool water as opposed to the dank brown variety from the water holes. When one leaves the bush, there is surprise and even delight in seeing water run from a tap, in starched linen on a well-set table, in all of the things one would normally take for granted—a hot shower, grocery shelves stocked with flour and butter and cans of cocoa, fresh beef and ham and fruits and vegetables trucked in from the farms. One fingers the cans of insect repellent and remembers steamy nights when huge and silent mosquitoes left arms and legs covered in knots by morning.

Air conditioning is suddenly a miraculous invention, and clothing and shoe shops a symbol of ease and plenty, however poor the merchandise may actually be. One remembers how many hundreds of miles a guerrilla can travel in one pair of oversized sneakers with their seams gaping open. I recalled asking one cadre about the problem of finding correct sizes among new or secondhand shoes donated to FRELIMO. He told me that there was no problem—"We make the feet fit the shoes."

Inside "the country," in the bush, one gradually adjusted and improvised. Diolinda made a neatly hemmed ribbon for me with which to tie up my hair, producing a strip of leftover material from a small tin box in which she kept her needle and thread. Everything is hoarded in the bush, for eventually a use for it is found. A potato sack with armholes cut in the sides makes a child's garment if there is no other. Each scrap is utilized, and the crates once holding arms or canned food are pulled apart and become benches or beds or wobbly chairs, their nails carefully pounded out and reused. Every piece of donated clothing is worn, however outlandish it may look or ill-fitting it may be. Food and water is carried and stored in pots made of clay, and cooking oil is extracted from the palm trees. There are no toilet rolls, so leaves are the substitute.

76

Baths are taken in the rivers or in secluded forest groves unless the village has a communal bath house. A small possession becomes a treasure because if lost, or gradually exhausted, it cannot be replaced. Diolinda had a bottle of scented coconut hair oil that someone had brought from Dar es Salaam. Unless her hair was parted into neat rows, like a field ready for plowing, then plaited and anchored down, it was wiry and unmanageable and to draw a comb through the mass without the aid of the oil was a noisy and painful process. She would begin the ten-minute ordeal each morning, before I was fully awake, her face screwed up and brown arms flailing. Occasionally a tooth popped from the comb under the strain. She poured tiny dollops from her dwindling cache onto each tuft and when fully gone through, it stood straight out like a starched Elizabethan ruff, each crinkle riveted in place, each rivulet stubbornly refusing to flatten out. Any attempt to comb it down and under only made the situation worse. With a sigh Diolinda would plait it, then don her casque. I never saw an Afro hair style in Mozambique and only one in Portuguese Guinea, worn by a guerrilla. He said that he had grown it to keep out the early morning dampness.

8

EXACTLY WHAT KIND OF PEOPLE ARE THE PORTUGUESE fighting in black Mozambique?

As I watched the guerrillas at rest, talking among themselves, off guard, or Cornelio as he went into one of his spontaneous dances, or half-naked carriers trotting purposefully down the trails, I was often to wonder at the resources that these people must have possessed to enable them to survive—undernourished, underequipped, a lifetime, perhaps, of self-denial stretching endlessly before them.

Time after time I had seen on Mozambican faces a quality of gentleness and patience and endurance that I had never encountered before. There was no envy or hatred or selfishness. Never did I hear them say that the "white man" is our enemy; rather it was the Portuguese government. It's not the people, they would tell me, but the government that had caused all of their sufferings.

You saw that there was no dejection on guerrilla faces, no loss of hope, few complaints, no self-pity. They were too disciplined for that, and all shared the same hardships.

Often I was to ask them: "How can you march so long, not knowing when you will eat or find water? What is your reward? Where is your relief? How can you fight when there is no end in sight? What sustains you?"

Always their answer was, "We are accustomed. We know that it will be long, but we are accustomed." I was to hear the same, later, in Portuguese Guinea—*"Nous sommes habitués,"* as we waded through swamp and mud up to our thighs.

Were the "big words" as one writer has called them, such as "freedom" and "liberty" and "independence" enough to sustain a people who had never experienced them before, enough compensation for the kind of effort and perpetual sacrifice that the guerrillas and villagers were called upon to make almost every day? When translated into practicalities and applied to their daily experience, perhaps they were. It is possible, once the hard, thankless early years of mobilization have been got through, sufficient attacks and counterattacks carried out to establish an unquestionable seriousness of purpose, and a democratic structure consolidated in the villages in which all can participate—a new and intriguing experience—that a revolution can take hold and sustain itself, propelled to some extent by its own momentum.

I recalled the words of the cadre friend—"We are not born revolutionaries, just people who could no longer support a situation. You get caught up in a revolution and then you see it through."

This is not to say that a revolution feeds upon itself, or that it is self-perpetuating; it needs constant guidance and replenishment from its leadership. One of the most important factors is morale, that hopeful and delicate state of mind that a good leadership takes care to reinforce. It is done in many ways; by instant exposure of enemy propaganda aimed at shaking village confidence in the movement; by truthful battle accounts whatever your losses (villagers are quick to sense a lie); by endless palavers with the population aimed at reinforcing their confidence and learning their practical problems—and very important, by example—the personal example of the cadres from the top down to the local village commissar-militant. A whiff of cynicism or defeatism can eventually undermine seriously the momentum of a revolution.

Another important factor is the continual assessment, criticism, and correction by a movement of its tactics, whether militarily or in its relationship to the civilians. This is done at top-level and is fed by on-the-spot reports from village committees, area leaders, district troubleshooters, and finally the provincial heads.

If FRELIMO's men in the field ever wavered before the task ahead of them, they never told their comrades about it, for it would do no good. A guerrilla force must possess not only guns, but also the ability to overcome their own weaknesses of character in a war such as this, to be a constant example to those around them and under their administration. It is incumbent upon them to be so, for they are dealing with a totally unsophisticated population in the Western sense, for whom they have assumed complete responsibility.

As I watched FRELIMO's men weld themselves to the population in countless ways, these khaki grafts whose impact had shaken the very core of village structure, I wondered how much more they would undergo before the weariness would set in, and if it ever would. Perhaps not, for they had a cause in which they utterly believed. It is a phenomenon, the "cause" syndrome, that somtimes fails. But when it does survive the erosion of time and cynicism, it is instilled so completely that nothing can shake it out, except perhaps the leadership itself.

The revolution had dominated these partisans, winding itself around their lives to the exclusion of anything else. Matter-of-factly, and with no apologies, it had demanded unquestioning sacrifice. For as long as they could remember, their lives had been a renunciation of comforts or stability or the solace of a home. There were no airs or posturings or subtle revelations of ego. They had gone beyond possessions or envy or malice. They were totally real.

They accepted, wore, or used whatever was given them, without question. One cadre appeared in a cast-off woman's blouse with a flower delicately embroidered on the collar. He was not conscious of any bizarre result and his eyes didn't even dare me to smile. It had not occurred to him. The time came when you saw the man or woman first, and later the rags. You noticed the eyes, the strength in the curve of the shoulder, how the long hands with their white palms closed over a burden or a gun barrel, and the set of their necks as they walked.

They had starved and survived and collapsed from fatigue and thirst and picked themselves up again and there was nothing left for them to overcome except "the enemy."

Our arrival at each village was always the signal for a presentation of arms by the local guerrilla and militia units, a welcoming oration, and speeches from the commander about FRELIMO victories or setbacks. Sometimes the groups would have already assembled and we would march straight off the path and into the grove where row after row of perspiring rebels awaited us. Among them stood the women militia in flowing *khengas,* those unruly lengths of multicolored cloth hitched securely over their bosoms as they hoisted their rifles into position.

"Ombro arma!" bawled Mijigo's adjutant. *"Apresentar arma!"* There was the scuffle of bare feet on the forest floor and the foreign snap of steel and metal as arms were whipped to waist level.

"Manda descancar!" and they were at ease, expectant.

A thin voice from somewhere in the back row would sing the first bar of the revolutionary anthem, which was then taken up by the rest. The words were in Portuguese and the melody in a haunting minor key. Written by one of the cadres, it was sung throughout the liberated zones and all of the villagers had learned it.

> FRELIMO will win, FRELIMO will conquer,
> A fight until liberty,
> FRELIMO will triumph.

The chorus told of African subjection by Europe and the determination of the blacks to force colonial governments out. Other verses forecast Mozambique's final victory and triumph, and eventually all of Africa's.

Many of the men were shabby and underfed and some had tied strips of rags around their bare feet. One man wore a pair of gym shorts and someone's cast-off evening jacket. Another stood in an undershirt and trousers, the bottoms of which had rotted off from knee to ankle. Next to him was a mustached cadre in knickers and a knitted cap with a pom-pom on top. Row after row of ill-clad freedom fighters in secondhand shirts and oversized trousers rolled up to avoid falling over the bottoms. They could not be cut down because someone else, a longer-legged man perhaps, might later be wearing them. This was FRELIMO's army in the bush, tattered, sworn to fight to the death, and very very lethal.

They sang with feeling and force, savoring every word as if victory were over the next mountain, yet knowing that it might take many more years of poverty and dying and endless miles across the length and breadth of Mozambique until the last path into Lourenço Marques.

And what of their opponents, those recruits from the motherland or sons of white Mozambican settlers called up to defend the colonies against the encroaching bandits?

On occasion, the guerrillas snared the enemy himself—often in the shape of a sweating little Portuguese corporal in stubbly beard to whom a black was a subhuman who worshiped totems and ate people. Strangers to the bush and the climate, the troops lived in seedy outposts in the heart of the wilderness, in crumbling forts roofed in tin and battered by rain and flies and enemy mortar. Sixty men to an armed tomb and outside, vipers in the underbrush and bandits on the wait. And always the heat. Capture was perhaps a relief.

I spent an afternoon with five Portuguese soldiers in a FRELIMO camp. They included three deserters and two prisoners from an inland post who had fallen into insurgent hands as they wandered unarmed through the forests toward what they thought was the Tanzanian border. An African peasant had warned FRELIMO of their proximity as they crunched through the underbrush flushing out birds and alerting those screeching forest sentinels, the monkeys. Their first encounter with armed blacks had been traumatic, for they had taken seriously their officer's stories about African predilection for human flesh.

As I sat talking with Simango, they had bobbed across the clearing toward us under armed guard, then stood at ease until invited to sit down. They were youthful, tanned, and dressed in the same clothing in which they had been captured. One carried a large comb in his shirt pocket; another had pinned a small cross to his chest which he said had been a childhood award in a Bible studies contest and was perhaps displayed as a precaution against some black Catholic's sudden reversion to cannibalism. They had been carpenters or shoemakers or masons in civilian life, and had names like Fernando, Joao, and Manuel. After so many days with the blacks, I was momentarily startled to see other white faces, and for seconds we stared at each other. They seemed curiously incongruous in the black world that I had grown accustomed to, and very vulnerable against the backdrop of the African forest. The guerrillas were the color of the teak and mahogany that surrounded them, of the gray-brown thatch of the huts in which they slept, and of the gourds from which they drank. What is the color of a *conquistador?*

Somewhere, five FRELIMO guerrillas were apparently wearing Portuguese army boots, for the prisoners were in tennis shoes. Two of the soldiers had been living in the bush with FRELIMO since their capture eight months before during a night raid on two Cabo Delgado forts. The three deserters had been prisoners for only a month after walking out of Mueda fort toward what they thought would be the frontier and political asylum 150 miles away. They had been interrogated for three hours that day by Simango and other leaders, and now they were to tell their story again.

Fernando Dos Santos Rosa, a 24-year-old lance corporal from the Chavez district in Portugal, told me that he had been captured when FRELIMO raided the post of Nambude during a rainy dawn. He had just gone off sentry duty when the guerrillas attacked with mortar and cannon. The post was grossly undermanned, he said, and the troops ran for cover despite orders of their platoon commander to fire back from the trenches.

"I refused, because the enemy was already spraying the trenches with machine-gun fire and we couldn't even get into them. The commander jumped in alone and was wounded. All around me men were getting shot up. I grabbed my gun and ran into my tent—the other buildings had already been blown in by mortars. Within seconds, FRELIMO men were in the tent and I raised my hands and surrendered."

He said that he had been well-treated since his capture, and often had better food than the guerrillas themselves.

"I had not expected this. Things are not quite the same here as our officers had told us. They said that the blacks hated the whites, and that their only reason for taking prisoners was to eat them. None of it was true. When I was captured, the security men found a bed for me and slept on the ground themselves."

Santos Rosa said that he had been surprised by the close cooperation of the peasants with the rebels, despite the hardship that they were undergoing because of the war. He also noticed that the guerrillas never took food from civilians unless it was offered.

The next prisoner, Joao Borges Gomes, told me that he had been captured while on sentry duty at Nasupaku fort and had been wounded in the leg by a guerrilla grenade as he raced toward the trenches with a light machine-gun. When he saw an adjacent building blown in by rebel mortars, he crawled from the trench and surrendered.

Gomes, with his thin body and pale, anemic face, looked like a 15-year-old dressed up for war. He could not walk long distances, he said, because of grenade shrapnel still embedded in his thigh. The worst aspect of his months as a prisoner seemed to be loneliness for his mother back in Portugal's district of Braga. (Mondlane later told me that Gomes would soon be exchanged on medical grounds through the International Red Cross.) FRELIMO had done its best to treat his wound, Gomes said, and had given him first aid while still at the fort, then carried him for three days to a rebel field clinic where he had remained to recuperate. But they lacked the facilities to operate.

The other three, all deserters, were admittedly misfits in the army, and had walked off into the bush because their officers had treated them "like dogs." Americu de Sousa, who had spent seven years in the Portuguese army before deserting from Cabo Delgado's Mueda fort, told a long story of discrimination and "abuse" during his army days.

"They gave us physical education and sometimes it was just too much. We were pushed hard, and if we couldn't fulfill the demands, we were punished. If we refused to jump a five-foot trench or a fence lined with broken bottles, they beat us until our teeth were knocked out. When we protested, they beat us again for insolence. I was finally imprisoned for disobedience and after my release was continually harassed by my senior officers."

When de Sousa had first arrived in Mozambique for

army duty, "I didn't even know its boundaries. They sent me to Nampula fort up here in the North, then to Mueda. I still didn't know why I was fighting. Eventually I decided that I just couldn't take it anymore and I decided to desert. I persuaded my two friends to come with me.

"After we left the fort, we remained in the forest for three days without food, afraid of both the guerrillas and our own army. African civilians ran if they saw us, thinking that we were part of a patrol. We wanted to reach the Tanzanian border but we soon realized that FRELIMO would get us first."

De Sousa complained bitterly of what he called the "lack of political life in Portugal," saying that any public criticism of the regime would mean prison. "Until today, the ordinary people are still poor and still hungry. Instead of schools and hospitals, the government is paying for this stupid war."

The two other deserters, both called Manuel, said that they had fled to the bush for the same reasons as their friend—they had not been "respected as men" by their officers.

Manuel de Jesus Santos, age 22, said that he knew nothing about the existence of guerrillas when he had joined the army in Lourenço Marques, where he had been raised.

"At Mueda fort they told us that we would fight the Cubans, the Russians, the Chinese, and the Algerians. We didn't know a damned thing about the blacks." The war was "all right for the officers, but not for the other ranks," he added.

The remaining deserter, Manuel de Silva Lopes, said that after leaving Mueda the group followed the forest trails by day and at night slept huddled together. They carried only a radio and did not know how to trap game or find water. When FRELIMO confronted them, they were near exhaustion.

Simango later told me that FRELIMO regarded the prisoners as "simple men, not excessively intelligent for the most part," and that the offer by some to work for the guerrilla cause once they were set free was regarded with some skepticism.

"After all, they *are* prisoners, and may feel that we expect this of them. They are in a difficult position and all of us realize it."

He thought that the men's statements did, however, help to confirm reports of unrest and rebellion within the Portuguese army, and in particular among the lower ranks.

Three years after the war in Mozambique had begun, the Portuguese government admitted that 15,000 men had dodged conscription within the previous twelve months, and that hundreds more were deserting the army either in Portugal or in the African colonies. In proportion to her population, Portugal has the highest call-up for military service in the world and, although regarded as the most impoverished and backward of European countries, spends over 40 percent of her annual budget on fighting the black guerrillas. Portugal produces comparatively little war material herself and even the guerrillas mistrust weapons made in the motherland—"They don't fire when you need them most"—preferring instead the Belgian- and German-made guns that are captured in the field.

Although most guerrillas said that they were content with any weapon they were given, some of the men, when pressed, said that the Russian-made "A-K" and almost any make of machine-pistol was ideal for most forms of guerrilla warfare. They were small, light, and their range was adequate. Because of the chronic arms shortage, however, the cadres fought with anything that fired, including old World War II rifles and machine-guns.

9

WE ROSE WHILE THE MOON WAS STILL UP, DRESSING AND packing by the thin shafts that reached through the open doorway of our huts. Our flashlight batteries, replaced only a few nights before, had died of humidity and I stumbled around the hut in a vain effort to find our laundry of the night before.

Diolinda, who can undoubtedly see in the dark, whisked it out of a corner and into our packs, feeling her way around the ceiling in case we had left something behind. Within five minutes we were outside where Mijigo and several others were busily sorting out the stacks of military packs and civilian belongings that had been piled throughout the night in the village square.

It was to be a long column because many civilian newcomers, seeking the protection of an armed escort, had filtered into the village to await our departure. There was a babble of voices and laughter and the sound of trampling feet as Diolinda and I, still drowsy, swallowed a cup of Carnation Instant Breakfast and stumbled over children who sat huddled under blankets in the darkness.

There was a call to line up and we were assigned a position toward the front, just behind a cadre carrying a bazooka. Mijigo shone his flashlight around the huts and under trees, continually discovering somebody's belongings left behind in the darkness.

"What's this? What's this?" he would call, sweeping the light over little knapsacks tied up and sitting lonely in the moonlight. Their owners would dart forward to retrieve them, leaping from the column while the rest shuffled restlessly and shifted their packs. The villagers had gathered around to see us off and they stood sleepily in the shadows wrapped in their cotton cloaks. In another hour they would be leaving for their fields.

Suddenly we were ready and organized and we moved briskly out of the village with Mijigo in the lead. It would be a fast march at least until the sun rose, for he wanted to exploit the predawn coolness to cover as much ground as possible. I kept one eye on the almost invisible ribbon of path and the other on the bazooka directly ahead of me. Its owner carried it over his shoulder and when he turned suddenly in the dark, its long steel barrel gave me a vicious clip on the ear. Tiny bush mice scurried across our feet, flushed in chattering fright from their nests at the edge of the path. There seemed to be large families of them every few yards and they raised a twittering din of protest as they hurled their little bodies across our shoes. Horned owls watched from the trees overhead and the amber eyes of tiny animals flicked on and off in the thickets.

It was a strenuous pace until the sun rose, Mijigo and the men marching in long strides, effortlessly. We came upon an overgrown crossroad, incongruous in this wilderness where one had become accustomed to trails only. Twelve Portuguese soldiers had died here in a FRELIMO ambush while traveling from one fort to another, and the men suddenly became quiet as we descended into the tropical valley just beyond.

The dried, closely packed elephant grass towered over our heads and I was warned that the Portuguese could be laying an ambush here. The men flicked their guns off "safety" and we marched rapidly, silent and watchful and waiting. I heard the occasional clink of metal against metal as water bottles struck against each other. Mijigo, annoyed, signaled the offenders to adjust their equipment. Reconnaissance men had already gone ahead. But had they missed anything—a suspicious parting in the towering grass as the troops moved forward, a careless cough in the distance, the sudden flights of birds, or the call of monkeys that would warn the men of danger?

Only the soft swish of our canvas shoes was audible in the eerie silence of the valley. Even the locusts were silent. Barefooted women with infants tied in cloth slings across their backs and bulging knapsacks balanced on their heads hurried forward to keep up with the column. The babies were round-eyed and silent, feeling the tension in their mothers' backs as they half-ran toward safer ground. None whimpered or cried as we quickmarched another five miles then veered up and out of the valley toward new foothills and a chain of mountains beyond.

Some of the cadres in the rear dropped back to rest.

"Vamos, vamos!"—"Let's go, let's go," snapped Mijigo and the stragglers hurried forward to rejoin us. Not until we were well out of the valley were the thermoses brought out as the commander permitted us a brief rest.

But he was not at ease, and he hovered about or circled the knots of resting men, his eyes sweeping the forest around us.

"We must move," he announced suddenly, and the column hastily reassembled and pushed ahead toward the mountains. It was an uphill march from then on and the footing grew more precarious as the terrain changed and well-worn paths disappeared. We scrambled up endless, almost perpendicular, ridges and wedged our feet onto rocks

90

and ledges, searching for a natural ladder. When the ground evened out, the women bounded along like brown deer, their thin legs flashing and their children clinging to their backs with tiny fists.

Oozing sweat and effort, the men with bazookas and machine-guns, their packs swaying, scrambled past us up the punishing mountainside, arm and leg muscles bulging with strain and blue veins standing out in knots on their brown necks. Mijigo, already at the top, was perched on a rock and looked down on us with amused sympathy as we stumbled toward the top. Although most of the men had loosened their shirts or slung them across their packs, Cornelio remained encased in his leather jacket and fur-lined cap, only his fogged-up glasses giving some indication of the intense heat that must be building up inside all of those layers. He jumped nimbly from rock to rock and hauled me up behind him. Trojan-like, Diolinda pushed on determinedly and in silence, all of her will concentrated in reaching the top.

"Cornelio," I said crossly, irritated by the heat and flies and the misery of the climb, "my arm is being pulled from its socket and you are going to die of heat in that jacket." He laughed and went on humming some *kwela* that I liked.

Cornelio had a fund of stories about the revolution and the people that he liked to tell me as we marched. Usually I was too preoccupied with reaching our destination to listen carefully enough and I always asked him to repeat them during our stops at the wayside or after we had settled into camp.

From Cornelio I learned, besides the more relevant information about the revolution, various tidbits about tribal life, including the fact that villagers didn't kiss but that town Africans did, that Moslems in Mozambique still maintained three or four wives, and that Makondes used a herbal anesthetic to pierce their upper lip during puberty ceremonies.

As we struggled up the mountainside, Cornelio started on the subject of cannibalism, which he and the other men thought an enormous joke when speaking among themselves, but which annoyed them considerably when outsiders took it seriously. I asked Cornelio what he knew about the subject.

"We Africans haven't eaten anybody in 500 years," he said. Besides, "that sort of thing happened only in West Africa."

I said that the West Africans insisted that it was an East African practice.

"Absolutely not," said Cornelio. "They don't know what they are talking about."

"What about Mozambicans?" I went on.

"We only eat people who cannot climb mountains," he said, and with a final pull we were over the top and joined Mijigo.

Our immediate destination was a militia center to be used as a base camp while touring the operational and training headquarters in Cabo Delgado, along with typical inland villages where I was to watch blacks living in cruel poverty listen attentively to Mijigo as he lectured about emergency precautions in case of napalm and poison gas raids. We trekked through green meadows and along the shores of a still inland lake. Its surface was broken by reeds and water lilies and it was used as a communal bath by militia and villagers. At the far end of the lake was a breeding ground for crocodiles. The cadres told me that neither side interfered with the other; if a crocodile did happen to stray out of his territory he was clubbed or shot to death, although the men were loathe to use up ammunition in this way.

Hidden away on the hillside, the militia center was like all wartime African villages that I had seen—so well camouflaged as to be impossible to find unless guided there. Invariably they were built of the same materials as their surroundings. Giant trees with overlapping branches formed a natural roof under the sky, a reason why Portuguese pilots preferred taking African informers along on reconnaissance flights.

The camp was under strong guard for several miles around and we passed knots of militia far from the entrance to the village. Some of their children carried bows and arrows, having shaped the arrowheads from scrap metal or spent bullets. I was told that a skilled archer could "pierce the abdomen" of the enemy at long distances and that adult militiamen, if short of guns, sometimes used them against raiding troops.

The militia camp was in a cool, tree-shaded village with the usual outdoor table and assembly ground nearby. Here the village elders, and later local guerrilla representatives with them, gathered for palavers (talks) that sometimes lasted a week. The men told me that when discussing a problem, African villagers will sit for hours, days if necessary, until a solution can be agreed upon. There is no time limit for speakers, which leaves everyone with the impression that he has gotten his point across, and all aspects of an argument are examined. Anyone may express his ideas, however irrelevant or nonconstructive they may be.

When the palaver is finally concluded, the participants are either exhausted or convinced into a line of action. Unanimity is sought but if this fails, the opinion of the majority is adopted and all are expected to conform to the decision. If the agreement later proves unworkable or dissident groups arise, another palaver under the trees is called and the process begins once again.

The Africans felt that this was a comparatively sane method of settling disputes and also insured that complaints did not simmer too long.

The members of FRELIMO's militia in the liberated zones are all civilians who can handle arms, although their training period has been shorter than that of a guerrilla.

Their main duties include defense of their home regions, reinforcement of guerrilla units should the enemy be planning a local attack, and the organization of supplies and information about enemy movements. Once the guerrillas have freed and consolidated a region under FRELIMO control, the militia are expected to replace them while they push on to new zones.

As part of the local civilian population acting as an arm of the political and military spine, they are also expected to help maintain the enthusiasm and morale of a people continually subject to attack.

The next day I watched FRELIMO organizers in action at a bush rally five miles from our camp. With our usual group headed by Mijigo was the village headman called Dadi Salimu, whose two wives had already welcomed us to the area with locally grown cashew nuts heaped on tin plates. The women were a comely pair, with large brown eyes and long legs. Each wore a necklace of tiny blue stones around her neck and her best dress. They accompanied their husband on the walk to the village and joined us on the benches reserved for guests of honor.

A makeshift stage had been constructed of bamboo and woven straw and around it in a circle on the ground sat over 200 Africans, the children in the front and the adults in tightly packed rows behind them. One child held a baby monkey which urinated copiously and flung its arms around its owner's neck when anyone attempted to pet it.

The crowd sat in silence, adjusting their rags around them and leaning their chins on bony, drawn-up knees. They had been waiting for some time and after the first burst of applause at Mijigo's arrival, settled back into a kind of weary torpor. Then Dadi Salimu went to work.

He ambled into the center of the circle, glared at the wretches before him, and suddenly laughed gently. There was a lone giggle from the back row and then silence again. The crowd shifted. Dadi Salimu leapt onto the little stage and shrieked the Makonde *"Mashala!"* and in one bound was back on the ground again. The adults stirred, aroused, and the children laughed. Dadi Salimu twirled his little knitted cap and hollered *"Mashala! Mashala! Mashala!"* The sea of black faces shrieked in answer, wiggling with pleasure as he leapt at them and raced back to the center of the circle, twisting and roaring as he went. He jerked his body into a kind of buck and wing and later through a shuffling dance as the crowd, shouting with laughter, clapped in unison and beat time on the ground with sticks. They had forgotten their hunger and all of their sacrifices and they could not tear their eyes away from the charismatic figure in the little woolen cap. It was as if all the children's bloated abdomens existed no more under their burlap gowns, as if the thin flailing arms were not their own as they pounded the ground with their fists.

Then, their enthusiasm reaching near-frenzy, they could listen for the next two hours with rapt attention as Dadi Salimu, Mijigo, and Raoul talked to them about FRELIMO, independence, and the eventual rout of the Portuguese. But in the meantime, the movement would need all the support that they could give to enable its guerrillas to succeed. This included a greater crop yield so that they could become more self-sufficient and improve their living standard, more volunteers for FRELIMO's supply lines, and most of all, the realization that the war would be long and that their courage must be maintained.

Mijigo then warned them to expect more air raids, especially with napalm, and quite possibly with poison gas which intelligence reports said might soon be introduced. If burned by napalm, he told them, roll in the sand until the flames are extinguished. If attacked with poison gas, "urinate on your cloth and hold it over your face." The children giggled.

As one speaker after another took the platform, the villagers began to glance worriedly at dark, low-lying clouds that signaled an oncoming tropical storm. When it struck there would not be the first warning raindrops, but a sudden avalanche of driving rain. The crowd shifted restlessly, shivering as they drew their rags tighter around themselves. The monkey burrowed further into its owner's arms, peering out apprehensively with eyes like amber discs.

But there were still their own problems to discuss and one by one, individuals from the crowd moved inside the circle to speak. There were cries of "Yes, yes," from onlookers and intermittent applause as a speaker touched a nerve. They began to chant and clap and an elderly woman shuffled toward the center where she stood, immovable, until someone led her away still mumbling. "She's insane," Cornelio told me.

Others leapt into the circle while guerrillas watched and listened. One middle-aged man suddenly stood up in his place and screamed to me: "We are hungry, Mama, we are hungry and there are no shoes. Look at us, Mama, send us shoes and clothes! Look at this child!"

He grabbed one off the ground, wrapped in a potato sack, and yanked it into the air. Its thin arms waved and its gray legs shot earthward for support. "Help us! Help us! Help us!"

"There's always one like you," shouted a chorus from the back. "Where is your courage? We must help ourselves first."

There was a mumble of scorn and assent and someone broke into the FRELIMO anthem. The storm struck as the last chorus ended and the crowd scrambled toward the trees for shelter, a rush of elbows and long, running legs, cloaks streaming.

Mijigo told me that African villagers were very susceptible to high fever when chilled, for they had no dry clothing into which to change and were often caught far from their huts during the sudden African downpours. These chills usually stimulated attacks of malaria, he said.

As we trudged back toward camp in the rain, our hair

96

and uniforms smelling of earth and humidity, I realized how distressing must be the task of FRELIMO's director of social affairs, a 29-year-old Makonde called Jonas Namashulua. I had met him just before crossing into Mozambique where we had dinner at a fly-blown restaurant a few hours from the frontier. His kind, deeply scarred face radiated continual concern for charges under him. His job was to find food, clothing, and shelter for African villagers shifted from one region to another because of the war.

Tanzania, he told me, has a refugee program on its own side of the frontier for fleeing Mozambicans where, with UN assistance, they are fed and sheltered in camps.

Inside Mozambique, however, there is no assistance from international bodies for displaced persons in any of the three fighting provinces, which means that FRELIMO must shoulder full responsibility with very limited financial resources.

"When a village is burned," Jonas said, "the people leave with nothing. We have to give them even the hoes for their new *shambas* (gardens) and organize volunteers to help them build new shelters. One mud and wattle hut can take six months to build if a family has much work in the fields. These people have to eat every day and have somewhere to sleep, especially during the rainy season. Imagine confronting a fresh stream of refugees, without even blankets, who have sometimes walked a hundred miles with their women and children and you don't even have a tent to give them. And they never have any food, not even a bag of rice.

"Although some of the socialist countries do try to help us in this," Jonas said, "we are trying to encourage our people to be self-reliant as well," adding that refugees outside the country are being urged to return to Mozambique.

Jonas is also responsible for sorting out housing and rehabilitation for the war disabled. A one-legged man, he said, can learn many trades including tailoring, shoemaking, and carpentry, these craftsmen being in short supply in the country. Unfortunately, he said, there was a grave shortage of essential teaching materials, such as proper carpentry tools, weaving machines, and thread—and one cannot make shoes and clothing without tanners and spinning facilities.

He said that church groups outside the country had so far refused help to Mozambicans in the liberated areas, as had international aid organizations in the West. There were certain private groups in the United States and Scandinavia which had given some assistance to these refugees, however.

But on the theory that outsiders help those who help themselves, FRELIMO was insisting that its people return from neighboring countries and help to reconstruct their country along with the rest, however pitiful the resources and depressing the implications of this task might seem. I also suspected that neighboring countries, however friendly toward the movement they are, have found the presence of so many refugees a nagging burden on their own underdeveloped economies.

I had talked at length with Eduardo Mondlane about these and other problems, including the price being paid by friendly border countries for their help to the movement.

Besides the occasional strafing of their own frontier villages and the resulting civilian casualties among non-Mozambicans, there were substantial risks being taken economically, and Zambia was a case in point.

Although technically independent since the crackup of the former Federation of the two Rhodesias and Nyasaland, landlocked Zambia must still channel much of her raw material and copper ore through hostile Southern Rhodesia for finishing or export via rail links with the Mozambican port of Beira in Portuguese territory.

Before Zambian independence, the entire system had been structured that way, with the nerve center in Southern Rhodesia where the Federation had its headquarters and where the majority of Rhodesian whites held financial and farming interests.

FRELIMO is dependent upon Zambian good will for access to the Mozambican province of Tete, when at any time Zambia's trade route could be blocked and her economy throttled by Portugal's allies in Southern Rhodesia.

There is no doubt that Portuguese interests coincide with those of white-run Rhodesia and South Africa when the question of black revolt arises. Any allied territory lopped off by the guerrillas in Mozambique brings the war closer to Salisbury and Pretoria, a creeping conflagration that would be better contained in Portuguese Mozambique.

With Eduardo I was to sense the same disappointment with the West, where he had been educated, married, and settled for several years. Eduardo came from the Limpopo Valley region in Southern Mozambique, about 50 miles from Lourenço Marques. He had grown up as a herdsman in a family of fifteen children and his mother, whom he called a "remarkable woman" had sent him at great financial sacrifice to a primary mission school. But as an African, he was later barred from government-run secondary education in Mozambique.

After teaching himself English, however, he attended a South African secondary school on scholarship, then went on to Witwatersrand University there. Eventually he managed a journey to America where he took a Ph.D. in sociology and worked for the United Nations Trusteeship Department.

He seemed as much a product of Midwestern America as of Mozambique, the impact of the American environment giving him a deceptively casual approach to complex problems, an American accent, and an easy rapport with Europeans. He understood them and was their bridge toward understanding Mozambique's misery.

For all of his bigness and bulk and sophistication, however, one felt that Eduardo was peculiarly vulnerable in the personal sense, and acutely sensitive to atmosphere. He had trained himself to speak in public after painful early experience. He told me that during his first public speech at the age of 18 he had burst into tears in fright and embarrassment.

I found this image a difficult contrast with the self-confident revolutionary leader who loped across the stage in Khartoum early in 1969 to tell a friendly conference of the moral and material help still needed by black African liberation movements.

He was interrupted only once, when a fuse blew like a grenade in a translator's booth, sending acrid fumes and blue smoke after the running bystanders. "I hope the enemy is not among us," quipped Mondlane as the tense audience relaxed. Two weeks later he was blown up by a TNT charge while working at his desk.

I had asked Mondlane about FRELIMO's political orientation and how he envisaged the state after liberation. What of his own ideology? He chose his words carefully.

"If I define myself as a progressive," Mondlane said, "it would mean different things in the East and the West. In relation to freedom for my own country, I am a radical. I want freedom now, and I am able to throw myself completely into whatever phase we have reached. A revolution has several stages, and in this one Mozambique is at war. Later comes the reconstruction on the mass scale that only the state can completely accomplish.

"We don't apologize for this war, for it is a fact. The Portuguese chose it. If there had been a possibility for negotiated independence we would have accepted it, and the Portuguese knew it. But this possibility does not exist and we cannot operate on the assumption that it might.

"We are a people's political movement, a fusion and not an alliance. I insist at this stage on a political line, but I am against a strict ideological line for its own sake.

100

"The political question is: 'Does a country stay under foreign control or is it given over to that of its own people?' The question is not one of socialism or capitalism, but the assumption that people want freedom. Once you assume this you gradually reach the second stage and educate them as to what kind of freedom is wanted."

His own ideas of self-determination included ". . . the reorganization of our economy to eliminate the use of our resources by outsiders without benefit to ourselves. The people themselves must control these through democratically elected institutions, which in turn distribute the gains and make available various services to the masses, such as schools and social services."

Mondlane believed that foreign capital could definitely play a role in the new Mozambique, but only insofar as it had been invited to do so by the "people's institutions." The role of foreign capital would be defined, however—to launch "initiative," but not to control the resources.

"I think of other African states which invite foreign capital from both East and West. There is no reason why we should not. If they tried to undermine us, however, we would act."

I asked him under what terms a peace with Portugal might be negotiated. "I would definitely reject partition or self-government under Portuguese control," Mondlane said. "And the Portuguese must be *out,* except for those who are part of Mozambique and who would remain there as citizens to be treated as any other."

Did he believe that white Portuguese Mozambicans would break away from the Portuguese motherland and declare unilateral independence if they objected to home policy on black overseas colonies? Mondlane was doubtful—there were only about 200,000 whites and secession from Portugal would propel a weak, local white administration even further under South African influence, perhaps to be eventually dominated by her. This would be inevitable because of South Africa's highly developed resources and efficient war machine, a necessary ally in the face of black revolt.

Further, it had always been South Africa's policy, he believed, to keep the shooting war as far as possible from her own borders and to use the Portuguese territories as shock absorbers, even to the point of sending her own troops there.

The stiffening of the Portuguese counterrevolution was not, therefore, a question of good neighborliness or white racial alliances, but one of calculated national interest on the part of South Africa.

Mondlane thought that her degree of direct involvement would depend upon her own internal security at the time, and black insurgent action within her own boundaries would certainly step up that degree.

What of the progress of the war from FRELIMO's viewpoint?

Mondlane admitted that "emotional and physical involvement" was currently more widespread in Cabo Delgado than in Niassa province, where depopulation had left only a quarter million people and distances between remaining villages were sometimes a three-day march.

The movement was concentrating heavily on Tete, the thickly populated key province in Western Mozambique thrusting inland along frontiers with Southern Rhodesia, Zambia, and Malawi. The guerrillas had already reached the area around the Cabora Bassa dam site, the Zambezi river in the hinterland, and had set up headquarters in its very heart. Supplies were still a problem, "but we always manage," he said.

One thought of the crippling tonnage hauled in on thin backs; dismantled iron cannons, heavy bazooka shells, steel ammunition cases, the spindlelegged carriers creeping through the lines by night and hiding in the woodlands by day, scratching out edible roots from the forest floor to conserve their meager rice supply. If the rivers were dry and the wells polluted, then weakened black bodies, malaria, and tse-tse.

I had seen a sleeping sickness victim, a wasted horror nodding in the dim interior of a low hut. There had been no drugs to help him and he sat crosslegged over a smoking calabash, drawing warmth from the flickering fire underneath. Four hours later, on our return, he had flopped over on his side, dying like a thin brown cat in the dark tunnel that was his hut. "The end of all things human," Marcelino had told me, and with a sigh he signaled me to join the waiting column.

10

MIJIGO'S HEADQUARTERS LOOKED MUCH LIKE ANY OTHER straw village in the Mozambican bush, except that sleeping huts were more widely spaced and there was an air of brisk military efficiency. Nothing more permanent than huts had been constructed because headquarters could be shifted at any time. There seemed more transistor radios than usual in evidence, and each three or four huts had their own dining table and clothesline.

I had already been led to one of FRELIMO's bush armories where, stacked in a clearing, recently captured arms had been displayed for my benefit. There were German-made bazookas, Belgian rifles, Mausers and Marcips, Berettas and old Lee-Enfields. They had been captured during ambushes or from the forts and Mijigo told me, "Our intention is to take everything the enemy has, including their helmets."

But captured camouflage kits went to the militia because they had no other clothing.

The man in charge of training both militia and guerrilla units in Cabo Delgado was a 26-year-old Mozambican called Joachim Manuel, a slender, dark-brown cadre in canvas shoes.

"Guerrilla warfare is conceptually one of hit and run," Joachim began. "Being far outnumbered by the enemy under normal circumstances, a fighter is taught to gnaw and jab at the opponent, to strike when he least expects it and to avoid direct confrontations whenever possible."

But if he nibbles at the enemy's flank, he said, or strikes at his fortresses, he must also be prepared for quick pursuit. This means that the guerrilla, already fatigued by the march toward the target, must have enough stamina in reserve not only to engage the enemy, but to disengage himself and run for long distances over unknown terrain, by day or night, after an attack has been completed.

The enemy, with his modern radio communications, spotter aircraft, and helicopter support, can quickly recover from an attack if his presence of mind has not been lost in the process, continued Joachim.

Despite the average African's staying-power, therefore, and his ability to cover long distances without apparent fatigue, the guerrillas are put through a gymnastics course even before entering basic training.

Then, with the militia who receive the same preliminary instruction as the new guerrilla recruits, the groups are put through a five-week program which includes armshandling, ambush tactics, and general strategy. In this accelerated course, they are also taught how to work if confronted when alone by an enemy patrol, how and where to hide, and how to disappear rapidly through the forests if pursued.

Joachim said that his recruits had to be toughened quickly, and trainers are told to march them across all kinds of terrain, under varied climatic conditions where possible. They are denied drinking water although wading across a stream, the object being to acquire enough discipline to forgo touching water that the enemy may have poisoned, however vague this suspicion may be.

The marches are organized daily, and at longer stretches, until the cadre can walk up to fifteen hours without a pause or, in the case of a forced march, twelve hours. This also means no food or water along the route.

Later, some of the more tireless cadres are assigned to communications work as "runners" from one base to another. FRELIMO field officers avoid radio communications because of enemy proximity, and all battle orders and other relevant information are carried by hand, he concluded.

A good runner can cover 50 miles in a day, through bush, sand, reeds, and jungle; he also acts as the local postman between villages if he can be cajoled into carrying private mail in his briefcase. This bush post is surprisingly efficient and a letter can reach the border from far inland in only a few days if the sender is fortunate enough to encounter a runner willing to carry it.

I often saw a communications man sprinting through a village and out onto the footpaths, pausing only to hand over a crumpled wad of correspondence and stuff another set into his briefcase for a destination farther on. Each base has its own liaison man who operates within his own sector and between the operations officers of other sectors. If a small-scale ambush is planned, each sector plans and carries out its own. For larger operations, however, the provincial commander will send runners to call in the commandants in all regions and together they coordinate the attack. The time necessary in planning an operation will depend upon the depth of reconnaissance need. If this is badly done, the attack will often end in failure, no matter how skilled its execution or how courageous the individual guerrilla involved.

Joachim said that in zones heavily overrun with FRE-LIMO guerrillas, the Portuguese troops rarely leave their posts except on patrols in the immediate vicinity, and never with a force of less than 24. However, they seemed almost ignorant of counterguerrilla tactics and if they did decide to encircle a FRELIMO stronghold their strength was rarely less than 150 men.

He attributed what he called Portuguese reluctance to mount all-out offensives to their fear of cutting themselves off from reinforcements by leaving the fort area, their lack of training in bush warfare, their low morale, and their inability to avoid black civilian vigilance.

Joachim set up a simulated bayonet charge for me to see, first distributing his trainees in the woodland around the grove where I was standing. It was almost dusk and in an instant their childish, gentle faces had disappeared into the bush, the muted green of their uniforms dissolving in the forest backdrop. Their arms became gnarled vines twisting up a tree trunk, their peaked caps the thrusting beak of a woodland bird. I was to be the fort, the enemy.

As I bent to examine a shoelace, the guerrillas burst from the bush in attack formation and galloped toward me with fixed bayonets, screeching *"Ciao!"* and *"Ya-a-a!"* and jabbing at the air and bearing down on me with murderous, twisted faces.

I had a strong desire to break and run, as wave after wave of contorted faces swerved around me and into the forest beyond, the force of the onslaught throwing up the earth and dust around me. It was over in seconds and I was speechless as they emerged grinning from their cover.

I wondered what the reaction of their enemy must be as they crouched in the carapace of their lonely forts, confronted with the spectacle of ragged and enraged guerrillas bearing down on them howling *"Ciao!"* in the middle of the night.

Normally, FRELIMO does not attack a fort with the intention of occupying it, but of forcing the enemy out permanently. The guerrillas then carry off anything portable and either burn the fort or permit it to decay naturally. If neglected for more than a few months in the fierce African rains, a structure quickly sags and crumbles. Occupying an abandoned fort is not necessary for FRELIMO's administrative purposes, and to do so would merely invite enemy bombardment when the movement's antiaircraft guns are needed elsewhere.

That evening, in a small camp built against the mountainside, I said a last goodbye to some of FRELIMO's officers, including Mijigo, who were to march farther inland to a fort that the Portuguese had just abandoned for no apparent reason. That same afternoon, reconnaissance men had arrived with sheafs of papers, including military documents, that had been left behind by the troops. There had been no recent attack against this post by FRELIMO—perhaps it was a trap, perhaps reinforcements were needed elsewhere.

Whatever the motive, it meant another chunk of territory falling into rebel hands, another block of African villages to administer, more homeless refugees turned back on FRELIMO with stories to tell and stomachs to fill—problems for the planning committees but an overall advance for the movement.

As our column prepared to move off for the long trek back to the border, I turned and saw Mijigo standing in the rain. I was suddenly filled with despair and cowardice on their behalf and Mijigo saw it immediately.

"Friends should smile when they say goodbye," he said. I nodded and shook hands and walked back toward the column.

"*Senhora*," he called after us, "we are going to survive."

Soon he and the camp had merged into the mountainside, swallowed in the protective strata of forest. Mijigo had told me that the return march would seem less arduous and I soon realized that he had been right—the now familiar bush, the fog lifting in the early morning over the valleys, the murmur of civilians and carriers as we threaded toward the frontier.

The trek was marked only by my first direct encounter with bush rats; one of the village huts occupied by Diolinda and myself during an overnight stop was infested with a lively family of them.

Mama and Papa rat had built a conical nest under the rush ceiling where the roof came to a peak. It looked like an inverted beehive and the pair had populated it liberally with tiny prodigy which slumbered through the hot afternoon with only an occasional squeak.

By nightfall, the nest bulged with activity and the scuffling of feet looking for a toehold. There were rasping sounds and muffled twitters of anger when the father plopped in with choice morsels. He apparently had assistance from relatives as fully grown as himself, for there seemed a steady column of furry gray rodents running across the overhead beams and I was certain that they couldn't all be the same rat. They grew larger as the shadows deepened.

Mealtime was apparently a lengthy affair up there for rending and chomping noises continued for over an hour. To my discomfiture, the extinguishing of our oil lamp was a signal, not for the cessation of activity by all occupants of the hut, but for a determined search farther afield for extra food supplies.

In the dark the crunching noises grew nearer and Diolinda's bottle of hair oil fell over with a thump, accompanied by the sound of running feet along the ledges. I sensed, rather than heard, a slight movement within my pack on the sandy floor beside me. As I turned over in my bunk, the rat scurried across the ground and up the bamboo walls. I could hear his nails hook onto the top of the nest and the furry plop as he landed among his chittering infants. A long silence followed and I hoped that he would be too intimidated to venture out again. It was already 2 A.M. and we would be up at six.

I had read somewhere that hungry rats are capable of attacking infants and even sleeping adults, first injecting a kind of anesthetic into the selected spot with their teeth; the victim realized what had happened only on awakening.

My problem was that I was covered with a somewhat short sheet which, if pulled over my head, left bare legs exposed from the knees down, an invitation to a rat if there ever was one. Ten toes to choose from and I wouldn't know my loss until morning. To cover my legs, however, meant exposure of my face, and I lay in the dark worrying about my nose, especially.

I decided that I could go through life without the toes but not the nose and pulled the sheet over my head. I had just begun to doze off when I heard the familiar sound of quiet groping on the beam directly above. Apparently the rat suddenly lost his toehold for he plopped onto my bare legs with all his furry weight. I was faster than he, for I was out of bed and across the floor before he had made it back to the nest, twittering with alarm all the way.

I grabbed for my flashlight and shone it onto floor, walls, and ceiling, the beam following fast-moving rats as they scampered for home. Diolinda, meanwhile, slept through it all, her face calm and undisturbed.

As I sat on the edge of the bunk, my bare legs folded under, I decided that there were four solutions to the problem: I could smoke them out of the nest, poke it down with a long stick, fire a burst with Diolinda's Marcip which stood in the corner, or pretend that they were not there.

If I did the first, I would wake Diolinda and possibly set the hut afire. The second solution might burst the nest asunder and bring an enraged colony of rats tumbling down around us, and the third would bring every guerrilla within five miles into the village on enemy alert, possibly dispatching a runner for reinforcements. The only solution lay in the fourth course and I rolled myself into a ball under the sheet, cramped but reasonably safe. By the time they gnawed through the material I hoped that I would notice.

Morning came without further incident and I was among the first out for coffee. A knot of men had already gathered at the all-purpose table, sleepy and unusually quiet. Raoul, whose eyes could barely focus, had propped his elbows on the tabletop and held his chin up in his hands.

I made no mention of the rats. The villagers had already given over their sleeping quarters to us and it was hardly the time for a lecture on the rat menace. This was the only village in which I had encountered them, and perhaps the inhabitants had hit upon some form of mutual tolerance.

The huts had been clean and swept and the bedding spotless, and to remind my hosts about the rats in their house seemed incredibly ungrateful. There was no pesticide to be had for several hundred miles around and perhaps, like me, they shrank from poking about with a stick.

Raoul then announced with a groan that he hadn't slept all night because of rat noises in his hut and had spent the entire time shining his flashlight around the corners. The other guerrillas also reported brisk activity with the exception of Cornelio who said that he had slept like a baby and, in fact, had never felt so refreshed in some time.

"Of course you were all right," I told him. "You probably slept in that leather jacket and cap with the earflaps down." He denied this indignantly and after I had completed my own tale said that, in anticipation of unexpected disturbances such as this, he always slept rolled up in his blanket, like a cigar, and kept his head under as well.

"Then how do you breathe?" I asked.

"Oh, I breathe," he replied, "I breathe." Cornelio, who had obviously worked out some system of his own for bush survival, was the brightest among us that day, his face glowing with rest and well-being.

Our last stop before the frontier was in a circle of huts which seemed inhabited primarily by women and children. The official greeter was a smiling, wide-hipped Makonde in her midthirties who, I learned, was the chief of a mobilization unit in her region. Her husband had been at the ever-shifting front for almost two years, and in the meantime she had become absorbed in the revolution.

In Raoul's opinion, she was one of the best mobilizers that FRELIMO had, a dynamic speaker and a tireless worker. She wore a scoop-necked flowered dress, gathered at the waist, which reached almost to her ankles.

She moved energetically among us with bare feet, shaking hands with some, slapping others on the back with bone-shaking verve. She had apparently rejected certain tribal traditions, at least the more obvious ones, for she had removed the metal peg from her upper lip. The result was a gaping hole through which the teeth and tongue were visible as she made her gregarious way through the group. In a country where the crippled and the maimed and the ugly are fitted naturally, somehow, into the social structure, this defect seemed so minor that it soon went unnoticed.

Her eyes were full of merriment and natural humor and she joked almost nonstop with the men, slapping her thigh and bending double at each witty remark, literally rocking with laughter.

Her eyes suddenly flicked sideways and she snatched up a hen as it ran past us bent on some destination of its own.

"Here's dinner," she announced, and one of the men carried it off toward the calabashes, grabbing an axe along the way. She decided that I must be tired after the march and, taking my hand, bundled me off to a hut for a predinner nap. There, a tiny lamp fired with palm oil burned on a bare wooden table beside a freshly made bunk.

She loomed large and efficient in its glow and perched on the edge of my bed as I eased my throbbing legs into the most comfortable position. She told me a story in Makonde, which I didn't understand, laughing gleefully all the while; then, noticing an involuntary twitch in my calf muscles because of cramp, sprang across the room for what turned out

112

to be a bottle of liniment which she indicated that she was about to apply liberally.

I remember being very grateful but she had hardly twisted the cap off when I was asleep. She thought this a tremendous joke on herself, apparently, for she told the story at dinner as we gnawed the last morsels from the unfortunate chicken's bones. Whatever remnants remained would be pecked at later by the other hens who had already gathered expectantly a safe distance from the table.

One of the more welcome gifts in a Mozambican village was a live chicken, for the flocks were not numerous. The meat shortage meant that they ended in the cooking pot almost before they began laying eggs.

Villagers traveling long distances often carried the night's meal, live, under their arms, and sometimes I saw guerrilla columns carry a hen or two along with the mortars.

At first I had not understood the significance of the chicken gift, a true indication of friendship, and promptly handed one back to a startled headman who had presented it to me in the name of some villagers during a little official ceremony one particularly humid afternoon.

I did not know how to handle hens, and sensing it, they usually gave me sharp little pecks in the hands. This particular one, a tiny white pullet, had set up a tremendous din as we stood sweating in a clearing and, grasping my fingers with its talons, had emitted loud squawks while its wings beat and the feathers flew. The moment the headman took it back, it snuggled into his arms, its frightened eyes drooping again.

Shortly after dawn next morning we had reached the border and the canoes, only a thin strip of winding river separating us from two wholly different concepts of government.

Our destination, on the other side, was independent Tanzania with its attempts to nudge its patient and fatalistic villagers from their Adam and Eve existences.

Numbed by generations in mud and wattle huts, they now sent their children to school and at the same time, through village cooperatives and industrial planning, were being urged to drag themselves through the social and cultural upheaval that survival as a nation in the twentieth century demanded.

Coaxing, threatening, demanding, commanding, Nyerere knows that there may not be another chance, and that if the parents cannot make it, perhaps the children can. Years of change and tiresome bureaucratic messes and poverty-line existence still lie ahead, enemies within and without; the trade problem, the Indian problem, the unemployment problem, and too few trained Africans yet to fill efficiently the administrative gaps. But the problems are national problems, black problems, pan-African problems, being coped with by black leaders.

In Portuguese-held Mozambique there are undoubtedly whites, as there are in South Africa and Southern Rhodesia, who sincerely believe that the average black African is a contented man, and that the colonizer not the colonized knows what is best for him.

The contrary opinion, of course, does not appear on the blank, closed faces of the black miner, the streetsweeper, the gardener, or the domestic. Dissension is quickly sniffed out and it could well mean unemployment, withdrawal of a pass, arrest on charges of sympathizing with an underground organization, or "resettlement"—that euphemism for banishment.

It is difficult to believe, moreover, that the urge to revolt would be so widespread if the picture presented by the paternalistic white governments was accurate. A mobilization team can talk endlessly, and with no effect at all, unless a nerve is hit, a familiar problem driven out into the open by those more articulate.

The mass, that most conservative of all units which, by its very nature, searches for its own safety valves, its own escape hatches—anything to avoid the physical and emotional expenditure which it knows in its bones is necessary to sustain a revolt—does not rise unless it has seen for itself the absence of any alternative except war to insure its own survival. It knows this by instinct, finally—but it needs the nucleus of a confident leadership to weld it together.

When the village headman ponders, then tells the mobilizer, "What you have said is true, but they are stronger than we," and the mobilizer, slowly and carefully and gently drives home the lesson of the staggering strength of a unified underdog, the first puff of rebellion blows among the calabashes and down the forest tracks.

Like insidious woodland spirits who appear when least expected, the *yirans* of revolt move as shadows in the tangle of the bush, nagging and crying on the riverbanks. They may disappear for a time, but every villager knows that they always return.

"But the natives are happy!" exclaims a white settler or businessman, for he has never seen their other face. He is safe in the knowledge of those gentle, contented tribesmen in their conical huts, or the black townsmen who remove themselves after work to some distant shantytown where they presumably dwell in contentment because "they are not accustomed to anything better."

After all, they have always preferred their own witch doctors, their own mealie, and their bare feet. It is quite true that they are not accustomed to anything better; they are, however, aware of something better.

And the next question is: after so many years of white government rule, with its pledge to civilize and Christianize its black charges, why are they *not* accustomed to anything better in Mozambique or Angola or Portuguese Guinea or in Rhodesia or South Africa? I can only wonder at the patience of their black populations who have waited so long to be "civilized."

What impressed outsiders like me was how quickly they

had "learned" in Mozambique's liberated zones—how appreciative they were of shoes, even of plastic sandals—and how much clothing was prized at the local barter shops.

What pathetic yearning for education they possessed, the gaunt adults in the guerrilla-held zones who sat mumbling their lessons from battered primary schoolbooks.

They looked like spent beasts of burden, living rebukes to a colonial system which had taken and never given. I wondered if they had truly understood what they had been deprived of, what opportunities they could have been given, what deliberate injustices they had been done, not in the day-to-day sense that their narrow experience had quickly taught them, but in the things that would dignify and give meaning to their lives.

I saw this knowledge, and the rage that follows, on only a few faces, usually within the leadership. For the rest there was the same benevolent calmness so easily mistaken for childlike simplicity, but which in fact is the final purification of a martyred race. They will win one day, by sheer endurance—ironically the only weapon that their governments have permitted them to develop.

Some nations, *in extremis,* turn in upon themselves in their awful misery. These people, by a quality of character shaped through centuries of nonpossession, seemed to have emerged from that trial with almost unearthly charity.

Those last miles to the border and my own familiar world again went almost unmarked by me. I had left Mateos, our platoon leader, in his billed cap and camouflage dress on the opposite bank, and somewhere in the blue outlines of the mountain chain far beyond were Mijigo and his men, Augustino and Pavlina, and the clearing where 200 intent villagers had to be told the drill when the napalm fell. I had left behind the bare feet and mealie and the perpetual hardship which these people took for granted with their wretched little knapsacks and mortality rates and dignity.

I was amazed at the sense of personal loss that came over

me, and the guilt that I felt for walking away from them, and from Diolinda and Cornelio who had coped and never complained.

How often I recall the law that no one survives guerrilla life alone. I know that I could not have survived it without them. But most of all I remember the faces, the trusting, expectant faces as they drilled and trained and sang their victory song on humid afternoons as the sunflecks shifted across the forest floor. It would be difficult to forget, for one day they had given me a small wooden statue of a gazelle, carved in the bush, and in it the maker had placed a tiny *yiran* of revolt.

Portuguese Guinea

11

ACROSS THE BREADTH OF AFRICA TO THE WEST AND UP THE
coast past the Cameroons, past the Ivory Coast, and beyond
Conakry lies the steamy little colony of Portuguese Guinea,
a mini-land of jungle, rice bogs, and Fulani stock grazers.

On a map of Africa it looks like a Portuguese
afterthought, an incongruous little slice of colonial pickings
snatched to the bosom of the motherland when the giant
shadow of bigger powers than herself fell across the continent during last century's scramble. Actually, the Portuguese got there first, over 500 years ago, but when the
frontiers were finally drawn they ended up with a wedge of
country shaped like the splayed paw of a many-clawed
dragon hooking out through the green swamps into the Atlantic.

The French got everything else from the ankles on back
and called it French West Africa. As a result, the Senegalese to the north write exquisite poetry in French and the
Conakry people in the other Guinea say *"ouay"* instead of
"oui" in their casual, loose-boned way, but they speak
French, all right.

Most of the blacks in Portuguese Guinea speak their tribal language or a corruption of the motherland's tongue called Creole.

Unlike the rest of Portuguese Africa—Mozambique and Angola—the little land of Guinea had never drawn many white settlers. It was too much like Graham Greene country and if the hookworm didn't get you the malaria would. Lisbon contented itself with an administrative grip on the major towns and a backstop of almost autonomous Portuguese *chefes do posto* assigned to fort-hamlets scattered deep into the interior.

Their lives were dull and uninspired and they were often cut off from coastal civilization by the long monsoons that washed out the skinny dirt trails and drove the crocodiles from the flooded riverbanks.

They were not expected to understand very much of the main tribes under their sway in the jungles or cattle-growing plateaus to the north, those thousands of blacks with their strange ways, their spectacular funeral dances, their barebreasted women with babies slung in cloth pouches across their backs—the Balantes, Mandjaks, Mandingos, Pepels, and Brames.

Perhaps easier to comprehend were the Moslem Fulas with their feudal structure and modestly garbed wives. Later, when the revolution burst, the Portuguese relied heavily on them as loyalists to shore up the trembling governmental infrastructure.

The Balante had been among the first to rise, for they were the majority, and from these jungle-dwellers had come much of the forced labor that hacked trade routes through the strangling creepers and linked one fort with another. From their malaria-infested villages came much of the beef and poultry needed by the fort administration, and their sullen passivity, poverty, and inability to pay their taxes seemed to bring down punishment on their ignorant heads more often than the rest.

119

From their swampy lowlands came rice that the administration-supported monopolies bought at prices fixed by themselves and later sold abroad at four times the amount. There were few tangible improvements back in the villages from these profits, yet monocultures such as this were enforced wherever possible.

Sometimes itinerant foreign traders hauled their wares to the larger hamlets, or there was an occasional call by traveling black hawkers; but most of the trade was done at the forts in shops run by Portuguese or Levantines. The blacks often walked two days to buy their essentials—soap, "cloth" for a dress or cloak, sometimes their own rice.

The brighter children whose parents had other plans for them could attend a handful of mission schools established by enterprising Christians in the interior, but pupils often left after the first year because funds back in the village could not cover the modest fees asked by the missions.

Thus the Balante fell away from Portugal's oft-declared purpose for holding on in Africa—her Christianizing and civilizing mission. On neither count, in fact, was the motherland markedly successful. Civilization in the European sense maintained only a fitful, self-conscious hold on a small minority of urban blacks and the remainder, living an essentially village life in their crowded African quarters, kept close tribal and cultural ties with the countryside. For European education was limited to comparatively few blacks.

Nor did the Christians make any spectacular inroads. Roughly 60 percent of Portuguese Guinea's blacks clung to their animist ways, the Fulas and Mandingos remained staunch Moslems, and the church held the cure of only 2 or 3 percent of black souls.

The Balante's tribal and political structure remained intact, therefore, as unchanging as the damp jungles in which they lived and died. Whatever foreign impact there was upon them came in the occasional form of salt and sugar, a

120

dress length, or a plastic bucket. They remained both unimpressed and isolated, and when they looked back over their lives they saw that the white crusader had taken much and given very little.

They were among the first tribes to be mobilized by a small nucleus of black revolutionaries who had earlier formed a new politico-revolutionary party in the colony's capital of Bissau a full six years before the shooting war began in 1962. The party was called the PAIGC, which translates into English as "African Party for the Independence of Portuguese Guinea and the Cape Verde Islands," and, as an exponent of independence for mainland Portuguese Guinea and the offshore islands of Cape Verde, was to be quickly driven underground.

After Portuguese security forces shot and killed 50 black dock workers one damp August day during a PAIGC-organized strike over wage disputes, the party took a long look at its tactics and decided to turn them upside down. Although the party was to continue clandestine operations in the towns from secret houses, it was clear that the peasant mass would have to be the backbone of any successful revolution, and that the force of the uprising would be felt from there. This meant pulling the bulk of the mobilizers from the towns into the forested interior where spies were fewer and the vine-choked jungles offered relatively better security. The evaluation proved correct, for by 1962 paid Portuguese agents had infiltrated into every African neighborhood, cinema, and meeting place in Bissau and the other towns and the party was virtually paralyzed. Then came the big crackdown; in a dawn swoop on a clandestine party center near Bissau, the security forces netted the PAIGC's president and some key cadres along with him. They have spent the past nine years in prison.

The party's leader was, and still is, Amilcar Cabral, an urbane and forceful African with a university degree from Lisbon who developed, as secretary-general, into a blunt and gifted tactician. A hardheaded realist who had early learned to winkle out counterrevolutionary plots from within and without, Cabral has gradually welded the PAIGC into a stable and efficient liberation movement whose leadership the man in the bush has learned to trust.

Now, with mobile guerrilla units spread throughout much of the country and its army in the North, the PAIGC is driving toward the coast in an ever-narrowing arc and hooking out the big forts enroute to the ocean. It already claims to hold three-quarters of the country while the Portuguese maintain the towns and an ever-slackening grip on beseiged fortresses in the interior.

Cabral credits these advances to the party's policy of collective planning and leadership rather than the brilliance or isolated effort of any single individual. He never signs a communiqué or battle order without first consulting his colleagues and listens endlessly to opinions and reports throughout a sixteen-hour day, including Sundays.

There is no doubt that the party is in firm control of the army and guerrilla forces, which it considers only one of many departments, all equally important, in a well-oiled revolutionary structure. "Democratic centralism," he emphasizes again and again, and the potential flowering of a field leader's ego is hastily dealt with.

The food grower, the local trade organizer, and the fourteen-year-old first-aider in the bush are made to feel as necessary to the cause as the armed guerrilla fighter. This pride is immediately apparent in the field and has helped to avoid the creation of military elites and armed local chieftains who may slip from party control and impose a subtle dictatorship upon the awed peasantry.

The problem had, in fact, begun to plague the party in the early days of the war when zonal guerrilla commanders were virtually autonomous in the mounting of operations. The PAIGC came down hard on the tendency by restructuring the military, both conceptually and in fact, and by following this up with some fast transfers. The mandate to do so had come from a vital party congress in 1964 which grouped all guerrilla forces and a newly created army under a joint command called FARP (*Forças Armadas Revolucionarias do Povo*), and also structured the party in such a way that political control would be maintained over it. The seven members of the war council which controls FARP are also members of the party's political bureau.

Just outside Conakry, the capital of the independent Republic of Guinea (formerly French Guinea) is the PAIGC's external headquarters, a busy complex of whitewashed prefabricated bungalows in neat, shady grounds. This office is a sixteen-hour jeep ride from the war zones across the northern border and is referred to simply as "the bureau." Its brisk efficiency is sometimes intimidating to visiting cadres who sit uneasily on long benches outside the front door and seem half the size they did in the bush, twisting their peaked caps in large brown hands.

These same hands, on the banks of steamy jungle lagoons scything through the rice-growing lowlands, had helped to tear the clumsy transport canoes from the sucking, hip-high mud when the tide suddenly fell; or brewed coffee in a tin can over an open fire while the gas beetles lurched across the village clearings.

Here at the bureau, the nerve center of the revolution, much of the overall planning and paperwork is done by the party's Secretariat and Central Committee staff who are in continual contact with the military via a communications truck parked nearby. The destruction of this bureau and the killing of its staff was one of the main objectives of an abortive Portuguese invasion attempt against the Republic of Guinea in late 1970, another aim being the overthrow of PAIGC sympathizer Sékou Touré, the Republic's president.

The bureau's tightly disciplined staff work a seven-day week and run the revolution like a business. There is a coolly efficient chief accountant, a supplies section, an information office, filing clerks and typists, and an unflappable woman secretary called Henriette who handles everything from appointments with government officials downtown to the sifting of voluminous correspondence from abroad.

There is one table fan to an office and for six years the PAIGC ran its revolution without a telephone. This meant long hot trips into town in the overworked office car crammed with sweating cadres all bound on separate missions—food buying, medical supplies, contacts with local and visiting politicians, and the frustrating hunt for spare parts to fit the organization's transport trucks.

These giant workhorses, often Russian-built, undergo spectacular punishment on their endless trips from the bureau to the frontier. Their interiors bulge with fighters and supplies and they rumble, squeal, and overheat across mile after mile of unpaved, empty highway. The occupants in the rear, unprotected from either sun or tropical downpour, bounce off the iron railings or crash to the floor as the truck smashes through bone-jarring ruts.

There is a brief but welcome remission at two wide rivers enroute when the truck is eased onto a pulley-operated raft whose tiny engine puffs and backfires toward the opposite bank. Its captain, stripped to the waist and wearing a billed cap against the sun, retires at dusk to his hut along the embankment and must be roused out with whistles and cheers should late-crossing passengers collect hopefully on the shore. Throughout the long afternoons, a mentally retarded villager sits on a smooth rock overlooking the river, a self-appointed sentinel wrapped in a gray cloak, watching the rise and fall of the tides.

On the opposite bank is another squat village over which looms a spacious, businesslike building of mud-brick with wide verandas—a former French administrative post now converted into a refreshment house. The refrigerator has been out of order for some weeks and it sells warm beer,

FRELIMO guerrillas and myself in Cabo Delgado province, Northern Mozambique.

Women are also included in FRELIMO's military detachments but their use in actual combat is avoided whenever possible. Pauline Mateos, age 17 (third from left, front row) is commander of a women's unit in Northern Mozambique. Her second-in-command, Criketa Joao, age 20, is at far left, first row, flanked by Fernando Raoul of FRELIMO's defense department. He later married Diolinda Simango (second from right, first row). To Diolinda's right is Cornelio Iboumila, one of my escorts during the journey.

FRELIMO recruits during basic training inside Mozambique.

Guerrillas and militia relax at base camp in Cabo Delgado, Northern Mozambique. Clothing for both guerrillas and militia members is still in short supply.

Children in a liberated area of Portuguese-held Mozambique. There are no sewing machines or adequate clothing supplies. Children are dressed in donated cloth lengths, old tablecloths, or potato sacks.

Carrying a loaded pack and machine-gun, a FRELIMO cadre negotiates a steep hill in Northern Mozambique.

FRELIMO guerrillas singing their national anthem, "Venceremos"—"We shall win." It was written by another guerrilla and the words are well-known in liberated zones.

Commander Calisto Mijigo, FRELIMO's military leader in Cabo Delgado (second from left) stops to converse with village women, accompanied by Mariano Matsinge (first from left) and Marcelino Dos Santos (center).

FRELIMO's civilian militia line up for inspection. Cabo Delgado province, Northern Mozambique.

The PAIGC's external headquarters is in close radio contact with its units in the Portuguese Guinea bush. Above, a PAIGC radio operator in the Northern Front. *PAIGC archives*

A PAIGC guerrilla with bazooka enroute to an attack on Cufar, a Portuguese for in the Southern Front, Portuguese Guinea.

A PAIGC training base in Portuguese Guinea. *PAIGC archives*

Streams and narrow rivers are often crossed by guerrilla-built bridges constructed of logs, Portuguese Guinea. *PAIGC archives*

Commandant Umaru Djallo's men cross a narrow stream in the Portuguese Guinea bush for an attack on the Portuguese fort of Cufar.

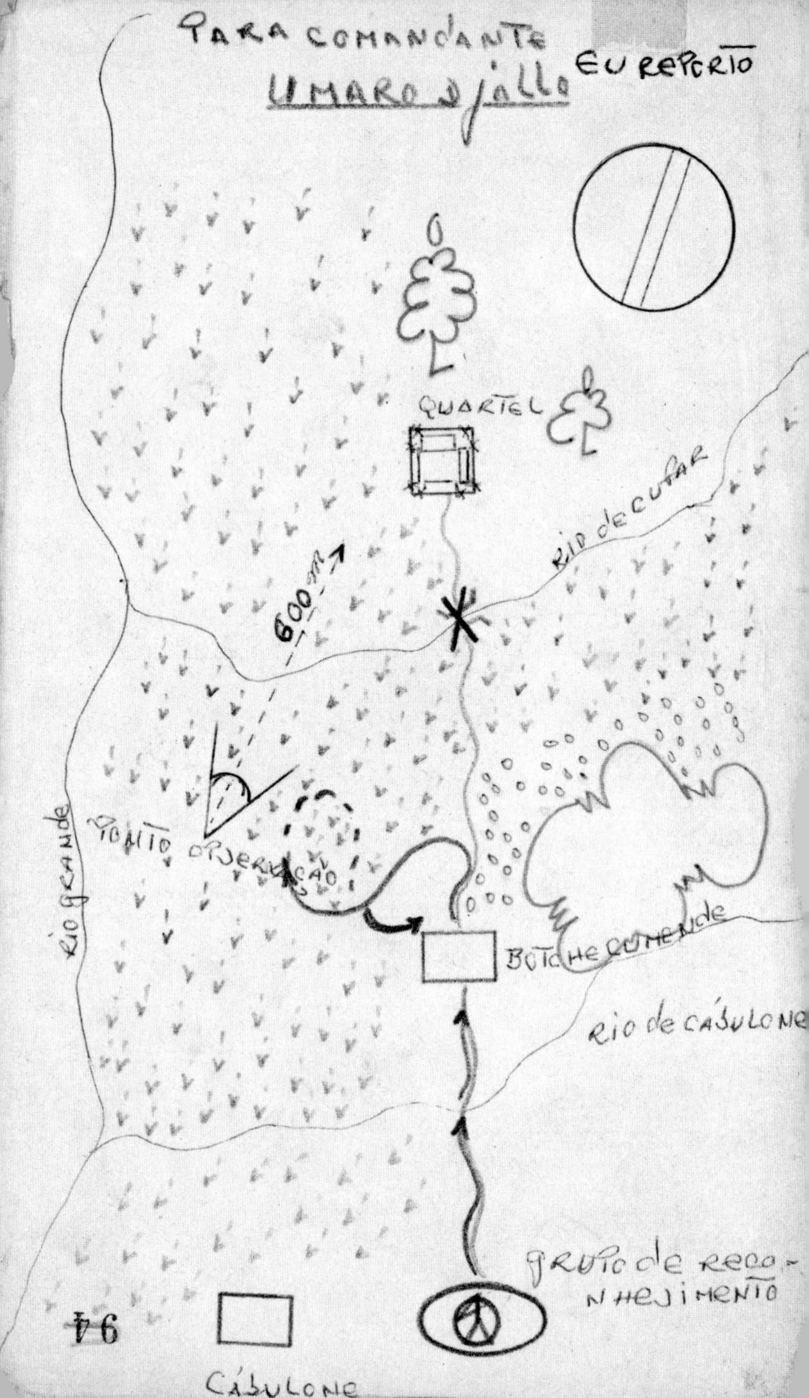

Para Comandante
UMARO DJALLO EU REPORTO

QUARTEL

600m

RIO DE CUTAR

PONTO OBSERVAÇÃO

RIO GRANDE

BOTCHE CUMENDE

RIO DE CÁBULONE

GRUPO DE RECO-
NHEJIMENTO

94

CÁBULONE

Members of a women's militia group in Southern Portuguese Guinea. All are members of the PAIGC. Many carried a child on one arm and a submachine-gun on the other.

African carriers transporting food into liberated zones of Portuguese Guinea. All are supporters of the PAIGC. *PAIGC archives*

The map prepared for Commandant Umaru Djallo by reconnaissance man, Philippe Saco, for the attack on the Portuguese fort of Cufar in Southern Portuguese Guinea and given to me immediately after.

TODOS SABEM
QUE OS BANDIDOS:

1. *NO MATO PASSAM FOME E FRIO*

2. *FURTAM AS BAJUDAS*

3. *FURTAM VACAS E ARROZ À POPULAÇÃO*

4. *TÊM MEDO UNS DOS OUTROS*

5. *VIVEM DOENTES E SEM REMÉDIOS*

6. *METEM MEDO ÀS POPULAÇÕES DAS TABANCAS*

7. *NÃO VÊM TER COM A TROPA PORQUE OS CHEFES NÃO DEIXAM*

8. *PROMETEM COISAS QUE NÃO DÃO E NÃO FAZEM*

9. *SÓ DIZEM MENTIRAS*

10. *QUE SE ENTREGAREM À TROPA SERÃO BEM TRATADOS*

A propaganda leaflet dropped by the Portuguese into liberated zones of Portuguese Guinea. It reads:

EVERYONE KNOWS
THAT THE BANDITS:
1. in the bush are hungry and cold
2. kidnap the young women
3. steal the animals and the rice of the people
4. fear one another
5. live in sickness and without medicine
6. terrorize the population in the villages
7. do not surrender to the army because their leaders do not permit it
8. promise things that they cannot give or do
9. only tell lies
10. will be well treated if they surrender to the army

ido Chefe das Forças Armadas
da Guiné Portuguesa

FAZ COMO ELES ▶

ERAM POPULAÇÃO QUE TERRO-
GUARDAVA NO MATO E QUE FU-
FOGE TAMBÉM E APRESENTA-TE À
RIDADE CIVIL OU À TROPA QUE DÁ
A, COMIDA, MEZINHO, PAZ E
DADE.

FAZ COMO ELES ▶

SÃO TERRORISTAS ARREPENDIDOS.
ENTA-TE TAMBÉM À TROPA. TAM-
ERÁS PAZ, COMIDA, MEZINHO E
DADE. SE LEVAR ARMA, TROPA DÁ
O. BANDEIRA PORTUGUESA É BAN-
A DE NÓS TODOS! AUTORIDADE
UGUESA AJUDA TODA A GENTE!
A DÁ PROTECÇÃO.

SENTA-TE COM ESTA GUIA

Portuguese leaflets dropped into the Portuguese Guinea bush urging the civilians and guerrillas to surrender. The illustrations show ragged civilians surrendering at a Portuguese fort and guerrillas turning in their guns to Portuguese troops, including African soldiers.

The leaflet depicting money offers cash awards for handing over arms to the Portuguese authorities.

1000   1000

HOMEM DO MATO

A TUA ARMA VALE DINHEIRO

APRESENTA-TE À TROPA

TROCA A TUA ARMA POR DINHEIRO E
PODERÁS COMPRAR ROUPA E COMIDA

1000   1000

(*Above left*) Boubacar Barry, my escort and interpreter in Portuguese Guinea, crossing into the war zone in the Southern Front. *PAIGC archives*

(*Above right*) Vasco Cabral, director of the PAIGC's commission for economic studies and planning in the Portuguese Guinea bush. He has a degree in economics from a Portuguese university.

(*Below*) Amilcar Cabral (right), leader of the PAIGC in Portuguese Guinea, with Joao (Nino) Vieira, commander of PAIGC forces in the Southern Front. *PAIGC archives*

Carmen Pereira crossing a Guinean river with her guerrilla escort. *PAIGC archives*

Schoolchildren who attend a PAIGC school in Portuguese Guinea. *PAIGC archives*

The mess hall of a PAIGC bush school in Portuguese Guinea. *PAIGC archives*

A commercial center in the liberated zones of Portuguese Guinea where guerrillas on a brief stopover mingle with civilians. *PAIGC archives*

Children in PAIGC elementary schools are encouraged to preserve their tribal dances. Costumes are made of forest materials, as are the children's bracelets. *PAIGC archives*

A court of justice in the Portuguese Guinea bush which is administered by civilians. Liberated zone, Portuguese Guinea. *PAIGC archives*

A young patient at the PAIGC hospital across the border from the war zone. Most medicine, hospital supplies, and bedding are donated from friendly countries and organizations abroad, but there is still an acute shortage of almost everything. *PAIGC archives*

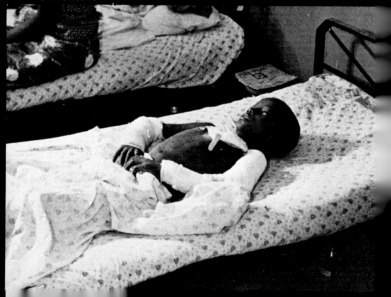

mango juice, and soft drinks, all bottled in "the Republic," as the cadres call former French Guinea.

This establishment had hoped to catch the civilian raft trade, but business is fitful and its proprietor watches gloomily as trucks crammed with PAIGC men slop up the muddy riverbanks below and roll on toward the north. The partisans never have money for luxuries such as this and must rely on friendly villagers along the way to refill their water canteens from farmyard wells.

Nor is there hope of food during the long journey until the guerrillas can reach their own *foyer* near the frontier. In the war zones, where the revolution feeds its own, there will be rice with red palm oil sauce, occasional canned meat, and sometimes game or chicken. There are mangoes and tiny lemons and wild fruit when in season, and occasionally even tea or coffee sweetened with gift sugar from abroad. But sometimes, on a long march or mission far in the interior, there is nothing.

Back at the bureau in Conakry, the diet varies little from that eaten by the fighters; often it is more monotonous for there is no game available and food prices in town are high. The bulk of donations from friendly organizations abroad, including canned food, cigarettes, sweets, or biscuits are sent directly by the party to the men at the front. These windfalls are great morale boosters to weary and hungry fighters who may see nothing but rice for weeks, and a bed on the forest floor is somehow less uncomfortable if a packet of cigarettes and a can of hot coffee is lying nearby.

Nor are living conditions at the bureau that much better, and many cadres on temporary missions there look forward to going "inside" again. The Secretariat staff, the teachers at the party's central pilot school, fighters returning for reassignment, and scores of others on permanent duty there, are billeted nearby in rented, concrete-block houses with cement floors and unpredictable plumbing.

Bachelors sleep six or eight to a small room and extra

cots or hammocks are thrown up on the narrow verandas should there be a heavy influx of fighters in transit. Married quarters are one room to a couple in houses set aside for families; if there are children, extra cots are moved in. Everyone, including Cabral and his pretty, Angolan-born wife, dines in a communal mess hall where meals are built around rice. Locally produced fruit and vegetables are expensive for revolutionaries, therefore carefully rationed out. A typical menu would be a breakfast of bread and jam or margarine, rice stew with fish or meat for lunch, and stew again in the evening. Those assigned to permanent work at the bureau visit Conakry town only on party business, avoid beer halls, restaurants, or nightclubs, and spend any free time either reading or visiting PAIGC colleagues.

As in Mozambique's FRELIMO, no revolutionary in the PAIGC is paid a salary or owns anything except what is provided by the party, including his soap and toothpaste. To save wear on whatever civilian clothes they may have been issued, the bureau staff often wear military fatigues.

If a cadre is sent abroad to attend a conference or on an enlightenment mission—all tasks and assignments connected with the revolution are called "missions"—his colleagues pool the best of their modest civilian wardrobe so that their representative will look his best. He is not expected to squander on trifles the little pocket money given him by the party for emergencies. A cadre abroad is often filled with guilt over the purchase of a bottle of beer for himself. Not only is he wasting valuable party money, but he risks damaging the movement's image. In some foreign quarters, the sight of a revolutionary over a pint of ale somehow arouses suspicions that the entire cause must somehow be going awry. The result could be the loss of that confidence so necessary for outside support.

Then, a cadre sent abroad fresh from the war zones will be secretly uneasy for eating the kind of food that his colleagues back home cannot have, even when the bill is paid

126

by another. If two guerrilla emissaries are together they will invariably, at some time during the evening, indicate this guilt through a casual comment to each other. Any luxury or abundance, whether a comfortable bed or a program of entertainment, removes a committed partisan in his own estimation from the sacrifices of his fellow revolutionaries, and by extension from the revolution itself. He is uneasy and temporarily adrift. Should the mission be of sufficient importance to justify the comparative luxury in which he suddenly finds himself, his guilt may be partly allayed.

But large quantities of food will always surprise him, and the removal from the dining table of half-eaten platters of meat is a shock. Guerrillas eat when they can and starve when it is necessary. This is hard on the digestion but armies such as these don't travel on their stomachs. A guerrilla in the bush will eat at any hour, depending upon his marching schedule and the proximity of food. I have seen a platoon eat a full meal at 8 A.M. and again at 11 A.M., then nothing until noon of the third day.

There are other adjustments necessary to guerrilla life, of course, and not always physical. Living in such raw proximity as they do brings the virtues—and the faults—of others into glaring perspective. This necessitates the development of a certain tolerance for annoying little habits that others may have. However idealistic and admirable one's comrades may be, guerrilla life is filled with coughing, scratching, snoring, loudness, clumsiness, and sweat. Then there are the other traits: carelessness, stubbornness, dullness, overzealousness. "We are not born revolutionaries, just ordinary people. . . ."

As in FRELIMO, the borrowing of another's pathetic little personal treasures lying in supposed safety at the bottom of his rucksack ranks high on the list of annoyances. This may be the remains of a carefully hoarded packet of tea from a mission three months before, a nail scissors, a battered can opener. The borrower has truly meant to put it back, and after all, the origin of any possession is usually the bureau's communal supply shelves.

"But you weren't here to ask!" says the startled culprit as the victim comes roaring out of a hut, his rifled rucksack still in his hands.

"I had five cigarettes left in that pack!" he accuses, "and now they're gone!" This was his small, hoarded comfort put by until the long march was over and he could flop onto a mat and watch the smoke blow over his weariness.

Yet the longer a man is in the bush, the more tolerance he has usually acquired for others' shortcomings. I was to notice on several occasions the patience shown by partisan leaders in the field to those less intelligent or self-controlled than themselves, and the accompanying distribution of duties in direct ratio to capabilities studied beforehand. I was to hear that phrase often—"within his capacities . . . those are his capabilities."

The ability to judge the potential of a man or woman is one attribute of a good guerrilla leader. His men sense it and rely upon it. An inept commissar can turn an entire village against them; a sluggish supply chief can cause many missed meals. A careless man on reconnaissance can kill them; a bazooka on the flank in the hands of a good man can save their lives.

A leader would tell his equal what a fool he thought the other was, but for the less intelligent who had botched an unimportant assignment there would be firm but kindly remonstrance, then another minor task for the crestfallen one to restore his self-confidence. For in a revolution of this kind, even the little dim one may find a niche and a successfully completed "mission" will cause him to swell with pride.

Carmen Pereira was a leader who understood this, and she was one of the most beloved of revolutionary figures among both guerrillas and population. I first met her at the bureau in Conakry, a medium-brown, oval-faced woman with whom, along with several others, I was to wedge into a

128

PAIGC jeep for the long, blistering journey to Portuguese Guinea's Southern Front. She was the chief political commissar there, a vast area bordering "the Republic" and one of the movement's three main fronts. Her visit to Conakry was the first in a year and she had come out of the bush to see her two children at the pilot school there.

Carmen had been a housewife and dressmaker in Bissau before the rebellion and had been drawn into the fledgling party through her husband's political involvement in the early 1960s. For an African in this Portuguese colonial capital, her standard of living had been comparatively high and her father's prestige as a lawyer had brought her into occasional contact with Portuguese families at clubs and dances.

Now 32, her role as the political representative and administrator of PAIGC directives in the southern jungles is so valuable that the Portuguese have put out a reward for her capture—she doesn't know the exact amount—and once strafed a village for six hours after inaccurate information that she was hiding somewhere in that tangled camouflage beneath their planes. The whereabouts of her base is still unknown.

She is elusive, mobile, and consistently unruffled, but as a townswoman, her adjustment to forest life had been difficult and exhausting, mainly because of the marches.

Her smooth features gave away nothing when I first met her, and like many African women, she seemed an enigma until very slowly the layers of some undefinable reticence peeled away. Perhaps it was the quiet observation of the female running its course, or perhaps she was wondering, as she watched me unobtrusively from a corner, how I would react to the journey ahead, the mosquitoes and stifling heat of the jungle at noon, the cramped agony of the transport canoes packed with human cargo, bazooka shells, and the inevitable hens. There was nothing in Carmen's eyes to caution or reassure, only a matter-of-factness that I could not read.

12

THE JEEP'S METAL DOOR BANGED SHUT AGAINST US JUST after lunchtime in Conakry, and for an onlooker the sight must have been reminiscent of the old Toonerville Trolley cartoons in which the total engorgement of a vehicle originally designed to carry some long-forgotten maximum of interrelated objects produces a near farcical situation both within and without.

Perched on hard leather seats in front were Carmen and the driver who were to take the brunt of sun and dust through the open windshield as we hurtled down the forest roads for the next several hours.

Ranged on benches in the back among bulging sacks and crates of supplies were myself, a good-natured guerrilla escort called Roger, a youthful but unidentified male passenger in a white sweatshirt who never found room for his feet, and a round-faced girl of thirteen called Awah. And of course the poultry. Under normal circumstances there would have been ample hen room, but the war zones needed continual supplies, anything on wheels was pressed into service and loaded to squealing point, and the human and animal factor in the revolution was resigned to discomfort.

"A real Mammy wagon," somebody said, as we reared off, recalling the battered old vans and buses that sometimes served as public transport in many West African suburbs and even ventured boldly beyond to career alarmingly down country roads from one village to the next. We swept by several of them going north, and I caught glimpses of desperate human loads clinging to doors and punched out windows while the spavined chassis sagged inches from the ground.

That they moved at all was a credit to the ingenuity of their owners who fashioned spare parts out of unlikely objects and nailed on sheets of tin where parts of the body had dropped off. They were widely purported to be held together with bits of string, but their occupants had preferred them to walking.

Our jeep suddenly seemed reliable and roomy, despite the fact that our supplies, although lashed together with rope and tied tautly to the metal frame, had worked themselves forward only a few miles outside Conakry, to poke and goad our perspiring, jackknifed bodies all the way to the frontier.

At one point they broke loose and like a ship's cargo cascaded onto our laps or hurtled past us onto the backs of Carmen and the driver. Metal ammunition cases slid wildly around the rear and pinched our hands in the ropes as we struggled to force them into place. A misstep brought outraged squawks from the hens who lay in a corner on the floor tied securely by their feet. What remained of their tailfeathers was a limp, sticky mass, the result of a can of pineapple juice that I had spilt on them just after Carmen, thinking it would refresh us, had passed it back.

I gave the remainder to the unidentified youth who neatly directed it from can to throat without touching the rim and who, in the meantime, had worked himself to the floor from his slippery pyramid of rice sacks. Despite the noise and vibration, he eventually dozed off and whenever we smashed through a rut, the layers that were his doubled-up body opened and closed like a bellows. Little Awah, whom I discovered later was a first-aider, sat stoically in a corner near the hens, her knapsack clutched to her stomach and a bandana wound around her head.

As the miles of washed-out highway went by beneath us, the poultry disappeared under the mass of shifting equipment and from time to time I peered worriedly in their direction, wondering how they would survive the appalling crush.

"Elles vivent, elles vivent," yelled Roger above the racket of the snapping canvas roof, and there was a reassuring squawk as he reached into a tunnel of boxes. As I surveyed the misery of the battered human cargo, I felt my concern somewhat misplaced. The hens were tougher than they looked, moreover, for when we stopped to collect drinking water from a village well they flew with croaks of triumph high onto a mango tree, having silently worked themselves free of their bonds.

"The chickens are in the mango tree," I said unnecessarily as Roger, already straddling the top branch, was scooping them down. We were to spend almost an hour by the roadside, for the radiator was boiling, and we, after fanning out discreetly in search of convenient *retretes,* had gathered around to watch the driver siphon gas from the auxiliary into the jeep's main tank. It was a noisy process, for whenever the flow was blocked he was forced to suck it out by mouth through the rubber hose, hawking and retching whenever the disagreeable liquid spurted into his mouth.

The smell of grease and gas fumes blended with the late-afternoon odors of the countryside, damp earth, river water, and cooking fires. We could hear but not see the awakening wildlife, the flutter of parakeets and toucans, the muffled cry of animals in the dense vegetation. An occasional military vehicle carrying troops of the Republican army sped by from Conakry, and at one point a jeep screeched to a halt some 50 yards ahead.

Its officer, rifle in hand, sprang from the door and into the bush, taking the roadside ditch in one jump.

"Lion!" he shouted, and in seconds was out of sight. His trained eye had apparently seen the animal as it flashed across the forest road, but I had noticed nothing. Recalling the vivid warnings culled from old books on the subject, I pondered the advisability of plunging alone into an unknown patch of bush after an unknown lion, but the man apparently knew what he was about and neither his driver nor our own group seemed unduly worried. When the officer and his jeep finally caught up with us at one of the river crossings later, I learned that the lion had escaped him.

By nightfall, I had almost forgotten what life outside the interior of a jeep could be, for by then we had all established unspoken property rights over our own cramped bit of bench which even permitted us slight shifts to ease the agony in our pounded tailbones. Biscuits were passed around, cigarettes glowed, and outside our headlights picked the way to the frontier.

Occasionally we passed a trembling Mammy wagon, still on the road, and whenever we neared a cluster of roadside huts our driver slammed on the brakes to avoid whole herds of small, round-bellied goats which trotted off reluctantly on short legs only after his repeated blasts on the horn. For some reason they preferred sleeping in the exact center of the road, perhaps to avoid snatch-and-run attacks by larger animals prowling the forest's edge by night.

"It won't be long now," said Roger. "That's our *foyer* ahead." This was a temporary shelter for guerrillas and other PAIGC members in transit to and from the interior, and as we drew up to the peeling one-story house, there were hails of welcome from cadres sprawled on the wide, concrete porch. They loomed up in the darkness, their glistening backs to the light, and cheerfully hauled our packs and supplies inside while someone went off to pump bath water from an outdoor well.

The chickens disappeared behind the house, and I glimpsed the blaze of cooking fires in the backyard. Voices and laughter rolled out through the threshold, friendly, enveloping laughter, and then we crossed into their guerrilla world.

The ancient *khans* of North Africa or Timbuctu must have been something like this, a crossroads, a brief meeting point in men's lives before they went their separate ways, perhaps to meet again on another summer's night next year. The main central hall was crammed with uniformed cadres and rucksacks and rows of iron cots, and beyond were similar rooms filled with voices and colliding bodies. There was an air of transience and urgency and the choosing of cots and floor space on which to lay a mat. Somebody's wife, an enormous woman in orange kaftan and turban, shifted on her bed in one corner and sighed in her sleep. A transistor crackled with Guinean drums and xylophones, and on a center table one of the men had taken a large radio apart for repairs. Some of the men were already dozing through the bedlam. Large brown guerrillas, stripped to the waist, filed in and out of the only bathroom, a towel flung over their shoulders and a demijohn of water in hand. The plumbing system had long ago fallen apart and there were no pipes on the market with which to repair it. Only the drains remained. After each bath, someone rushed in with pail and mop and the next occupant entered, pushing a large stone across the door against intruders. Just outside, a wooden table served as an ironing board where guerrillas pressed their jungle-green fatigues, humming under the shadeless light bulb.

Yielding to our hunger, the radio man gathered up his

134

nuts and bolts and our chicken and rice stew was eventually set before us on the table, with apologies for the lack of serving bowls. Normally, everyone prepared his own food, but I was a newcomer and someone else had volunteered to hunch over the backyard fire. Coffee was brewed in a tiny kitchen at the rear and a jug of fresh drinking water came along with it. We were fortunate in having eating utensils, a glass, and plate, for there was a chronic shortage of these refinements and many drank from tin cans.

"Is the water safe to drink?" I whispered to Carmen, feeling citified and fussy. She had never experienced any ill effects, she said, but had probably built up resistance to local microbes. Her own problem was malaria.

Camp beds had been put aside for Carmen and myself, and I was billeted in a small back room with an African nurse from the PAIGC's frontier hospital where the volunteer staff worked like navvies and were fortunate in having a morning off.

She showed neither surprise nor irritation when awakened by loud scraping as my bed was set up on the concrete floor next to hers. Her guerrilla husband was at the front and she had been assigned a permanent room at the *foyer* until alternative accommodation could be found. She was an operating room nurse and her life, except for occasional visits from her husband, was made up of interminable hours over bombing casualties, fractures, and mine victims carried in from the interior, many of them civilians.

Her only sanctuary, the tiny back room, was now being invaded by an unknown foreigner. In one corner she kept her small store of food, including a lidded casserole containing sugar and a packet of coffee. There had been attempts to alleviate the bleakness of the little room with a homemade bedspread, pictures, and mementos of student days in Russia, including a folk-art candelabra which stood on a side table. The wooden shutters were closed against

135

mosquitoes and as in most homes in Guinea there were no windowpanes for the weather was never cold enough to warrant them.

Next morning, as she lay in bed flicking her transistor from Senegal to Freetown and back to the PAIGC's *Radio Libertaçao* broadcasting from Conakry, she told me between the pop music and the war news that her nursing scholarship had been offered her through the movement. In prerevolutionary days, she said, she could never have expected to study. In the five centuries of Portuguese rule, only fourteen blacks had attended university. During eight years of revolution, the PAIGC had managed to send several hundred cadres abroad on foreign scholarships, trained over 350 nurses and auxiliaries, and were expecting their first black medical school graduates. In the meantime, they had relied on outside volunteers to help staff Solidarity Hospital where she worked, a whitewashed compound of cement-block wards of which they were extremely proud.

Built by their own cadres with help from the Republic of Guinea, Yugoslavia, and the OAU, the hospital treats guerrilla sick and wounded, serious civilian cases from the liberated areas, and is also equipped with X-ray and laboratory facilities. As always, the problem is transport. War casualties are carried through the bush by stretcher and canoe, then by truck to the first hospital that Portuguese Guinea's blacks have ever considered their own.

Its African administrator, a serious, bespectacled cadre in his midthirties who had helped mark out the site when it was still desolate, stony ground, said that the certainty of Portuguese aerial attacks had precluded its location inside guerrilla-held zones. He insisted on a full tour of the scrupulously clean buildings, including the laundry block—"one of the most important areas in any hospital"—then a lightning doorway view of the sterile operating room. "Can't have anyone walking about in there," he said and hustled me down the corridor.

136

Although the site had been chosen for its open, comparatively breezy aspect, I was already breathless in my heavy cotton khaki because of the chronic humidity. Besides the more direct discomforts due to the wet heat, there were side effects as well which I found so debilitating eventually—the edema of hands and feet, the distended, queasy stomach, the malaise which made very simple tasks into mountains of effort. I wondered how they ever got the rice crop planted.

We were soon joined by another staff member who, I noted, was similarly affected by the wilting humidity. He was the hospital's chief surgeon, Dr. Zivorad Josipovic, a 45-year-old volunteer from Belgrade. Although fresh from a nap and shower after an all-night operating schedule, he was perspiring profusely after the short walk from his small house across the compound.

For his work in the tropics, where the humidity reading often rose to the level of the temperature, he had obviously chosen for his dress the coolest combination of style and material that modesty and the free circulation of the sluggish air would permit—a V-necked, collarless shirt of sheer muslin with tiny sleeves over trousers of the same white color and material. But as we moved around the compound, they clung damply to his streaming back and legs.

During operations, one nurse was occupied almost solely with swabbing rivulets of perspiration from his face and neck lest they splash onto the patients, for there was no air conditioning and the high-powered surgical lights turned the operating room into an inferno. Sometimes during night surgery, the weak generators failed abruptly and flashlights were brought out.

He moved slowly and deliberately, as if wary of a climate which might sneak up and divest him of whatever reserve energy he might have. The flesh on his tall, spare frame was almost transparent, and as we moved among his patients, I wondered how long he would maintain his own health.

For cross ventilation purposes, the wards had been built

to a depth of only one room, strung out in a chain along the compound with covered verandas running the length of each side. Inside there were burn victims, amputees who had lost arms or legs to mines and lay sweating on their bandaged stumps, childish bodies shattered in forest accidents or by shrapnel, bandaged guerrillas with chest wounds, and in another block, rows of tropical disease cases.

"We have just operated on this one," the doctor said, hauling up a bandaged leg. "Elephantiasis."

In the isolation ward lay a calm young woman in a white gown whose tropical illness was finally to prove incurable. She had been one of the nursing staff and she watched us with round, curious eyes as we followed the doctor from bed to bed.

There would be other victims like her, the staff knew, until the ignorance and neglect that had encouraged these diseases for so many centuries could be remedied. The appalling list read like a textbook on tropical medicine: leprosy, typhoid, yellow fever, bilharzia, tuberculosis, cholera, amoebic dysentery, ancylostomiasis, tick-borne fever, malaria, vitamin deficiency diseases . . . and never enough medicine to treat them.

There would be no miracle cures here, and preventive medicine was still in its early stages. Only a state has the means to drain swamps, stamp out epidemics, or hammer home the principles of balanced diets and personal hygiene on a nationwide basis. And how do you blithely tell a people to eat plenty of fruits and vegetables when there aren't any, or educate them overnight out of centuries-old habits when most cannot even read?

13

THE SOUTHERN FRONT, THAT EARLY HEARTLAND OF BLACK revolt in Portuguese Guinea, is mainly Balante country and in addition to the visible impact that the war has had upon them, the Balante also live in unseen, spirit worlds.

Although the largest in a country of divided tribes under the Portuguese, they were always among the least developed, both economically and socially, and to discourage thoughts of revolt, the Portuguese had imposed loyalist overseers from smaller tribes upon them.

But the Balante had resisted with glum and prolonged stubbornness any attempts to alter their internal structure, and as a result have maintained intact many of their old customs and beliefs.

They have always been a "society without chiefs, without castes, and without classes, and with the family at its center," says a PAIGC document. Unity was maintained through their communal, animistic religion and tribal mores, and a council of elders handed down justice. Land was considered the property of the tribe in general, but each family was given enough for its own subsistence. Although the status of women was comparatively higher than in most other tribes—Balante women also worked on the land—there was a tendency toward polygamy which answered the problem of female protection in hostile surroundings.

For the Balante, theirs is still a country of spirits, good and evil, and it is not difficult to understand why. The jungles, choked with trees intertwined with their own climbing roots, seemed almost to breathe. One *knew* there was always something going on inside those unseen depths; gnarled old hands breaking away from rotting trunks and tumbling to the forest floor, grasping creepers twisting the life from weaker vegetation, fearful screeching noises— man, beast, or *yiran?* They gave off a rich mixture of moss, decay, and crushed foliage, ebbing and flowing and undependable in the abruptness of their change. From dark, wet surroundings engulfing everything that passed, the jungles suddenly became arid, grinning expanses of brittle underbrush; and while trudging down the paths one could never see more than a few feet into their secret dimness.

The forests in Mozambique had been gentle and serene; these jungles were dynamic, and I wondered if the psychic impact of the landscape had somehow shaped the characters of the two peoples. In Mozambique I looked behind only to see what I had stumbled over; in Portuguese Guinea I was conscious of each contortion in the twisted climbers, each hiss and scurry. One could comprehend the necessity for a well-disposed *yiran*.

Curiously, at night I was to feel a strange comfort from the forest, as if all its creatures and its *yirans* were, like me, gathering strength in their beds of straw or moss, content to leave the jungle to itself. The Balante did not agree with this notion, especially about the *yirans,* for their spirits were at work around the clock and especially after midnight.

After long experience and the absence of credible evidence to the contrary, the *yirans* had been firmly established in Balante minds as the elements largely responsible for personal blessings or misfortunes.

Although they accepted the notion of one God—as fetishists they thought him embodied in a rock or peculiarly shaped tree, however—it was the *yirans* with whom they dealt on a day-to-day basis.

If a canoe were caught in its moorings, or the tide was slow in rising, it surely signified the presence of a mischievous *yiran* somewhere downstream. They also haunted certain belts within the forest, and only a fool would venture through these sections.

Illness was caused deliberately by one of these spirits, and a pacification ceremony would be immediately organized as a good will gesture. At the same time, the villagers had great confidence in the modern medicine introduced by the PAIGC, especially in the form of injections. I thought it paradoxical that the same power which caused the illness was not invoked for the cure until I realized that outside aid had always been sought. The villagers had always called in the services of what foreigners called "witch doctors" who had dispensed cures made of forest herbs and who had passed down their secret knowledge from one generation to another.

This was a world totally removed from anything that a Westerner might know, and only through the lesson of example combined with the means to dominate one's surroundings can primitive beliefs such as these fall away. Slowly, the party was trying to educate the villagers away from their *yirans,* but a people do not easily surrender their spirits and would probably invent something else to take their place. At this stage, occupied with more important problems, the party was not pressing the point; its object was national liberation, not religious reform.

I was to encounter an entirely new set of guerrilla faces that night when tired and hungry we walked into a base

141

camp set snugly in the center of thick jungle. This was the Southern Front and here the language was predominantly Creole, Balante, and sometimes Portuguese; even the French *"ouay"* that my companions had unconsciously spoken in the Republic of Guinea had narrowed into *"oui"* again. The camp was filled with tall, relaxed men with heavy pistols slung low from side holsters, and down a narrow path beyond the sleeping huts there was laughter from the moving shadows over the calabashes.

It was a comfortable camp, spacious and well-supplied, protected from sun and spotter planes by giant, wide-branched trees and close-growing jungle bush.

Around its thinly wooded clearing was a circle of huts which spilled back into thick foliage and overhanging branches. Their sides of woven raffia were supported by thin, rough poles, and heavy bundles of long, dried savanna grass formed their low, sloping roofs. These swept out and beyond the walls as an overhang to lend protection from sun and rain. A two-foot gap had been left between ceiling and roof for air circulation all around, but their interiors were always dim because of surrounding vegetation. The huts were entered by a low doorway in the center over which a curtain was sometimes hung for privacy.

Each hut contained two or three bunks with cotton mattresses stuffed with straw. The mosquito nets suspended over each were lowered and tucked carefully around at sunset.

There were two large beds in the hut assigned to Carmen and myself and on each were fresh white sheets, pillows, and dainty cotton bedspreads, a startling sight in a guerrilla encampment. It was obvious that someone had made careful preparations for the ladies, for the previous occupant's belongings had been hauled out and stacked unceremoniously at the rear. The sand floor had been swept clean of footprints and the small wooden table, normally strewn with guerrilla bric-a-brac, had been cleared. A single candle stood flickering on a saucer, and a curtain hung from a string across the entrance.

The only intruder during our four-day occupancy was to be a very large white duck which slept under my bed each night and most of the afternoons. If we attempted to expel her—for she made almost continual clicking and blowing noises with her beak—she waddled off indignantly to within a few yards of the hut and always sneaked back when we weren't looking. Eventually I was to relent and permit her to stay, for she was miserable without her shelter and I grew accustomed to her scuffling and sighs. Sometimes I forgot her existence altogether until, sitting on the edge of my bunk, I felt her feathered body brush past me enroute to the door.

"Have you seen the helicopter?" asked one of the new faces, as I joined them in the clearing for dinner. In the center of our table, just beyond the weak light of our oil lamp, was a beautiful insect with large, blade-like wings set into the upper half of its body. It was larger than a mammoth butterfly and it lifted off abruptly and vertically with a great whirr, fanning our hands with wings as delicate as rice paper. It seemed hypnotized by the flame and flew again and again into its heat, finally crashing into a singed dead heap off to the side. We watched its inevitable demise with regret, and then formal introductions were resumed.

Opposite me was the commander of the Southern Front, 30-year-old Joao Bernarde Vieira. As military chief for six years in this vital zone adjacent to the friendly Republic, he is known to his men simply as "Nino." Because of its strategic importance, his area is under frequent and intensive Portuguese bombardment, while guerrilla counteroffensives against the remaining forts here are frequent and deadly.

Beside him sat one of his key men, a 26-year-old Balante called Pansao Na Isna who was the only guerrilla whom I was to see in Mozambique or Portuguese Guinea wearing an Afro hairstyle. He wore thick metal bracelets on his upper arms which had been given him by his parents and he wore them for luck. Pansao, who was chief of one of the eight sectors under Nino's command, sat silent and glowering over his rice stew, a bush knife on one slim hip and a pistol next to the other. He was proud and withdrawn and his disciplined, jungle-trained body hung loosely under his watchful, stalker's face. I thought him one of the deadliest men I had ever seen, yet he was shortly also to prove one of the gentlest.

Then there was Boubacar Barry, the 27-year-old cadre from Bissau, who had grown up in the revolution and who was assigned to me as escort and interpreter through much of my visit. He had the fine-boned delicacy of his Fulani father and the deep brown of his Mandjak mother, and he taught me about *yirans*. The year before he had narrowly escaped death during a bombardment, and the shrapnel was still embedded in his back.

There was José Araujo, then the chief of the PAIGC's information section—"We are militants, not militarists"—who had just arrived mud-caked and bone-weary after six weeks in the interior, where he was later to become a political commissar. He was the devoted husband and father of a family back in Conakry where his wife worked at the bureau.

I was introduced to Pedro Ramos who, like Nino, had been one of the earliest PAIGC cadres and had narrowly avoided capture in a Portuguese dragnet while still living in Bissau. He was a supplies chief who had helped to open the Northern Front by organizing and leading arms-carrying human caravans past Portuguese bush patrols. His brother, Domingos, had been killed in battle in the East and was a national hero.

And of course Antonio, the camp cook, who could serve bully beef with a practiced flourish if there was nothing else, brewed tea from forest herbs, and made coffee for his be-

144

loved fighters when not engaged in noisy disputes with them. These altercations usually centered on the quality of his cooking which was admirable when one considered the limited choice of ingredients and the steamy little lean-to in which he worked. When mealtime came around, Antonio's mournful, craggy face looked over us with barely contained glee, his thin, buzzard shoulders hunched forward, hopefully anticipating some ungrateful aside on which he could pounce.

I was later to find that there were always subtle differences between one guerrilla camp and another, although their outward appearances might be almost identical. This was due to a combination of factors, such as position, proximity to water, the personality of the man in charge, and the capabilities of the cook.

A guerrilla camp on higher ground was often cooler, more spacious, and its water supply often cleaner. Those sited in the core of thick jungle, without a clearing and with huts built closely together, were usually stifling and fly-blown, the hovering forest drawing out whatever sluggish air there might have been. Water in these lowlands was usually in short supply during the six-month dry season and was carried for long distances from exposed wells shared with villages in the area. This meant that both cooking and bathing water were rigorously rationed, and laundry day was a nightmare of bucket-hauling down jungle paths in sweltering heat.

Although the PAIGC maintained certain permanent bases for supply, rest, and military coordination, their number had been minimized for tactical reasons as the war had progressed: fixed bases make fixed targets, a tired cadre is tempted to linger longer than necessary, and the proximity of a base could seriously undermine a guerrilla band's fundamental characteristic—constant mobility.

In some areas I was to find no base camps at all, only

temporary bivouacs which ambush units and coordinated attack groups set up for a few days, then immediately abandoned after an offensive. They were often nothing more than a rough lean-to and a triangle of charred rocks to contain a cooking fire, with the men sleeping on groundsheets in the open with mosquito nets hooked onto the branches above.

Life in the jungle at night was miserable without these nets, for the mosquitoes bit silently and savagely until dawn. Some of the nets were circular and could be hooked directly onto a bough. They had been cut on the bias and fanned out over the groundsheet beneath, giving adequate protection to its owner if carefully tucked under at twilight. Others were rectangular and were roped to adjacent trees. Tears or rips were immediately repaired because, however small the opening, the insects managed to find it. When hung in place, or taken up in the morning, the men first shook them out to eliminate any hidden mosquitoes, for a determined one would often lie quietly in the folds until the camp slept and then feast undisturbed on his snoring victim, having survived an all-day journey in the bottom of a rucksack.

There was always a shortage of nets and the unfortunate men without them were not only more susceptible to malaria but spent sleepless nights swatting into the darkness all around them. There was no mosquito repellent and the straw fires which produced the pungent smoke to drive them off burned brightly but briefly.

We sat up late that night over Antonio's coffee while Carmen and the men caught up on each other's news. It might have been a pleasantly tired safari party reminiscing over the day's hunt except for the crump of bombs across the jungle and very occasionally bursts of sporadic fire.

"They're bombing the Kinera region again," somebody said, and the conversation went on. This was a rich agricultural region and a frequent target of Portuguese aircraft.

Sometimes there was a series of explosions, identified as Portuguese gunboats escorting their river transport carrying supplies to outlying forts.

"They shoot ahead into the embankments all along the way, as a matter of course," explained one of the men. "They can't see what they're shooting at, but they do it in case we are waiting in ambush. They have lost a lot of men on the rivers, and once a boat is hit out there the chances of escape are small. If they do make it to shore, they walk right into us. We find a lot of drowned men afterward."

Both the guerrillas—and the Portuguese when possible— use the country's many rivers and canals to supply their men, and each prey on the other's boats. If guerrilla activity effectively blocks these supply routes, the Portuguese drop food and ammunition to encircled forts by helicopters and small aircraft, and sometimes carry out entire troop rotations this way.

One of their forts, which I was soon to visit, had been supplied in this manner until finally abandoned. Pansao said that in many regions the guerrillas had far less direct confrontation with the enemy than before, although every attempt was made to flush them out.

"We attack them often," he said, "either with mortars or cannons. They respond to our shelling, but they won't come out on foot to enter the forests."

Pansao, who had been trained in a Chinese military academy and later distinguished himself during a ferocious, four-day battle on Como Island which helped to change the course of the war, said that in his opinion the Portuguese were "not very good fighters. They lacked the heart to fight."

He was immediately interrupted by another cadre who disagreed, saying, "They also have some brave men in their ranks."

Pansao conceded that a small number had been "brave"

147

enough and some could even be considered "good" as jungle fighters. "But most are not," he insisted, attributing this to low morale caused by conditions in the encircled forts and the nature of the antiguerrilla war that they were fighting.

"We get a lot of their deserters who tell us that their conscience had bothered them, or that the war was too risky. Usually they had been told that we were bandits, and they resented being sent from home to the bush for this purpose."

The construction and defense system of Portuguese forts was similar to that in Mozambique, Pansao said, with the size of the post varying from 200 yards to a mile. The larger forts included an airstrip within the barbed wire fence. Beyond this lay a chain of mines against guerrilla incursion. There was usually a single entry gate and the buildings stood in the center protected by sandbags and another two rows of barbed wire. African civilians and prisoners were housed in huts to the rear, while machine-guns mounted on sandbagged platforms in all four corners looked out to the forest beyond. Numerous trenches had been dug inside the compound.

All approaches to the post, either by road or down the forest paths, were mined and when the Portuguese abandoned a fort the mines were left in place. In addition, they often booby-trapped the interior of the buildings knowing that guerrillas would eventually come looking for abandoned equipment.

I slept soundly that night, unaware that I would be in the middle of a minefield myself the next day. At 6 A.M. we were awakened by the swish and clump of *pangas* cutting away the brush near our hut. Some of the men had risen at dawn to build a bath hut close by, using bundles of straw to form three high walls. A groundsheet served as door and inside was a small wooden table to hold towel and soap. This was the ultimate in luxury under guerrilla conditions and it meant that baths could be taken in privacy at any time of day, an important point for guerrillas in transit who wanted a brief rest and bath before moving on.

That morning I left camp with Barry and a platoon led by Pansao for an abandoned Portuguese fort where we were to rendezvous with a mine detail who had been working in the area since early morning. We carried water bottles but no food. It was a brilliantly clear Sunday morning and we were to take a roundabout route through the forest to inspect the wreckage of a Portuguese aircraft shot down with machine-gun fire during an all-day bombing raid that had pounded the sector not long before. The trek was exhilarating for the first hour, for we passed noisy families of monkeys and brilliant toucans fluttering in the branches. The toucan, a large and multicolored tropical bird, can climb to great heights with the aid of its big feet and hooked beak, so large in proportion to his size that one wondered how balance was maintained. They screamed and whistled when we passed underneath and, filled with suspicion, hoisted themselves onto higher branches to watch our retreat.

We crossed old and abandoned elephant tracks, skinny paths almost grown over now. The forest became dryer as we crunched farther into its heart, and the rich greens had taken on a yellow tinge. The paths were dustier and dead branches crashed without warning from giant trees within, causing an explosive sound that never failed to startle me. One could sense the shortage of water here and the struggle for survival among the trees. Their own roots had pushed themselves out of the earth to climb the parent tree again, sometimes choking its life out as they worked toward sun and air. Others had loosed their hold and fallen to the ground just before they reached the top.

Another hour and I was gasping for air. It was as if the jungle were paralyzed, for not a leaf moved nor a bush quivered in the vise of the noon heat. Swarms of gnats tormented our perspiring faces and we poured water down our necks and backs.

"That's a caiman's cave," said Barry, pointing to a jagged hollow at the base of a tree. "It's abandoned now." I glimpsed a broad, deep shelter, subterranean and cool. "He has gone to live closer to water, a sign that the streams have dried up around here."

A caiman is a species of African crocodile which sometimes reaches six meters in length; their heavy carapace can resist bullets. Although formidably quick in water, their tank-like bodies are cumbersome and slow on land. The situation must have been desperate for this one to have heaved himself from that merciful coolness for the long pull to the river.

Pansao, Barry, and the rest walked effortlessly in the heat, and seemed to perspire far less than I, who had hoped that my earlier marches in Mozambique would have toughened me for the ordeal in Portuguese Guinea. But I was as nonathletic as ever as I wheezed down the paths. This was probably accounted for by my reversion to normal patterns on my return home from Mozambique and also by the fact that I was a heavy smoker. Most of the guerrillas smoked only occasionally, if at all, and I recalled a long lecture on the smoking question that Cabral had once given me.

The immediate problem was heat, however, and I was relieved to find that our vanguard was resting around the next bend. Barry and another cadre had cut leafy green branches from a small bush to form pillows for us, and as we sprawled gratefully on the ground, someone dragged up more branches with which to cover our bodies. We lay like a row of leafy mounds, protected from flies and gnats and basking in the cool air as it filtered through the layers. As I dozed, the mounds that were Barry and the nearest guerrilla suddenly sprang up, scattering leaves in all directions.

"A gazelle. Let's go," said Barry and in a flash both men

were off into the bush after it, stopping only long enough to snatch a lightweight rifle and the pistol from Barry's holster. If they brought it down, there would be gazelle meat back at camp that night. Because of bombardment, much of the game had migrated into other regions and the men let few opportunities go by.

Through gaps in the underbrush I glimpsed a large, brown animal standing absolutely still; abruptly it sprang away at right angles. There was a shot, and another and another, and shouts of "He's ahead!" and then more shooting. And finally silence.

The dying gazelle had collapsed in a clearing and one of the men had quickly slit its throat with a bush knife. It was sleek and well-fed and under two years old, but Barry was ashamed of its many wounds.

"A clear shot in these forests isn't easy," said Barry, "but it died hard and we don't like to hurt an animal unnecessarily." He covered the head and bloodied throat with leaves; it would be collected on our return. If left unprotected, the scent would attract flies and possibly other game to feed upon it.

There would be another six hours trekking ahead of us, and we had already run out of water. There was a hasty palaver and Pansao went off alone to search out a water source that he remembered ten miles away. We would join him on the approach road to the abandoned fort, and in the meantime I was to see the downed aircraft.

It lay in a patch of savanna, in three parts over a wide area. It was a Fiat jet and its Portuguese pilot had died instantly.

The downing of an enemy aircraft was a considerable morale booster in guerrilla and civilian eyes, for the planes caused devastating losses in civilian lives, destroyed whole villages, and flattened the food-growing areas. It also represented a visible victory over a force far more technically advanced than the guerrillas could ever hope to be. Having

151

already driven the Portuguese from much of the land, the men were now knocking them out of the sky, despite the serious shortage of antiaircraft guns which necessitated dragging them from one region to another wherever needed most. The PAIGC had no aircraft of any kind, which meant that, unless there were antiaircraft weapons in the gunpits below, the enemy were unchallenged during aerial reconnaissance or strike missions, and except for lucky machine-gun fire, could drop their bomb load almost with impunity before flying back to Bissau only twenty minutes away.

Portuguese pilots flying reconnaissance missions were told to pinpoint unusually large concentrations of people near villages or crossing open fields, which to them signified the possible presence of mobile guerrilla units below. Then the bombers were sent out.

The Africans were convinced, however, that the Portuguese often practiced free bombing with no purpose other than to shake civilian support of the PAIGC by blowing whole villages out of existence, at the same time picking off symbols of PAIGC enterprise such as local schools and field clinics. It did not seem to matter how many civilians died in the process.

Viewed from the ground, the tactics seemed absurd against a revolution which had reached the irreversible point that this one had. This was no local, unfinished rebellion; and although the bombardments certainly terrorized the population, they were by no means driven to repudiate the liberation movement which fought in their name and now controlled three-quarters of the country. And by control was meant not only guerrilla presence, but the existence of an administrative system with all that this implied.

On the contrary, every overflying aircraft was a winged bully, and every bomb which tore up a village or maize patch was a symbol of a Portuguese paternalism that never was.

It is difficult to convince a population which you are intent on disemboweling that you are concerned only with its well-being, a proposition advanced frequently in Portuguese propaganda leaflets so ill-timed that they sometimes fluttered down in the wake of the bombardments themselves. The object was to imply that civilian sufferings would be over if only they surrendered, but the blacks were often too busy burying their dead to look at the pictures.

"The fort is about a mile ahead," broke in Barry, as we emerged abruptly from the forest onto an unexpected country road. It was wide enough to take a truck, and had once been used to supply the fort until guerrilla ambushes had closed it off.

"The mines have been cleared out of this patch, but don't stray off the sides, just in case," he warned. For the first time I found no difficulty in keeping up with the men, and forgot all demoralizing thoughts of hunger or thirst or fatigue as we trekked past innocent clumps of greenery growing from the shallow, sandy embankments.

In twenty minutes we had reached the rendezvous, a small stone bridge spanning a dry riverbed. Perched along its low walls were some fifteen armed guerrillas, including the bomb disposal expert whose task was to recover the enemy mines. The group had also drained the last of its own water supply, and we sat in sweaty pools along the bridge, consumed by the sun and wearily picking at our damp trouser legs. Then someone sighted a tiny figure moving jauntily toward us on the road. It was Pansao, who strode up grinning broadly under his wild mass of hair. He carried two large glass globes filled to the brim with clear water, and had walked a total of seventeen miles through the bush to bring it. There was an orgy of splashing and replenishing of water canteens and the men were alert and cheerful once again.

But there was to be no savoring our new sense of well-being for it was already late afternoon and we must move immediately if I was to see the fort before dark.

We formed a column just beyond the bridge, and Pansao and the demolitions expert swung into the vanguard. The rest of the men, their weapons and water canteens hanging from shoulders and belts, dropped silently into place ahead and behind me.

This was no loosely bunched, casual trekking formation, with the occasional quip or snatches of a song, and I wondered at the unexpected imposition of strict and apparently unwarranted caution. The fort had been abandoned, after all, and there were no Portuguese patrols in the area. Although the men marched steadily onward there was an imperceptible hesitation in their well-muscled bodies, an unusual lightness in their tread.

"The road is mined from here onward," said Pansao. At first I thought that it must be some ghastly mistake, but then recalled that the Portuguese had always mined the approaches to their forts.

"We have been lifting them out of here for some time," said Pansao, "but we started on this part only this morning and we cannot tell how many are left."

At this point, the demolitions man pointed to a metal slab along the roadside on which lay rows of small, dark objects, like square iron cakes on a confectioner's tray. Each was topped with a tiny, plastic button like the decorative blob on a petit four. Just underneath lay the attached detonator and if stepped upon the explosion could tear the legs off or rend the crotch or split open the abdomen, depending upon the angle of the victim and at which point he had stepped.

They were "antipersonnel" mines and because of their plastic caps could not be sensed through the headset of a normal mine-detector. Instead, the expert used a simple metal probe with which he prodded the ground ahead, inch by inch. Barry told me that some of these men possessed an uncanny sense which warned them of the presence of buried mines even without the use of a probe.

As we inched toward the fort, the men absolutely quiet, I was gripped not with fear, surprisingly, but with a steadily rising sense of an evil so awesome and proximal, a peril so acute, that it blocked all emotions of terror or despair or panic. There was only an all-pervading and insupportable tension which seemed to originate in the calves of the legs and unfold in layers as it rose, like a large, black rubber flower, finally to settle in the brain where it lay flopping and breathing.

"Walk where the terrain is hard," cautioned Barry. "Follow exactly in my footsteps. Don't go near any loose patches of earth. Step exactly where I step."

I saw nothing except the ground directly ahead, every square inch of it, with a concentration so intense that my vision on either side had shut down and the world was only the treads which Barry's canvas shoes had made.

"There's one over there," called the specialist, pointing a few yards to his right. We stopped in our tracks and watched him circle his quarry. There was a tiny pillow of soft sand about an inch high and the cadre, on all fours now, crept up on it with caution, his eyes driving into the terrain close by. He was looking for a second mine which may have been planted to booby-trap rescuers arriving to pick up the casualty from the first should it have been set off. There was nothing suspicious, however, and he now lay spreadeagled on his stomach, carefully blowing away the little sand pillow like an archeologist whisking the dust from an ancient find.

Just underneath was the plastic button and with infinite patience he blew a tiny trench all around, then lifted out the mine and carried it back to the tray. Just then there was a loud bang from the roadside where a group of guerrillas were examining a small object. A detonator had inadvertently gone off but no one was injured.

"*No bai*—Let's go," said Pansao in Guinea-Creole, and the column moved on.

"Ask him how much farther the mined area extends," I peeped to Barry. The strain had apparently affected my vocal cords, for my voice bled out as through a filter, in thin, volumeless cheeps. This startled me and added considerably to my distress, for I was certain that I could maintain my nerve in these circumstances only through a calm and detached façade, mainly for my own benefit at this point. Once I humiliated myself in my own eyes, I would capitulate to the coward fluttering around inside. Now, my own voice was betraying me. I already knew that just below the tension lay the instinctive fear, and beneath that the dread which, if permitted to take hold, would send me racing back to the safety of the bridge. I had considered this prospect earlier, during a moment of rising hysteria; but one doesn't simply excuse oneself from a guerrilla column and there was also the possibility of treading on a mine during my miserable retreat.

We passed a three-foot crater in the road and embedded around the rim were the remains of a blue and white shirt once belonging to a civilian. He had stepped on a mine there the previous month while hunting in the area. It was a pathetic and unnerving spectacle and the men glanced back without expression as we passed. I had been privately speculating over the apparent sanguinity with which the men reacted, not only to the unseen danger buried under our route, or its more visible consequences around that jagged hole, but to the audible all-day bombardment in the next region which at any moment might be extended into our own.

Later, when I learned more about them, I was to realize that their coolness was due, not to lack of imagination or tension or even fear, but to a strictly observed code which prohibited the overt display of normal emotion in a situation of mortal danger.

To do otherwise would be to acknowledge that every casualty was a crippling blow to the revolution itself, or every mission a potential death trap, a notion which could quickly demoralize and intimidate an entire guerrilla unit and finally the nation itself. This is not to say that the dead were not mourned or honored or revenged, simply that a perspective was kept and ranks were closed. For their part, the guerrillas took normal precautions, were audacious when necessary, and insured that Portuguese casualties outnumbered their own.

I watched the demolitions man with greater attention. He had a bland, cheerful face and he worked with apparent casualness. Actually, he was extremely cautious and the patience with which he removed a mine indicated the degree of respect in which he held it.

I had been too engrossed in Barry's footsteps to notice our objective, the abandoned fort of Gandambel which loomed up at our right without warning. It was a decaying building of whitewashed mud-brick and its surrounding yard was already overgrown with weeds and brush and part of its corrugated iron roof had been knocked off.

It looked like a large, rectangular warehouse, not at all conforming to my expectations, and it was encircled by a barbed wire fence. It had been abandoned only three months before, yet in its neglected state seemed to have been deserted far longer.

It stood bleaching and flaking in the center of a bare field for all trees and high bushes had been cut down during its occupancy, allowing a clear field of fire for its defenders and also handicapping guerrilla penetration without warning up to its very doorstep.

Despite its state of decay, there was an unexpected air of durability about the graceless structure, so incongruous in this jungle land of straw villages where lives were lived in such fragile truce with the surroundings.

Perhaps the inclusion of doors and windows and its ugly iron roof gave it its aura of defiance against the encroaching bush. It was clearly a transplant from an alien world, however, for while an African villager may coexist with the bush, he will never challenge it. I also suspected that the village huts with their sloping rush roofs and air vents would be cooler than the interior of this fort.

Would I like to accompany Pansao and some of the men inside? The answer was no, for I was certain that in my present state of fumbling ineptitude I would surely be booby-trapped. In retrospect the prospect seems unlikely as Pansao or Barry would have prevented my touching anything remotely suspect. But the coward within was howling with dismay. I had somehow pushed my luck far enough.

I have often regretted the decision because the interior of a building can often yield valuable clues as to how its inhabitants had once lived, even if all furnishings have been removed.

What was the condition of the floors, and were the walls whitewashed or painted?—a possible indication of the expenditure that the military had been willing to make on one of its remote outposts, and also of the degree of permanency which it had expected.

What facilities had been provided for the men, if any, and how were they billeted? What were the washing and latrine facilities, and where was the garbage dump in an area thick with mines? Small things, but a hint as to the degree of smartness—or slovenliness—that had been maintained.

As it happened, the fort may have proved comparatively safer than the road, for ten minutes later I came within a hairsbreadth of setting off a tripwire which, if stumbled onto, would have caused a series of explosions immediately under and around us.

While Pansao reconnoitered the fort, I had continued the march with another group, my relief over leaving the immediate area having caused an unusual degree of talkativeness on my part. As I gabbled on, I caught sight of a thin black wire running under thickly growing creepers lying across much of the road, an innocent jungle plant which grew profusely in the region. In another stride, my toe would have hooked through it. I froze in midstep and Barry, who had seen it the same instant as I, reached out to steady me. Somehow, the men ahead had missed it by fractions of inches, but they would have also died in the resulting explosions.

We stepped over it carefully, warned the men behind, and continued on. It was dusk now, and in the rapidly waning light the road became difficult to see, the firmer terrain merging with the loose patches, and creepers and bush plants intruding from the forest sometimes obscuring our route altogether. In a few months, the road would be completely overgrown, for the first rains had already begun.

And after the monsoons, when the earth would dry completely again, the road would harden into a solid surface and no longer betray the softer parts under which the mines lay. When originally placed, the soil over the mine could not be firmed because the weight of a hand could have set off the detonator.

The guerrillas had also learned to use mines against the enemy, often those that had been taken from Portuguese supply depots or dug up around forts. The heavier types were used to blow up transport trucks on the link routes, or to ambush troop convoys moving from one area to another. When the convoy halted in the confusion, the guerrillas waiting in the forest attacked quickly, inflicting still heavier damage and often capturing arms and ammunition.

I saw the remains of one of these trucks at a junction in the road, a burnt out rusting hulk which had once carried over twenty men. All had been killed during the attack.

Pansao rejoined us here, reporting that except for a few old tables left behind, the fort was bare. Antipersonnel mines had been "planted like potatoes" on the unpaved driveway, haphazardly, and very close together. They were also placed at the entrance and under the windows.

Once clear of the zone, we trekked steadily back to camp and arrived several hours late for a dinner which Antonio had saved for us. It was grilled river fish, freshly caught that evening.

In the meantime our gazelle had been carried into camp from its hidden clearing by the militia who had waited until sundown to reduce chances of spoilage. It would hang all night from a tree behind Antonio's cooking shelter. As we sat over our fish and palm sauce, one of the carriers appeared from out of the darkness and held out a swollen finger for us to examine. With frightened eyes he explained that something had bitten him as he reached into a clump of bushes, and he was uncertain whether it had been a small animal or a poisonous snake. We saw a small puncture at the swollen tip and one of the men, who had the only anti-snake serum within miles, raced into his hut for the precious vial while I fumbled in my pack for a hypodermic syringe. Just before slamming our terrified victim down on a bench and removing his trousers for the injection, however, we examined the bite again. The swelling had not spread upward from the finger, which had been already bound at its base, and on further inquiry we learned that the incident had occurred over half an hour before.

He showed no other symptoms of poisoning, and I announced confidently that he would have been dead already if indeed bitten by a snake (I learned later, to my chagrin, that this is not always true). But the carrier, a spindly, middle-aged Balante in plastic sandals, seemed greatly reassured and we decided to save our only injection for confirmed cases.

Next morning our patient was walking cheerfully around camp, a spot of iodine on his bandaged finger which had been applied by one of the PAIGC's less excitable first-aiders. Later, I was to dine with a Balante witch doctor who had his own secret remedy for snakebite, but that was to be many canoe journeys away. In the meantime, I was to hear about the development of the war from the military point of view.

160

14

THE PAIGC'S MEN IN THE FIELD, INCLUDING THE MILITARY, had a marked socio-political view of the revolution which had not only short-circuited the warlord syndrome very early on, but had also expedited the shifting of men from guerrilla units into varying noncombative duties and back again with little disruption in attitudes or behavior patterns.

An important reason for this was the presence of a political commissar at the elbow of every unit even remotely connected with day-to-day revolutionary tasks. Each front had its chief commissar, and under him a widening pyramid of commissar-cadres which reached to the very foundations of this jungle administration—the five-member committee in every *tabanca* (village) in the liberated zones. The commissar was a combination mobilizer, political mainliner, complaint department, troubleshooter, father confessor, cheerleader, and advisor, and there was no doubt that in the field, the political superseded the military.

"We are a political party, not a military organization"—they told me again and again, in case I had forgotten, and lest they themselves should forget.

Every guerrilla unit had its commissar, and he often fought alongside the men on ambush missions. There was one in every first aid post, every bush school, every training camp, and militia group. Often he had been drawn from the ranks of early mobilizers who had gained valuable experience of peasant psychology and habits.

He was the spark which had encouraged the population to defend besieged villages with bows and arrows when arms were few, and to fell trees and dig pit traps across the roads to disrupt approaching enemy convoys.

As the direct link with the party and its political bureau, he was the grassroots spirit of the revolution, the black "man on the spot" in Portuguese Guinea, who slept in peasant huts and ate peasant rice, marched with the fighters and slept on the ground as they did.

Through ceaseless contact, reinforced by attitude and example, the notion was implanted that the guerrilla was only a militant with a gun, a civilian turned inside out. Their unarmed brothers, their comrades, made equally important contributions and were to be as highly respected as themselves.

The idea may have been deflating at first, but guerrilla motivation had to be based upon solid concepts which generated admiration, not fear. For terror was a Portuguese product, they reasoned, and to the peasant it would have made little difference who imposed it; should this principle be ignored, support would be gradually withdrawn and the movement would have found itself without its peasant prop.

There is no guerrilla elite, therefore, and none of the gunslinging which might be possible in limited rebellions or in amateur bands. To the armed PAIGC fighter, his life was neither outstanding nor unusual, and the risks that he took were no more remarkable than those taken by the oft-bombed civilian, his contribution only as valuable as that of the unarmed rice grower who cultivated for the cause.

If there is one *gaffe* which a PAIGC guerrilla fears to

make, it is affronting the peasantry. A unit on the move and seeking food or shelter for the night, or extra carriers to help haul their loads across the forests, will deal directly and only with the *tabanca* committee, whose civilian members are elected by the village itself. This avoids unseemly altercations with any recalcitrant elements, saves considerable time, and pinpoints responsibility squarely.

The PAIGC had early discovered that a sense of responsibility is an acquired trait and one often overlooked in the character-molding efforts which accompanied Portugal's mission in Africa. This was, therefore, another new notion to be patiently reinforced at bush level, and painful though the results could sometimes be, there is no African within the revolutionary structure who is not "responsible" for something. And the word has been carefully chosen—there are no bosses, no directing elite in khaki, simply "brothers" and "sisters" responsible for something. The results have been generally encouraging, and the principle also reaches to the very core of the guerrilla.

Military leaders on all levels are respected, and followed, because of a demonstrated sense of responsibility along with their fighting experience. Should they prove no longer able to lead or to take initiative, they are quietly transferred or replaced.

There are no military insignias or badges, no saluting, and in general no rank strata in the military branch. Although men leading whole regions or sectors are called "commandants" those heading small mobile attack units are referred to simply as "leaders." In battle orders, the tight little squads cooperating in major attacks are cited only as "Comrade X's" group.

The subtle deference shown men like Nino Vieira, the military commander of the Southern Front, grew out of respect for qualities that he had demonstrated over a long period—fairness, coolness, and his assumption of responsibility.

He seemed equally as commanding in mufti as in combat uniform, and around camp he usually wore a tee shirt and Levis. His hut was in a group of three set in a quiet grove 100 yards from the main camp and on his tree-shaded conference table strode a brilliantly feathered baby toucan which perched on the spread of papers and upset the coffee mugs. Nino's only sign of rank was a large, square gold ring inscribed with his initials and a wristwatch with three rows of luminous dials, including a stopwatch and the date. The watch supplies were usually limited to those whose jobs required a knowledge of exact time, such as military leaders, reconnaissance men, and coordinating administrators.

For the rest, time was a rough estimate, the position of the sun, or the signal to move off. Nino also possessed a flashlight which the men were continually borrowing, and a sturdy transistor which brought him African and foreign newscasts.

He had powerful arms and shoulders and an unexpectedly small waist, and his open face was uncluttered by dilemma or calculation. He was the product of fourteen years of revolutionary planning and practice and had long ago learned to pare away the nonessentials in his life.

Although not much older than the average cadre, there was an air of seasoned maturity about him, and beneath the uncomplicated manner was a steadiness which the men relied upon. He smiled easily, talked freely but not unnecessarily, and treated his men with quiet respect. They called upon him naturally and on many nonmilitary occasions, and I once watched him leave his place in a truck's crowded rear to direct its extrication from a water-filled trench.

There was a misleading informality in relations between military leaders like Nino and their men, yet a strong element of discipline which made disobedience a rarity. Nino ascribed this to the "fraternal" nature of the party, and the "strong sense of mutual respect between the men." To me, it all seemed too simple, too idealistic, and asked much of

164

the average man's "level of consciousness" which they talked about so often. Yet the men believed in it as did so obviously Nino, and the fact remained that the average PAIGC cadre was a dedicated component in the revolutionary machine, responding freely to tasks which called frequently for personal sacrifice and intense physical discomfort.

There was no crude brainwashing, and the original decision to join the revolution actively was never imposed from without. In fact, the PAIGC had more guerrilla volunteers than they could handle. But once inside its ranks, the recruit found that discipline was applied indirectly, both by the example of colleagues and by the presence of political commissars who, in explaining the reasons for the war in the first place, also stressed the necessary development of "self-discipline" within the fraternal structure. For the first time, the average black Guinean was made conscious of social needs far outside his immediate tribe or village, and of a vision so revolutionary in concept, so stunning in its personal implications, that to interfere with its dynamic and almost tangible momentum by an individualistic act of egoism seemed a shabby display of gross selfishness. More important, the shame which resulted would be generated from within.

The result was, said Nino, that "we can fraternize very much with our men without affecting their response to orders during enemy engagements."

What about recruitment and training? What were the qualities sought in the guerrilla?

The movement, he said, looked especially for men of "good behavior, courage, and intelligence." On the surface, it seemed usual recruitment poster material in any Western country, except that this was no conventional war and its aims profoundly affected each new recruit personally.

Normally, guerrilla training is done inside liberated areas and consists of two to three months of basic training in camouflage, principles of bush warfare, deployment, weaponry, and marching. Concurrently, there are courses in simple political theory and revolutionary aims. Further experience is gained in actual combat, and if a man seems exceptionally good leadership material, he is sent abroad for further specialization.

Having already had personal experience of the rigorous pace set on many of the marches, I questioned Nino further on this point; since even the women and children seemed able to cover long distances without apparent effort, why the necessity to include it in basic training?

"Although the average African is a born walker," conceded Nino, "a soldier must learn what we call disciplined marching. This means reaching a level of nine hours daily, nonstop, for four days, at four miles an hour with arms and pack. He must also learn to go hungry at the same time."

This meant 36 miles a day strapped to pack and gun, on an empty stomach, through jungle, woodland, and fields, across streams and rivers, and in heat and humidity so persistent that clothing never really dried. And at the end, there must be sufficient stamina remaining to engage the enemy if necessary.

Although small-arms supplies in the PAIGC had now built up to a "fairly satisfactory" level in bush war terms, the quantity had been so limited in the early days that commandos were often equipped with only three weapons per group. These bedraggled assault forces sometimes reached as high as 30 to a band, and their main purpose at the time was to attack small enemy convoys to capture their weapons.

Since the blacks were so poorly armed for these forays, their only source of protection seemed to lie in their own agility and their recourse to the tribal magician-medicine man. According to a PAIGC document, the animist elements among the men had sometimes asked party money to finance ritual ceremonies before a confrontation with the Portuguese.

"That was the role of the magician in the revolution," the report states somewhat wryly. "In most cases the men would get the money for rituals because they were so poorly armed it was fair to assume that they needed a source of strength.

"Later," the report goes on, "when the party had acquired enough weapons and ammunition, anyone asking money for rituals would be handed a machine-gun by his leader and told 'this is all you need now because this is what the Portuguese have. From now on, this is your god because your life will depend upon it.' "

Gradually, as weapons supplies increased and large groups became unwieldy, the normal guerrilla unit was filed down to 21 cadres with submachine-guns, one heavy machine-gun, and a bazooka. They were led by a group commander and the twenty-third man in the party was the political commissar.

There were also problems other than arms shortages, recalled Nino. There were no maps in earlier days, and men from other regions did not understand the layout of the land. Local civilians acted as guides, while their families helped to feed the men. Until food supplies could be organized on a steadier basis, however, this had always been an acute problem for the population itself was underfed. Another problem was uniforms, clothing, and boots. A heavy cotton uniform lasts an average of three months in the bush, and a guerrilla fortunate enough to be issued one had no replacement when it fell apart. His personal clothing, if he possessed any, would then be substituted and this, too, was quickly destroyed.

"Fortunately," said Nino, "at the same time that civilians were helping us increasingly with food, friendly countries had begun to contribute more arms and uniforms."

There is still a considerable shortage of boots, however,

and entire guerrilla groups sometimes go to war in sea-green plastic sandals, pausing enroute to repair broken straps or whack out mud collected in the soles. Inconveniences such as these are not permitted to hamper the war effort; a main concern now seems to be sufficient clothing for the civilian population.

All supplies, military and civilian, are lugged into the interior by carriers and sometimes by canoe in regions such as the South which are crisscrossed by rivers and canals.

All carriers are militia and village volunteers and include men, women, and teenagers who have already been mobilized and regard their work as a service to the revolution. During these "missions" they are fed by the movement unless they carry their own rice supply.

The PAIGC had opened its first front in 1963 in the South, and within two years had opened two others in the North and East. They are demarcated by two main Guinea rivers, the Geba which flows to the Atlantic past the capital of Bissau from the country's heartland as far as Bambadinca; and the Corubal which splits down from the Geba to snake across the shoulder of the Southern Front and up through the Eastern Boé region. From these rivers break hundreds of uncharted canals and lagoons—low-lying, mosquito-infested, and hung with trees.

The Portuguese still hold a considerable chunk of the Northeast and certain enclaves inland; but they are encircled either by contested zones or those completely controlled by the PAIGC. They are also entrenched in large, claw-like areas along the coast including the portion containing Bissau and the old capitol of Bolama, and further south in the offshore Bissagos islands where live a tribe of the same name.

There are guerrilla raids within 20 miles of Bissau, sabotage operations at the airport, and incidents in the main towns. There is also growing underground agitation in the archipelago of Cape Verde, a triangle of ten, formerly volcanic islands lying in the Atlantic west of Senegal which are still Portuguese-held.

Their link with the Guinea mainland reaches back to the fifteenth century when their position on an important maritime route made them a natural receiving and processing center for black slaves from the mainland. Until Portuguese occupation, they had been deserted except for occasional Senegalese fishing parties.

Later, when slaving ostensibly ended, the white Cape Verdian *"seigneurs"* who had entrenched themselves there turned to farming, this time using mainland blacks as unpaid field hands and cattle herders.

Sexual liaison soon developed between male Europeans and black women, and as a result most of Cape Verde's population of 200,000 are now blacks or *mestizos*. Because of their mainland ethnic origin, the PAIGC regard them as an integral part of the Portuguese Guinea revolution, and I saw several Cape Verdian revolutionaries in the bush who appeared as white as I, and who are accepted in this predominantly black movement without question. The eventual liberation of Cape Verde is also among the main aims of the party, of course, and the "C" in the PAIGC is there to stress the point.

On the Guinea mainland, guerrilla ambushes and raids are mounted day and night in relentless efforts to keep the enemy off balance with attacks on his garrisons, his trucks, boats, and bush patrols. Besides the countless harassment operations, at least four very large-scale attacks, often involving as many as 100 guerrillas, are carried out each month against key installations. In the process, says the PAIGC, the Portuguese are suffering heavy losses which are rarely publicized abroad. In one month alone, guerrilla attacks on Portuguese forts and transport cost the enemy 239 confirmed dead, including 28 found after special commando forces blew up two gunboats on the Geba and Cumbidja rivers.

In reprisal, the Portuguese destroyed twelve African villages during bombardments which killed fifteen civilians and wounded thirteen—again PAIGC figures—attacked a field clinic and dropped 30 napalm canisters on an African primary school on the Eastern Front.

Reluctant to announce guerrilla casualty figures for the benefit of enemy ears, the PAIGC will only say that they are "far less" than their opponent's. The party attributes this to guerrilla mobility and relative compactness, and familiarity with the bush. Moreover, the casualties caused when a ship or truck carrying large numbers of troops is destroyed are almost certain to be heavier than those inflicted on a strike-and-run guerrilla band with the advantage of surprise on its side. And the fact that Portuguese patrols unfamiliar with normal forest hazards suddenly find themselves thrust into a bush war can be quite demoralizing.

African civilians are fond of saying that "although the enemy march with uniforms and strong boots, they fear the serpents and the animals and the forests," a notion which gives the blacks, barefooted and bush-wise since childhood, a valuable psychological advantage over their opponents.

Then, the guerrillas are a normally careful lot, insisting on careful reconnaissance before attacks and holding their mine casualties to a minimum by either pinpointing or removing them before all-out raids against the forts. There is a vast intelligence network in the bush which depends upon the surveillance skills of militia members and trained civilians who report troop movements and mine-laying operations to the nearest village committee commissar. Unseen eyes are always watching from the bush.

In Nino's opinion, the average Portuguese soldier "does not want to fight. They demand immediate air support when in trouble although they usually far outnumber us, and they disperse quickly after very brief combat." They had apparently had some degree of antiguerrilla training, he went on, which included ambush tactics, mine-laying, and the use of helicopters in bush warfare. But they lacked "initiative" he said, their morale was low, and they seemed uncertain about why they were fighting in the first place. From the guerrilla viewpoint, their main danger lay in their aircraft, helicopters, and minefields, but even so the casualties they caused were frequently civilian.

15

THREE DAYS EARLIER, CARMEN HAD LEFT FOR HER BASE IN the interior where I was to join her eventually on foot and by canoe. She had taken Awah and a small escort with her, and besides the replacements to our own column, I was also to be accompanied by Pedro and Boubacar Camara, the latter a youthful liberal arts graduate who had joined the revolution only a year before, had made the difficult transition to bush life, and now wore his sidearm with pride.

We numbered about fifteen, including volunteer carriers who milled over heavy loads of rice, fruit juice, canned meat for emergencies, cooking pots, and live hens which had been lured into six-cornered baskets placed in the shade.

By way of a pleasant announcement, the men told me that much of the journey would be undertaken in a *"pirogue,"* the translation of which I had misunderstood, and for some time I wondered hopefully if it were some amphibious, Rube Goldberg contraption that the men had contrived as a cunning substitute for walking.

Actually it is a French word for the type of fast African canoe carved from a tree trunk and driven by long, fixed

172

paddles handled by a varying number of crew. When its meaning was eventually explained I was doubly delighted at the prospect of cool river breezes fanning our cheerful, up-turned faces as we shot past darkening mangroves, and perhaps even a hearty river chant or two from the Balante paddlers. Equally important, it would mean conserving our energy for the long overland treks which the humidity rendered so exhausting.

The revolution was suddenly very remote, and even the bombardment in the distance seemed unreal, as if there were no villagers below and no one was really under fire. We left camp after lunch, allowing ample time to meet the 8 o'clock *pirogue* at a prearranged anchorage along a thickly wooded embankment. It would take us far into the interior and save at least a two days' march.

We covered the distance rapidly, there being no lagging on my part because of good times ahead, and also because Nino was escorting us to the canoe. He might cut me out of the column and order me back to camp should I falter along the route. I threaded my way robustly through wooded meadows and wide fields still littered, in parts, with spent bullets and large, twisted sheets of burst shells. The territory had been dearly won.

We reached the anchorage just after dark. African canoes rarely travel before dusk, being easy daylight targets for swooping jets patrolling the waterways. Many of the civilian canoes carrying food and barter goods for the liberated zones—called "production canoes"—had been previously blown out of the water and the boatmen were taking no more chances. We were to travel overnight for two nights by canoe and would rest by day near villages close to the shore.

I was to learn that waiting for a *pirogue* in an African jungle is somewhat like waiting for a Mediterranean shuttle-bus; its route is open to negotiation, its arrival time dubious, and its contents unpredictable. I was also to learn that a *pi-*

173

rogue's time schedule is utterly dependent upon the *marée,* the French word used by Barry to mean the tide. The *marée,* moody and whimsical in its rise and fall, was to rule our lives for much of our journey into the interior.

We waited almost two hours for our first *pirogue* that night, crouched in the bush and talking softly. Beneath overhanging trees, another canoe already moored swayed gently with the undercurrent, its outlines barely visible in the moonlit darkness. The region was thick with creepers and mosquitoes, and the damp jungle earth smelled of swamps and the fat, skittering bugs which swarmed about on frantic missions of their own. They were referred to as gas beetles and gave off an overpowering stench of decay when stepped upon, a kind of revengeful last gasp which swept through the immediate vicinity and hung on the night air for hours.

A single lantern glowed dimly in the bushes to guide our canoe, and there was an occasional dull splash as an animal slipped into the water. I could hear the rhythmic creak of fixed wooden oars as our *pirogue* neared, and their pull against the locks when lifted. There were voices and female cries from the darkness and an answering call from the sentry. Then it skimmed up triumphantly with the tides and veered toward our embarkation point, rolling in the current only five yards from shore as flashlights snapped on.

It was a water-borne Mammy wagon, and I watched fascinated as passengers of all sizes and shapes tumbled out and waded to shore in the pale light. It was a produce canoe, and its occupants were struggling up the embankment with large woven baskets of kola nuts, rice, chickens, and eggs, their soft voices hailing friends on shore, and their children tied to their backs.

Originally built to carry some twelve passengers in relative comfort, I was certain that double that number had wedged themselves into the oval-bottomed barque.

Many of the Balante women were barebosomed—dark

brown women hung with amulets and headscarves, iron bracelets clinging to their upper arms. From the waist down they wore a wrapover length of cloth reaching to their calves and fixed into place with a deft twist—no knots, pins, buttons, or hooks. They could walk miles through the bush without mishap, carrying children on their backs, water buckets in their hands, and swaying baskets on their heads.

As they waded to shore, bending and calling with the moonlight on their backs, they looked like bright jungle spirits washed up with the tide. Their men, in rolled trousers and ragged shirts stood to their knees in water and handed up the children left sitting in the canoe, then unloaded the heavier baskets while the women made camp under the trees. There would be an overland march for most of them the next day, and they would sleep until dawn.

Guinea women seemed taller, slimmer, and stronger-willed than their Mozambican counterparts, and unless there had been a marked Christian or Islamic influence, were usually bare from neck to waist. There was a jet-black oiled arrogance about some of them, and a subtle core of personal independence which the men could not define but profoundly respected. It was my impression, too, that the West African man did not particularly regard the female breast as an erotic symbol, but rather as a functional part of the anatomy, like an elbow. Rather, it was the legs that mattered, and I noticed that the women kept them modestly covered and as they bent over cooking fires tied their scarves around their hips to prevent skirts from riding up. It made me wonder about all of those Mother Hubbards donned by Christianized African tribeswomen in the past, when all along their menfolk were peering gravely at their shinbones.

When the last kola sack was carried to shore, the men hastily loaded our supplies into the bobbing barge and placed our food stores in the second canoe. Crashing and sliding in the darkness, I was half-carried down the steep, slippery bank and, feeling somewhat like a pampered passenger on a one-fare cruise, was set down with a flourish in a *bonne place* near the bow. My water bottle and raincoat were placed nearby, and alongside them my rucksack and headscarf. In the meantime the men were examining the rough wooden perches which served as seats, for if not fitted well to the curving sides, they would roll under on themselves and flip their occupant backward. To replace the spavined ones which sagged alarmingly amidships, extra lengths were cut from nearby trees and whittled into shape on the spot.

Eventually we were all in place and heading toward midstream, the *pirogue* thrusting forward with the tide. Besides our original column, there were also extra passengers squeezed in among us. To my right sat Boubacar, with Pedro hunched against the narrow stern, just behind the oarsmen. Ranged between us were over twenty other cadres and civilians sitting two across on their precarious perches, guns against their legs. Under our feet from bow to stern lay tightly packed rows of live mortar shells, the weight of which brought the barque within inches of the water line. There were only two crewmen, powerful Balante rivermen with bulging arms and knitted caps. They stood fore and aft, their great shoulders stretching in rhythm as giant paddles strained into the rising river. They rowed barefooted with their trousers rolled to the kneecaps and from ankles upward were deep tears and healed scars from a thousand night canoe trips.

They rowed ceaselessly and silently for hours, down the winding black river and past moonlit shores choked with vegetation and grasping branches, past burnt out fields still smelling of wood ash where plantations had been cleared. Decapitated trees stood like grotesque spines in the darkness, distorted shadow figures pointing toward the bush.

We sat in near-silence, listening to the full, steady ram of

176

wood against wood and the breathing of the paddlers, more labored now. We had all become tired and very hungry and secretly longed for our rice stew and straw bunks and the cheerful evening talks in the camp clearing. At every thrust our wooden perches sawed into the seat of our trousers, and we longed to ease our cramped legs. There would be little sleep until morning and nothing to eat. I swallowed a few mouthfuls from my canteen but the water tasted of gas beetles for we had filled it from a well near the anchorage.

"Is the river water clean?" I asked Boubacar hopefully, for its swiftly running surface was cool to the touch. He shook his head and I thought of crocodiles and lapping lions. I smoked a cigarette and stared at the dark banks and wondered what lay beyond them. From the shore came an occasional screech and flutter and bushes shook.

The men, silent and thoughtful, gazed at the tangled mass of shadows which groped out over the water to brush our *pirogue* as we passed, or reached down to snatch at our sleeves and caps. On several occasions we narrowly missed ramming a floating log or the branches of a fallen tree lying just beneath the surface. We sat closely packed with knees drawn up and backs aching, shifting imperceptibly to ease our tortured bottoms. Heads nodded and shoulders sagged forward and the men began to hold their faces in their hands, lulled to half-sleep by the rhythmic creak and dip of the oars. We were surrendering to the discomfort now, detaching ourselves from the limb or muscle which ached so dully. I pitied the bulge of men behind me, their great long legs confined in tiny spaces and feet twisted under. Some had slowly dropped sideways, angled, their heads coming to rest against the *pirogue*'s splintered rim where hard, unyielding edges cut into the sides of their necks. But they dozed on, their faces turned toward the river.

I wanted to sleep, too, to escape the throbbing cramp that had become my body, but I had not yet learned to doze sitting up. I had lost my headscarf somewhere at the bottom

177

among the mortars and the black ooze that had collected there. As I fumbled around for it the barque wobbled and the men jerked awake, groaning. I stared back with hollow eyes and wan face, a chalk-white *yiran* looming up in the African night, perched on the bow of their *pirogue* like some winged nightmare in midflight, its hair a stiff mass in the humidity. As I tried vainly to find a comfortable position, Boubacar fixed a narrow bed for me of raincoats laid over the rucksacks and shells, spreading my retrieved head-scarf, reasonably clean somehow, under my head. This was the signal for the men to shift into prone positions also, and they were eventually a tangled mass of arms and legs hanging from the sides, their knees hooked over the perches and backs against the mortars. Water and ooze gurgled around the bottom and seeped up past the shells, but we slept on until the tide fell, like a boatload of huddled refugees, silent in our misery.

Abruptly there came the scrape of sand along the hull and then I was the only one in the *pirogue* and the banks had risen high above us on each side. The men had slipped over the side and were lifting our canoe over the sand traps. They stood hip-high, then to the knees in the receding water and finally we scraped to a halt. There was insufficient water to refloat the barque and the breeze, too, had stopped. It had happened in only a few minutes, like someone letting the water out of a bathtub. We sat drooping and dozing in the boat, literally high and dry, and when the tide began to come in a few hours later it sounded like water trickling into an empty tank. Then the trickle became a stream, bubbling and alive again, and our *pirogue* rose slowly and miraculously from its marshy trap. One could feel the pull of the current on the boat like unseen hands along the bottom. It carried us on effortlessly for another few hours until we put in at a near-vertical embankment of ooze, its wet shiny wall daring us to the top. It was not yet dawn and in the darkness far above I saw moving silhouettes with flashlights and rifles.

We slopped to shore and the mud quickly tore off my canvas shoe and a sock, then sucked me under to the knees as I stepped into the embankment, then to the thighs. Throwing his gun to another, one of the men hauled me up behind him and finally, reeling and plunging, carried me through the vise beneath and over the top on his back.

We lay exhausted, craving only water and sleep, but there was a five-mile walk to a village inland. When I stood up to join the forming column, one of the men wordlessly picked up each of my feet, removed shoes and socks and washed each foot thoroughly with water from his canteen, also doused the shoes and socks and just as wordlessly put them back on. It was a precaution against hookworm which lies unseen in warm moist soil and often enters the body through the feet and legs of its potential host. If untreated, it can cause anemia and sometimes death. Scraping mud from legs and clothing as best we could, we plunged up the inky path behind our waiting guide. We were soon joined by a panting carrier with news that our food supplies, which arrived soon after by the second canoe, had been misdirected into still another barque which was now punting heroically against the tide in the opposite direction. With it went our coffee, tea, cigarettes, sugar, and even the hens. At this point we were too tired to care and as we climbed to higher ground the men moved like sleepwalkers with their heavy packs.

We stumbled after our guide, our smarting eyes on the smoking flame of acrid straw which he burned to light our path. He held it aloft as its sparks burst back at our feet like a catherine wheel. When its flame died, he grabbed another bundle from the pathside. The smell of cooking fires from the evening before signaled a settlement ahead and there were goats and a cow tethered off the path. It was a rambling village and when we reached its dark, sleeping heart the column halted before a one-room structure of mud and wattle. There was one door and a small window, both firmly closed with solid wood against mosquitoes. There were several raps and the door was opened by a sleepy African clutching at a cloak. He stood blinking in the torchlight and through the door beyond I saw several figures moving about sleepily and mumbling. There was a hasty conference and we swung back into line. There was a safe shelter another four miles up the hillside, he said, a local primary school in a wooded grove to which one of his relatives would lead us. No use bedding down in the village, he said, for enemy bombers were expected later and we would shift to the forest at first light anyway.

We filled our canteens and wearily pushed on, flailing our robot bodies uphill in speechless exhaustion. A night such as this was quite normal in a black revolutionary's life, and though his whole purpose was geared to that exquisite *raison d'être,* engagement with the enemy, the fact remained that much of guerrilla time was spent in overcoming physical discomfort only indirectly connected with armed confrontation. A main element in protracted bush life, I realized, was its sheer inconvenience and unrelieved discomfort.

We reached the school, a large thatched lean-to with earthen floor, like a picnic shelter in a national park. Some of the men slid promptly onto the benches, leaned over the wooden tables before them and were instantly asleep on their arms; others sprawled against the wooden supports, knees bent, their rucksacks and guns propped alongside.

For me, Boubacar detached two planks that served as benches, dragged them into a corner and over them placed an air mattress and mosquito net. I slept until midafternoon while the warm sun advanced across the floor, awakening to find the others still drowsing and a line of village women gliding up the hillside with water jugs and rice jars on their heads. We were sodden with perspiration and after hasty

180

baths we sat down and ate like boas, many of the men rolling the rice grains in cupped hands directly from the communal bowl.

The younger girls stood shyly at the edge of the grove while their mothers busied themselves around the school, their long breasts hanging like empty skin bags, almost to the waist. The Guinean habit of carrying babies in cloth pouches with the ends tied tightly across their chests eventually broke down the breast muscles after years of childtoting, an unfortunate disfigurement to otherwise athletic bodies.

Pedro, aware of the eleventh-hour difficulties that I always had with my rucksack, always gave me advance warning of our departure. We were to leave for the river at 5 P.M. Bissau time, he said, to rendezvous with another *pirogue* for the continuing journey. There was always a certain confusion about time in the bush, for both "Bissau" and "Republic" time were used, despite the one-hour difference. The latter was maintained because of continual contact with Conakry headquarters and the frequency of border crossings by the cadres. "Bissau" time, of course, underlined the fact that they were on home ground.

To avoid misunderstandings, the guerrillas always specified which time was meant when rendezvous were set. As in Mozambique, my rucksack problems were always caused by fruitless attempts at neatness in a shapeless, bulging carry-all. And not only must I identify my belongings in the dark, but packing techniques differed according to our accommodations. Life in a *pirogue,* for example, required other articles than those needed in a bivouac, which in turn differed from those used in the more settled existence of a village hut where one could spread out a bit.

Because the rucksack was literally one's house, there was a curious sense of disarray, of needless complication, when articles were misplaced or lost, like someone continually moving the furniture around. And it is not very considerate to keep an entire column waiting while one searches for one's clean socks.

I had already discovered that laundry must be secured separately in a plastic bag, immediately ready for the unpredictable moment when water could be found for this purpose. It was useless telling yourself that piled-up laundry could be done when the base camp was reached in two days' march, for the stay there might be unexpectedly brief.

Ideally, uniforms should be changed twice daily in the wet heat, but clothing often took 24 hours to dry and longer during prolonged rains. If placed still damp in the rucksack it would mildew the entire contents within a few hours. Men with only two changes of clothing were therefore in trouble, but they always managed to look less bedraggled than I. Barry, Boubacar, and Pedro were among the neatest cadres I had seen, and after an all-day march through mudholes and swamps seemed almost as well-pressed as when we had started. Although the question of personal cleanliness is somehow contrary to the general image of unwashed liberators threading down the jungle paths of Africa, the fact remained that the majority of guerrillas hated being dirty. This aversion was so ingrained that, as in Mozambique, footsore commandos would detour miles for a bath, and seized any opportunity to launder their clothing. Even the villagers, however unhygienic in certain other habits, maintained a surprising standard of bodily cleanliness under the primitive circumstances in which they lived. Long before the introduction of commercial soap, they had learned to extract a substance from jungle trees which the men told me was "very strong" and irritating to tender skins. But it did the job and at the same time soothed sandfly and mosquito bites. At one production center, the PAIGC was now manufacturing blocks of soap made from palm oil and soda.

16

WE DEBARKED HURRIEDLY FROM OUR *pirogue,* LEAVING
little hollows amid the piles of equipment which had held our
bodies like canvas nests. The bombardment down river had
already begun and we were clear targets in the soft, early
morning sunshine. There was no mist on the river and fog
patches had already lifted from the fields which we were
soon to cross. Only a few hours before we had sat like wet
birds in the bottom of the boat while a fierce storm had sent
sheets of water against our bowed bodies and soaked us
through despite our raincoats. Our clothing had dried
against our bodies in the early sunshine, its comforting heat
very welcome then.

There had been heavy fire in the area over the past few
days as the guerrillas struck back at Portuguese aerial incursions. But only when an occasional spotter plane droned
directly overhead, hunting for targets that could well include one's own column, did the war become immediate
and very personal. How vulnerable one suddenly felt,
scrambling from the bobbing canoe and racing for cover as
reconnaissance planes circled low, ready to betray us with

some routine radio message about suspicious movements along an obscure riverbank near the Guinean village of X.

Until then it was somebody else's war, an occurrence about which one heard, the devastating results of which one saw, whether with pity or anger or apathy. But it was still somebody else's war. With sudden clarity one now comprehended the existence of a force far superior in arms and equipment which was using this advantage to hunt one down with deadly intent. The transition from the theoretical to the actual had been abrupt but there were no more doubts as we scurried to safety among the leaves like the gas beetles one carelessly tread upon. I was to find that the initial shock was replaced by an unexpected sense of acute annoyance, a bizarre feeling of intrusion which so offended the spirit that one ultimately responded with outrage. I was to experience other emotions, of course, such as alarm or sudden passivity, depending upon how well-camouflaged I supposed myself to be, or how bone-weary I had become.

In my case, exhaustion seemed to produce a vague sense of unreality and a dangerous tendency to underestimate the lethality of enemy intent. It is at this time, I thought, that a guerrilla band or a patrol can become careless and stumble into situations for which they are not psychically prepared.

These reactions are very personal, and are on a purely physical level. Only later, when the immediate danger is past, does one consider again the broader principles involved in black revolution and the "big words" which are invoked. I wondered what the average black villager thought when, going about mundane chores, he was suddenly trapped in a maizefield by encircling helicopters or, when the jets struck, was driven into one of the deep trenches skirting every village—if there was time, of course.

There are no commercial airline flights over Guinea war zones and overhead aircraft could only be Portuguese, and then only helicopters, spotter planes, rocket-spewing jets, or troop transport. These are readily identified by sound, and whatever it is, one heads for the trees until it has disappeared. If already protected by forest camouflage, one listens and watches, immobile, through the gaps in the tree-tops where the sun filters through in yellow shafts and turns the leaves to emerald and blue-green again.

We are now enroute to Carmen's home base on the Southern Front, and we race across open ground between two expanses of forest.

"Their planes can hurt us," I remember one guerrilla saying, as a small aircraft buzzes in the distance, then flies slowly overhead, banking. But we are already in the trees and the sound of its engine recedes. We watch it climb higher, nosing through small patches of cloud. I wonder if it has sighted us, its pilot already radioing back for jet strikes. Only minutes to Bissau, I remember.

We have neither slept nor eaten since yesterday afternoon and as we trudge on I am suddenly dizzy and very warm. Pedro removes the raincoat from my pack and spreads it on the ground, wringing out my scarf in our precious water and patting my face. I sleep for an hour; the men are spread out and dozing against the trees. There are four sentries, and they put up their guns when we rise. We plunge ahead, hurrying, for it will rain soon and the trees are already a deep blue-green in the overcast. But I stumble and falter and fall behind, finally, and they slow the pace. Pedro watches me closely. Suppose I fall and refuse to get up?

They are responsible for me.

We cross great open fields linking one forest to another and I trip clumsily over roots and easily negotiable hillocks. Nothing seems in very clear focus and the humidity lies across our backs like a sodden load. We walk down unending footpaths past unending trees and out into fields again. There are nasty little bridges to get over, narrow little tree trunks thrown across wide, water-filled ditches, and we inch over them, lurching and teetering across bark slippery with mud. The men guide me over, sideways, reaching for my hands, then lead me onto skinny ledges to cross the sunken ricefields. We thread across, single file, plunging and sliding and watching the sky for reconnaissance. Thorn bushes rake our arms and ankles, ripping through our clothing, and we turn back, exasperated, to retrieve wrenched-off shoes from the deep mud.

Is this country really worth fighting for? a visitor, an outsider, would ask himself at moments like this. Is it deserving of such human effort, such unrelenting hardship, where much of the time was spent in simple human survival. Insufferable heat like a fat, clammy hand pressing against the neck and head, the old West African joke—"we have two seasons, hot and very hot"—and oozing rice bogs and dirty water and canoes and humidity and mosquitoes.

Can they seriously consider living here, or fighting over it? I remembered a mention about Portuguese Guinea in some Western guidebook. It rated three lines and the author's ship hadn't bothered to dock at Bissau. Nothing much there. The Portuguese lived there, or something, and there were blacks in the interior who grew rice and peanuts and ran about naked. Just another sweatbox along the old slave coast.

I wanted to return immediately to Conakry and eat cool pineapples on ice and sleep in a bed again and squirt everything with insect repellent and stand in a cool shower all morning and then sleep again. A nonrevolutionary, probably a counterrevolutionary; I wished them well, of course.

It began to rain, in hard, driving torrents which bent the towering oil palms and flattened their finger-like fronds and almost knocked us from our feet. Rain and sweat merged on our exhausted bodies as we toiled through washed-out fields and lumbered over ravines, the deluge driving at our backs and down our necks and into our packs.

"Nous sommes habitués," they had always said, when their bare arms were laid open by thorn bushes and equip-

ment was an aching burden, or while they crouched silently all night in tortuous canoes, or there was no food and the water stank.

"Nous sommes habitués." And now they were thinking it again, that matter-of-fact, stubborn acceptance on their faces which blanked out any notions of surrender or compromise.

They were proud of their humid little country with its choked jungles and rolling grasslands, and of how they had fought and sweated for it, and later drew charts and graphs showing the upward creep of agricultural production and new bush schools and medical units. After centuries as non-people, they were now discovering the worth and charm of themselves, already talking about reconstruction after the war and how they would drain the swamps and build highways and modernize agriculture. The present battle for the land was only phase one, and they were aware that, in some respects, reconstruction would be harder than the war and would demand as much of them.

They had an inordinate interest in their children, anybody's children, and treated each one like some rare jungle plant to be fed and watered and schooled, little brown shoots in donated clothing who would one day bloom into scientists and writers. For themselves, the adults, there was only infinite physical effort ahead, their patient acceptance of sacrifice to be redirected into reconstruction when the shooting war had ended.

In the meantime they would trot out all of their wretchedness for me to see, their backward, primitive tribes and monotonous diet and diseases and asked only that they be judged by their dreams and in relation to what they were before the revolution had begun. And I was not to weigh them by Western scales, but by theirs, for they offered as much to me—these bush bandits.

Carmen was waiting for us on a trail leading to her camp a half-mile away, a smiling brown figure in a sleeveless

187

khaki dress. A sentry had seen us long before and sent news of our arrival by runner. As we walked up to the neat range of straw huts that was her base, the sun came out and we sat on wet benches and devoured rusks spread with processed cheese which she had prepared. No cocktail canapé had ever tasted quite so good, and we suddenly laughed with delight.

The base was well-organized and spacious, with lanes of hard-packed earth between the huts and the underbrush cut low under vast, protective trees. We ate and bathed, and Carmen offered me her bed. In her sleeping hut there were signs of a town woman adapted to bush life: a few cotton dresses hanging in one corner, a can of talcum powder and a glass on the bedside table, a four-poster of rough, solid wood with crisp coverlet and sheets. I slept through the afternoon under its voluminous netting, rose for dinner and slept through the night again, awakening at midmorning to find the camp seized with bureau-like activity. There were *ad hoc* meetings of incoming guerrillas in secluded groves, rows of party officials bent over papers piled high on planked tables, stacks of equipment being sorted alongside the huts.

The camp was a halfway station on the teeming life line through the interior, and Carmen's motherly presence lent an element of homeyness to essentially migratory lives when she herself was not on a mission.

One of the current visitors was Vasco Cabral, an amiable and bespectacled Central Committee member in khaki and sturdy walking boots who had been trekking through the region for the past weeks and was billeted temporarily in one of the huts. The party already had a full-blown commission for economic studies and planning with 42-year-old Vasco as its head. His job included routine visits to local production units and from him I was to gain further insight into the importance which the party attached to long-term economic planning. From Carmen I was to learn the hazards and rewards of a woman revolutionary's life in the jungle.

Many PAIGC cadres disliked discussing their personal lives. Although they would spend hours over general problems and tactics connected with liberation, they seemed overcome with reticence, almost embarrassment, when the conversation shifted to another, more personal plane.

It was not a matter of revealing their identities or positions within the movement, for these were freely given since the party was not clandestine in the liberated regions, and the PAIGC news bulletins about "life and war in Guinea and Cape Verde" which were sent abroad often carried names and photographs of guerrillas and party officials.

But they had been for so long grafted to the revolutionary structure that suddenly confronting themselves as separate entities seemed to require an immense effort, a visible struggle to recall themselves as they once were when living under circumstances in which these questions would normally arise.

They had ceased to regard themselves individualistically, for in the interests of the revolution the worm of ego had long ago been supplanted by the positive denial of self. They were not flattered, only startled, when interest in their personal reactions or contributions was shown, and their response always entailed a halting, unaccustomed venture back to some barely remembered time.

There were moments when I was to observe certain unexpected similarities between the religious mystic and the seasoned black revolutionary, although their aims and their cosmotheory were essentially diverse.

The mystic is shaped by a conscious effort of will, essentially a one-man operation with mankind to benefit by extension; the cadre by an uncorrupted revolutionary process which destroys not the man but the ego, a mass effort culminating hopefully in mass benefit. But there are arresting character similarities which develop enroute, one of them being the voluntary suicide of the "self" to achieve certain ends.

Then there is the absolute commitment to a cause and the moral discipline which it exacts, a kind of awesome self-lessness and patience, and the ability to withstand physical deprivation without complaint. Sacrifice is a word very prominent in a black revolutionary's vocabulary.

For the new breed of African revolutionaries, self-sacrifice had become a life style. But it had not occurred overnight; only through the gradual modifications of character during a protracted war, and the guidance of a leadership which expected—and exacted—the best of what its people could give.

The party had always kept a gimlet eye on the development of potentially beneficial or harmful "tendencies" within the structure, even though they might appear innocuous at first glance. In fact, these superficially innocent trends could often make or break revolutionary momentum.

While acknowledging work well done and issuing regular, minutely detailed *mots d'ordres* liberally dosed with encouraging "do's," there was also frank criticism couched in no uncertain terms which the guilty readily understood and to which they were expected to respond.

At one point in the early development of leadership material there were obviously snags, and the following instructions were issued, being typical of PAIGC exhortations:

> Stress that those in responsible positions involve themselves seriously in study, that they interest themselves in problems of life and war in their fundamental aspects and not only superficially.

> Oblige each responsible person to improve their knowledge each day, their culture and their political awareness. Persuade each that nothing can be known

without learning, and that the most ignorant is the one who "knows" without ever having learned; to study life and learn from our people, from books and through the experience of others. Always to learn.

And then, more pointedly:

Those responsible shall put a definite end to the spirit of childishness, of irresponsibility, of frivolity, and to the tendency toward postponement . . . to regard life seriously and with full consciousness of responsibilities, guided by the preoccupation with the fulfillment of duties in a spirit of camaraderie based upon work and duty accomplished. All of this is not in opposition to the joy of life, the love of life, spare time, and confidence in the future which must animate our actions, our struggle, and the work of each.

Outwardly, Carmen Pereira was the most noncommittal of women, whose smooth, oval face expressed only bland detachment as she plodded down the jungle trails, calling out to the escort in Guinea-Creole or grappling with some administrative problem in a village gathering.

Except for the colorful woolen cap perched atop coarse black hair, she would pass unnoticed in any African market town, just another ripe, smooth-shouldered woman gliding down humid, sun-washed streets on some domestic errand.

Her knitted cap with its blue and white design was similar to that worn by scores of PAIGC members, including party leader Amilcar Cabral, and was part of their dress not only in the hot Guinea bush but also on missions abroad. Her plaited hair, sectioned and tied off into tails, reached almost to her shoulders. Small golden earrings tightened securely into pierced ears framed her creamy face and around her neck and wrist she wore linked metal chains.

Until she smiled, there was the aloof, high-cheekboned

191

dignity of an Indian in her features, perhaps some Brazilian forebear surfacing in Portuguese Guinea after the slaving era.

She was a bourgeois townswoman from Bissau, a member of that small, privileged group of blacks in the capital, who had severed herself from its narrow but predictable rewards to join the bush bandits.

I asked why had she done it. She was surprised by the question, believing the answer so self-evident. For moments she pondered over the reply, reaching back and recalling the motivation behind that irreversible decision, straining to put it into words.

The reply, finally, was simple enough. "Although my own life was not unpleasant, I could see the sufferings of my compatriots all around me. At the same time, my husband had become a secret member of the party, and eventually I was drawn into the revolution myself.

"I had felt myself gravitating toward revolt, but the question for me had been how to contribute to the fight like a man."

This was the period of dawn swoops into African houses by the Portuguese security police, then called PIDE, and finally, in 1962, Carmen knew that it was time to cross the border into Senegal where the PAIGC had already established a somewhat shaky exterior base from which to operate. There was a communal house crowded with cadres, and almost no money at all.

"The movement was so poor then, and we all offered whatever help we could. I prepared meals for them, took in sewing, and treated our wounded brought in from the Guinea war zones across the frontier. We had no money for hospital bills in those days. I was looking after my own children at the same time, for I had no other place to leave them."

Finally, when the war escalated in 1966, Carmen went with the fighters into the Guinea bush.

192

"My first responsibility was for health," she recalled, "but I also had my own problems in the beginning. I couldn't march for more than a few hours and I didn't know the village people. I needed about three months to orientate myself, to adjust to the life here.

"The next year I became a political commissar and I walked all over the Southern Front. My only companions were men because we had so few women members at that time."

As a lone woman, how was she regarded by the men?

"They treated me as carefully as a doll. I think that their attitude under these circumstances would always have depended upon my own behavior. I gave and took respect."

At one point Carmen contracted malaria which still plagues her with recurrent attacks and once put her in a Conakry hospital for a month. She is also anemic and moves about the jungle fortified with iron pills.

Along with the medicine in her briefcase, she carries party documents, a notebook, and transistor, and in her rucksack the bush uniforms and eating utensils that she will require. She is never without an armed escort.

"Food is supplied at villages along the way and I eat whatever the people can give me, the same as their own. I couldn't eat special food, you know. Sometimes this is difficult because the food is bad, or there is only rice, and sometimes there is no place to sleep except the ground.

"But I have lived so long in the bush now that I am fully accustomed to it. It is home and sometimes I stay inside for a year at a time, never seeing a town."

Carmen has found no handicap in being a woman among traditionally patriarchal tribes—"they accept me as a party authority and directives given through me are always carried out."

As the chief commissar, her job is to control, to replace, and to reassign, to know all of the problems and to get across to the people through her deputies the aims and

193

orientation of the party. At the same time the villagers are urged to speak freely, to learn how to govern themselves.

Like most cadres, her life is usually migratory—strange beds, new villages, familiar faces along the bush paths, sometimes the run for life when the bombers swoop. Part of her value to the movement has been the rapport that she has established with primitive jungle dwellers who sense the respect in which she holds them and respond accordingly.

Because of people like Carmen and Vasco Cabral and the veteran arms-runner Pedro Ramos, the movement now holds three-quarters of the Guinea mainland.

But it is not enough merely to sit on conquered territory while fending off enemy take-over attempts. Until independence, therefore, what was the PAIGC doing?

The answer was threefold: basic economic reconstruction as they fought, massive education efforts, and the parallel evolvement of a purely revolutionary party structure into an administrative one, so that when the sudden shock of peacetime came and "Freedom Week" celebrations were only a pleasant memory of visiting dignitaries and street dancing, the foundations of a stable government would already be there—no administrative loose ends to tie up, an experienced staff conscious of rural problems, and a hundred projects already in the planning commission.

If the PAIGC was anything it was anticipatory, and it had no intention of creating governmental voids into which old enemies might crawl, or permitting the emergence of postrevolutionary ennui to siphon off the well of constructive energy so painstakingly built up through a decade of revolution.

Now, night after night in the bush, planning groups sat up over kerosene lamps while mortar fire thudded in the distance, filling up files and drawing blueprints for their new Guinea.

It would be the kind of newly independent state in which

footsore official guests would be ushered proudly from one small industrial unit to another—canning factories, processing plants, each looking much like the last, and with only the bush bandits fully comprehending their cost.

In the meantime, the movement was getting a head start on economic planning, along lines as modern and extensive as guerrilla warfare and current trade links would allow. The process was often cumbersome, snag-ridden, and at a painfully fundamental state, but that it functioned at all, and seriously, in terms of a population majority still bare-footed and housed in straw huts, was an indication of PAIGC make-do and versatility.

Vasco Cabral, the 42-year-old Guinean from Farim who headed the economic commission, holds a degree in economics from a Portuguese university and had spent six years in a mainland prison as a political agitator. Released under restrictions, he eventually fled to Conakry and joined the movement there.

Vasco had a patient, donnish air and seemed to be pondering somebody's thesis as he frowned over a shaft of neatly written reports and carefully columned figures spread before him on the outdoor table. He was surrounded by clucking hens and stray goats, and puffed continually at a pipe which he kept filled with a hair-raising variety of local tobacco which he mixed with a hoarded foreign brand to make it last.

Beside his pile of notes was a printed census form headed "Liberated Zone—Guinea Bissau," with the results still coming in from cadres who walked from village to village to gather information for its columns. In the process, they learned much about the people they were liberating, and for the cadres involved this was an important educational mission.

The object of his commission, Vasco said, was the countrywide orientation and control of scientific research and planning carried out by the party in connection with economic growth and food production. For the first time there would be planning on the village level.

His own group was closely linked with a national reconstruction commission which in turn handled education, health, economy, and public information. Together, the two bodies were a vital part of the country's present and future.

At this point in the economy, internal trade is entirely on a barter basis, a system with which inland villages have always been familiar and which has been made further necessary because the circulation of Portuguese currency within liberated zones is forbidden.

At party-run barter shops in the bush, local agricultural produce can be exchanged for clothing, shoes, and other essentials still not manufactured locally, which were purchased or bartered for abroad with whatever local surpluses exist, such as oil, peanuts, kola nuts, or hides.

The money earned is either plowed back into the war effort or used to replenish import goods bartered off in the jungle shops—and sometimes for products specially requested by village customers. The Balante, for example, set great store by ceremonial garments, and for morale purposes the party occasionally brings the luxury cloth although it privately prefers bartering for more essential items.

Like every other process in wartime Guinea, the system relies heavily on human effort, and every sack of rice and every article of clothing exchanged for it has been carried inside on the backs and heads of men. There is even an occasional, pedal-operated sewing machine resting importantly on the thatched veranda of a jungle shop, while potential customers mill about estimating its value in rice kilos.

The higher the agricultural production, of course, the larger will be the selection and quantity of goods, a principle which has been painstakingly explained to the population.

Through local zonal committees responsible for production, the commission could encourage not only greater yield, but diversification and controlled experimentation with new varieties of rice and cereals. Concurrently, there is the development of animal production and beekeeping on modern lines.

"We not only teach the people the value of work, but also how to approach it scientifically, using whatever resources we have," said Vasco.

As a result, there have been marked increases in the production of rice, tropical fruit, oranges, bananas, manioc, and potatoes. And it has all been done with crude farming implements. I never saw mechanized equipment on the Southern Front.

In addition to the land owned by the individual villages communally and which continues to be cultivated by them, the party is also producing crops on plantations abandoned by blockaded Portuguese landowners or Africans who joined the enemy when the war broke out. These are often experimental in nature and used not only as teaching centers but also contribute toward feeding the guerrilla army.

"Under the Portuguese," Vasco went on, "there were two great monopolies for all farm products, and our people could sell only to them. Ground nuts and rice, very valuable export products, for example, were handled by these companies with great profit to themselves. Not to our people, of course. When the villager wanted to buy back his own rice, he paid three times the price that he was originally given. These firms have now closed because their supplies from the interior are completely shut off. As a result, the Portuguese in Guinea must now import their rice. They're in trouble while we, on our side, can cover our own needs."

Further schemes in the PAIGC development program include an iron foundry in the East, agricultural cooperatives, and bigger exports of animal skins (including crocodile), artisan products, handicrafts, and African masks.

Later, the party will take a closer look at bauxite deposits now under the movement's control in the East, and at possible oil reserves still under exploration when the war broke out.

Besides the responsibility for the economic well-being of a liberated area, there are other problems which must be faced by a movement such as this, one being the evolvement, in the absence of a state, of an administrative body to take its place.

This must be foreseen long before the actual liberation of an area, for to dither about with eleventh-hour attempts to fill this void can cause appalling failures in consolidating revolutionary gains. Who will assume responsibility for economy, trade, justice, public health, education, and internal security if not the movement? These issues must be dealt with even on the day-to-day bush level, despite the exigencies of guerrilla warfare and enemy reprisal.

If villager "X" stabs villager "Y," there must be somewhere a tribunal to judge the case; if villager "Z" cannot barter his rice crop because transport facilities to other regions have broken down, if sick peasants continue to die through lack of clinics, or clothing supplies dry up, what then is the position of the movement as a liberating force? And what of the chaos which such shortsighted policies could cause? Besides being a liberating factor, a serious movement is also expected to be a stabilizing one.

Anticipating such eventualities, the PAIGC functions as a jungle administration through an exquisitely conceived apparatus of interlocking party committees on various levels. Its anchor is the locally elected, five-member village committee (which must include two women in its make-up), which operates vertically through the sector, the region, the interregion (both the Northern and Southern Fronts are interregions), and ultimately reaches to the Central Committee.

At each link in the chain, the PAIGC urges peasant participation whenever possible, and considers the local committees as a good training ground in government.

Whatever structural form the administration finally takes after projected independence, one point is already clear—it will be geared to a unified nation, and the party already foresees the dissolution of the administrative structure in its present, interim form. It will be, in fact, phased out.

Says a PAIGC document: "The moment that there will be a clear distinction between the party and the State, and when the services of that State will be constituted independently of the services of the party, and when the political domain will be separated from the administrative one, the territorial aspect of the interregion will cease to exist."

17

OUTSIDE, AND DOWN THE WINDING PATH LEADING TO THE
bush hospital, an orangutan coughed in the underbrush,
watching the glow from our kerosene lamp as we talked in
one of the huts at the edge of the compound.

This was Guerra Mendes hospital, so named for the peasant hero who had been killed, along with two other guerrillas, in a Portuguese encirclement operation which had
stretched into five days and cost the enemy some 50 lives.

Built high against rolling hills, and protected by a ceiling
of thick forest, it had seven beds and a doctor and nursing
staff who treated guerrilla casualties and civilians from the
region.

"It's a mobile field unit, not a hospital in the European
sense. I would like to stress that," said Abilio Duarte, turning up the flickering light. Abilio, a former Sorbonne student of *beaux arts* and now a member of the PAIGC's reconstruction committee, is responsible for improvement of
public health and sanitary conditions in the villages.

He spoke quick, articulate French, and illustrated particular points he wished to get across by tracing imaginary diagrams on the cane tabletop with his forefinger.

"I'm responsible for public health. Yes. For example, Africans here will bathe daily but will eat with their hands from the same pan. It's not only a question of lack of utensils, but of habit." He picked up some imaginary rice grains and popped them into his mouth. *"Voilà."*

"About our hospital here. We know its deficiencies. But we must work with what we have, utilizing everything. Take our huts. We can put up four in one afternoon—somebody promised us some tents, but they never came. So we do without. We cannot use anything more permanent, in case the Portuguese bomb us and we lose whatever we have. They're always looking for our hospitals and we cannot justify having any expensive equipment out here in the bush."

I thought of the five-bed ward in a thatched hut down the path. The patients lay on wooden bunks with blankets folded double over a straw mattress. In the center of the earth floor stood a lone bucket of water in case of a napalm attack. There were two guerrillas with leg wounds, two civilian hernia cases, and a child burned by hot palm oil.

The hut was tidy and swept and African nurses in face masks and green hospital gowns hovered with dressing trays. In the women's ward, a new mother sat by triplets, her admiring relatives crouched nearby.

Under the trees there is an outdoor operating room swathed in netting, with a metal table at one end with various attachments ranged on a shelf above, to be bolted on when needed. It stands on the forest floor, and in a row on either side, precious medicines are stored on benches in covered metal containers. There is no refrigerator, no autoclave, no electricity, and saline drips are suspended from a bamboo fiber.

"And our people," Duarte went on, "they have all the diseases—malaria, pneumonia, parasites, tuberculosis, sleeping sickness . . . everything found in underdeveloped and neglected countries—a legacy of Portuguese rule.

"The Portuguese administration had no interest in the life of the people. They took everything we had. They never developed our sanitary facilities or taught us how to improve our living standards.

"They did have some isolated health posts in the forests, but these were usually without medicine. Actually, they existed in name only. In the countryside, there was never a public health service, never an attempt to stop contagious diseases or epidemics. We had to use our own forest medicines. And there was so much malnutrition caused by bad eating habits. Nobody knew any better.

"There was a hospital in Bissau," Abilio continued. "But in reality only those who could afford it had attention or operations. And the cost of prescriptions was prohibitive for most Africans. Our people died because of these things.

"Today, the population has more assistance than they ever had, so you can imagine the conditions before the revolution."

The health service has already carried out mass inoculations against smallpox and cholera, trained mobile public health teams for teaching missions from village to village, and are attempting to drive home the importance of a more balanced diet—more fruit, and the value of cow's milk and goat cheese, for example.

But old habits die hard, the party has found, and it is dealing with an almost totally illiterate population.

"That's why it's so important that they learn to read . . . our job would be far quicker then."

As Abilio talked on, our hut filled up with listeners, including Barry, Pedro, and our escort. Although they were not connected with public health problems directly, they listened with interest to Abilio, sitting on the edges of the bunks or on their packs.

This particular hut was an unusually large structure, with

a bathing cubicle attached and, some yards away, a closet of woven reeds containing a deep-trench latrine with a sand floor and wooden cover. It was the only privy I was to see in the bush, and since I had been assigned a bed here, it had a considerable effect on my sense of well-being. Not only could it be easily found in the dark—just up a vine-covered pathway—but this refinement meant a temporary end to crashing about the bush at night. In the back of my mind was the orangutan waiting in the underbrush. I knew that wild animals usually fled at the approach of humans—in fact it was very difficult to see them at all—but after an ominous hissing from close quarters one dark night, an incident which was fading only slowly from my mind, I was very dubious about venturing out.

Since the incident, I had devised an advance warning system which would communicate my imminent arrival to any animals or reptiles lying about in the underbrush. It consisted of talking to myself or humming when alone in the bush, hoping that purposefulness might give pause to the dangerous animals and scare off the cowards. But there are some experiences that no person can be expected to survive, and for me, it would have been an orangutan staring through the parted bushes as I mumbled by in the dark.

As Abilio talked on there were rolls of thunder in the distance, not the all-night cannon fire this time, but another tropical storm. Later, when the rainy season began in earnest, the men would be swimming across the fields in water over their heads, holding their guns and equipment above them. There were raindrops on the thatched roof and we heard the pad-pad of the orangutan's feet as he lumbered off into the forest for shelter.

The storm struck swiftly, carried on strong, humid winds which swept across the forested hillside. Within minutes it had flooded the drainage ditches around our huts and the rest of the compound was invisible in the wall of gray water.

It seemed endless and dangerous in its intensity and bore down on the frail rooftop with huge, destructive fingers. I waited for our hut to be torn from the earth and hurtled across the clearing. But, like African hens, they are tougher than they look and the sloping roof with its wide overhang and heavy thatch stood firm. Tall, brown men crashed through the doorway carrying steaming tins of coffee, their ponchos dripping rainwater on the sandy floor. They joined us around the lighted circle and dried their hands over the lamp.

I asked Abilio about education schemes for the black children in liberated zones. As a reconstruction committee member, he was also responsible for schools. I had already seen two of them, similar open shelters which the children had helped build.

Their bundle of school supplies was limited to pencil nubs and a well-thumbed copy book. When a lesson was well-learned it was erased and the next one written in.

Except when an area was under intensive bombardment, in which case the children stayed home, they walked miles under escort through the forests to these heavily camouflaged schools. Their teachers always carried submachine-guns against ambushes, and enroute to the hospital I had met one column of eight-year-olds being ushered through the forest by Carmen's younger brother, Joao. Attacks on schools and bush clinics particularly infuriated the party, and when this occurred guerrilla reprisal operations were immediately ordered. Scores of children had been killed or left permanently maimed in napalm attacks, and once a school was pinpointed it was immediately abandoned and rebuilt elsewhere.

As I had watched the children, some of them painfully thin with malaria and an inadequate diet, I thought of their "study" conditions at home—a rush mat in the corner of a fly-blown hut, heat, humidity, and chickens scratching in the doorway.

"Illiteracy was probably the worst aspect of Portuguese rule," Abilio went on. "If an African child did manage to attend school, he learned the names of all the rivers in Portugal and of all the kings, but he did not know his own African rivers or his own mountains.

"It was a great destruction of our culture, a mental perversion. Our people learned nothing of other African countries. Now they do," he said, "along with the alphabet, reading, writing, arithmetic, geography, geometry, science, and world history." Although the bush schools currently reach only the fifth primary level, they are a vast improvement on total illiteracy. Then, the more promising students are given further education at the "pilot" school in Conakry.

Creole, which is widely spoken throughout the country, has now become a written language, but the stress is on learning Portuguese, a decision taken by the party because "we want the fastest progress possible for our people," said Abilio.

"We want to rid ourselves of Portuguese rule, but not of their language which will open more cultural doors to our people than would Creole. That's realism."

Until now, only that small percentage of black *"assimilado"* children in the towns—those to be totally assimilated into the Portuguese way of life, severing all ties with their African traditions—had been effectively taught that language. Usually they found posts later as government civil servants.

The village children had relied solely on the mission schools in the interior, if any existed in their area.

"There was a great deal of praying and singing going on," said Abilio, "but they did teach the children basic reading and writing if they could remain in school long enough."

In general, both in Mozambique and in Portuguese Guinea, I found a somewhat ambivalent attitude on the part of Africans toward these long-closed schools in the liberated areas. While recognizing the good intentions of the individual missionary, many blacks felt that the Catholic Church of Portugal, having been entrusted by law with African education in the countryside and receiving government subsidies for the purpose, had felt it incumbent upon itself to reinforce attitudes of loyalty and docility to that government among its pupils. Ironically, scores of PAIGC cadres were Catholic-educated or were products of Catholic families.

"The political consciousness of our children is now very high," said Abilio, "because they are growing up in an intensely politico-military situation, and the awareness which this brings. Already there has been a profound cultural, technical, and social revolution as well—which is actually what national liberation is all about."

The rain had stopped, but the clearing was still a muddied pond and the tall, lithe girl called Tambo brought our dinner to the hut in covered casseroles. There was also French coffee brewed in a blackened kettle. The coffee was strong, thick, and heavily sweetened; but for the intervention of Barry, there would have been extra sugar added on the spot. For, like many Africans, Tambo had an inordinate craving for sugar as a quick energy-giver and it was assumed that liberal spoonfuls of this scarce commodity would be welcomed by all. There are many Africans in the bush who have never seen candy, sweet biscuits, or cake. Honey was relied upon to fill in the gap but this, too, was in short supply still.

Tambo had been assigned to our column as a temporary cook along the trail and as a female companion for me. She was a quiet Balante girl of sixteen and had volunteered for first aid training a few years before. She knew all the arts of jungle cookery and firebuilding, which snakes were poisonous, and always carefully counted all of our cooking utensils and other supplies every night before the camp slept, dragging them in and out of my hut where they were kept. Like every African girl, she carried the large, triangular scarf which served so many purposes—turban, childtoter, laundry basket, egg carrier. She also beat the bushes for me when I went out to bathe in the forest and then stood guard some yards away.

One night, after we had left a village along our route, I noticed that Tambo was unusually quiet, but occupied with other matters I did not ask the reason.

Later, Barry told me that her brother was dying in the village after a long illness but being on a mission and "responsible" for me, Tambo had not asked to remain behind. The men did not know the nature of his illness, only that it was incurable.

Before the war, the Balante could rely only on their "witch doctors" for medical help, and a surprising number of Portuguese in the bush had also gone to them.

One such doctor, who had offered his services to the Guerra Mendes hospital was a 46-year-old Balante called Patrao Barboza. He told me that he had joined the movement because "our people were so tired," and confided that before the revolution he was sometimes taken to Bissau to "assist" in certain cases there.

When working in the bush, and among villagers who believed strongly in *yirans,* witch doctors like Patrao were the only means of reassuring patients that the evil spirits which had caused their illness were being effectively dealt with. As every modern doctor knows, psychological reassurance is often half the battle and African witch doctors were fully aware of this.

At the same time, the herbs that they use are occasionally the basis of certain modern pharmaceuticals, and the rate of cure, therefore, was sufficient to establish village confidence in them, especially when there was no alternative.

Patrao wore Western dress and a stocking cap to which he had pinned a PAIGC button. On many occasions, he had been the bridge between primitive patients and the movement's modern medical team. In the early days of the war when pharmaceuticals were almost nonexistent, Patrao gave the first "health assistance" to guerrillas, he said.

A main danger to bush-dwellers had always been poisonous snakes and in the absence of antisnake serum, the men had been forced to rely on doctors like Patrao and their herbal remedies.

According to him, these herbs produce beneficial vomiting, while poultices applied to the point of the bite "to draw out the venom" and to the head—"this affects the nervous system"—were used in combination.

But like any self-respecting witch doctor, Patrao refuses to divulge the identity of the herbs which he secretly collects, even to the party. Witch doctoring, he said, is a family trade, handed down from father to son and the secrets are always closely guarded. Otherwise, he confided, the forest doctor would soon be out of a job.

I asked his opinion of modern doctors and their drugs and his creased, little leprechaun's face was both thoughtful and guarded. It was obvious that some internal struggle was going on and that privately he thought his own skills as effective. But he also realized that witch doctoring, too, must move with the times and that some form of coexistence could be worked out, with the foreign trained doctor inevitably fitted into the health scheme.

"I think that both kinds of medicine work," he said magnanimously. "For example, if a person has a fracture, both kinds of doctors can fix it."

To set the break, Patrao said that he first immobilized the injured limb and, using a herbal anesthetic, eased it into place. He believed in getting his fracture cases moving as quickly as possible, placing a rope above their beds "so that the patient can always experiment with movement and work himself up to a standing position."

His medical supplies were kept in a row of wooden bowls

along one side of his hut—pulverized substances, dark clumps of roots and leaves, an oil mixture, mortar and pestle, all ready against the moment his services would be asked by some village traditionalist.

His hut smelt vaguely of moist earth and crushed leaves, like a root cellar. There were aphrodisiacs, tranquilizers for the mentally ill during their "violent spells," and remedies against headaches, stomach disturbances, worms, toothache, and vertigo. He could also remove bullets in the absence of a surgeon, using herbal antiseptics and locally made thread.

Although trained doctors were much appreciated by the tribesmen, especially when giving injections rather than pills (they believed that tablets ended in the stomach whereas injections reached all the corners), there were some occasions when the services of both were asked by a patient, just to make doubly sure. PAIGC doctors had no objection unless harm could be caused, the party realizing that to wrench its primitive population from its witch doctors too rapidly could impair morale among the more elderly patients.

In the meantime, they believed that the witch doctor would eventually become an anachronism as the advantages of modern medicine slowly became more apparent. There was no intention of letting his knowledge of herbs die out with him, however, and the party hoped that before long witch doctors like Patrao would reveal the source of their cures. It would all be done in the interests of scientific research, the importance of which Patrao had already heard. As he considered himself a medical colleague, not a competitor, he thought that "someday I may decide to help in this research with my secrets."

But he was also a practical man, unsure of his future in the new scheme of things, and heedful of ancestral warnings against loose talk. For the time being, therefore, the identity of his herbs would remain locked away.

What of appeals to his better nature? "What of those who cannot reach you in time?" I asked. "Suppose I were a villager bitten by a snake while alone in the forest, miles from a witch doctor. Since you cannot reveal which herbs might help in this case, what would happen to me?"

"You would die," he said immediately.

While Patrao returned to the grinding and pounding which occupied much of his time, I visited the rest of the sprawling compound. There was a staff of 25, including the African surgeon, two operating room nurses, a mobile public health team, a pharmacist, a nurse-commissar, a first aid instructor, and several of her pupils who also helped with hospital chores.

The surgeon was the only doctor in the region and any spare time was spent on sick calls in the villages. Along with the rest of the staff he lived in one of several huts on the premises and as in most bush hospitals was often handicapped by the shortage of supplies. Replenishments for used stocks must be ordered weeks in advance because of transport problems and the distances involved, and often the required medicines were simply not available. Antibiotics, antimalaria drugs, anesthetics, bandages, and cotton were always in short supply, and medical stocks for the treatment of tropical diseases were still very low, one reason being that these drugs were not manufactured in large quantities by many countries sympathetic to the movement. They were not often included, therefore, in other donations. For the party to purchase these drugs on a large scale itself meant considerable depletions in funds earmarked directly for the war effort.

18

THEY WERE BURYING AN OLD AND VERY REVERED BALANTE
woman near a jungle village that night, and we could hear
the chanting of the mourners from a half-mile away.

Since morning we had been bivouacked outside a mud-
brick hamlet in the heart of the rice-growing region,
sleeping through the gnat-filled afternoon on straw mats
spread in shaded groves at the edge of the field. Not far was
a similar civilian encampment thick with palm-roofed shelters where entire families cooked and slept each day along
with their children, their chickens, and an occasional nim-
blefooted dog. There was a diligent thump-thump of women
standing over wooden containers like butter churns,
pounding coarse corn into mealie.

To avoid air raid casualties, the black population usually
moved to the natural camouflage of the bush during daylight hours and returned to villages or fields only after
nightfall. Barry told me that the entire rice crop was often
sown and harvested by night in regions under intense enemy
attack, the farmers working by touch in eerie darkness and
plunged to the thighs in black ooze.

I had noticed a column of schoolchildren ambling by our encampment at twilight, their arms laden with circular skirts, necklaces, and ankle bracelets all fashioned of straw. They were to be the principal dancers at the old woman's funeral that night, and we were invited to attend.

She had died of natural causes and chants as old as the tribe told of her good works and begged the intercession of the *yirans* for the peaceful release of her spirit. Smoke drifted across the forest from some great fire and I thought that her remains were to be burnt in full view. The Balante bury their dead, however, and the fires were to illuminate the rituals which followed the burial.

I could hear the rhythmic pounding of drums, an occasional whistle toot, and tentative female voices, high-pitched and atonal; then, as we broke from the trail into a rolling meadow, the funeral ceremony crashed into life.

Smoke and flame from three great bonfires leapt to spectacular heights while around each a wide circle of perhaps 300 Africans swayed and clapped, their dark, animated faces and naked chests shining in the heat and light of the fires.

Goaded by the quickening tempo of small, skin drums wielded by intense, sweating hands, the tension rapidly rose to unbearable heights, driving the crowds to shrieks of protest. There were loud screams, whistles and shouts across the clearing, and a rising babble of Balante.

Then pandemonium as the schoolboy dancers sprang into the firelit center, their thin, bony bodies festooned with straw bracelets, their grass skirts flying up over their khaki shorts. Screaming, roaring excitement as they took up the leaping dance, their bare feet crashing down in whirls of dust at the last drum beat, bony elbows bent like plucked birds' wings. Then a pause and it began all over again, led by the fury of the drums.

There was a joyousness in the women's voices as if carrying the old woman's soul along with them, yet pleading too, trying to call up the *yirans* somewhere in the woodland. The quality of the voices seemed unimportant to them; what counted was volume and they sent out earsplitting choruses in quick, four-beat time, using the drum as an anchor and sliding from major to minor key in midchant. They sang with great concentration, gazing at some fixed point in the distance and ignoring the rest of the crowd.

Their music did not call up images of impenetrable tropical jungle and primitive rite, but of tribes wandering lonely in some desert wasteland. It was not so much primitive as primordial.

The faces of the dancers were like frozen masks, all of the expression concentrated in their wiry bodies. For all their knobbly arms and legs and narrow, shapeless torsos, they had become beautiful in the grace of high, perfectly executed leaps, their elongated necks arched backward as they landed on half-bent knees and outstretched arms. They drummed the earth with their oversized, adolescent feet, like bush birds measuring an opponent, advancing and retreating, then recognizing the drummers' abrupt change of tempo with a plunge and twirl that coiled their bodies taut again.

Into the circle leapt the Balante magician, a dazzling figure in an ankle-length coat, wearing sunglasses and what appeared to be a woman's hat. Aloft he held an opened umbrella and waving it wildly, raced around the circle blowing blasts on a whistle, running in opposite directions to the dancers.

The guerrillas from our column stood on the edge of the circle as spellbound as I, for they were not all Balantes and it was a spectacle rarely encountered by them.

We watched for another hour, until the women's voices had grown thinner and the schoolboys walked tiredly off into the bush toward their huts, drums muffled and straw skirts swaying above their bare feet.

Next day, when the dancers were back in geometry class,

the magician with the umbrella and feathered hat would be discussing revolutionary politics with the local PAIGC commissar and neither would find the subject out of joint.

As easily as the Westerner might separate church and state, so the Balante could comprehend that neat division between the traditional *yiran* and the revolutionary process, and when viewed in the context of the jungle environment, it could be even more readily understood.

Tribal life is based upon getting around the clock with the least possible complication, and what cannot be explained away can always be ascribed to the *yirans*. The notion fits very well into the tribal life pattern, and while not encouraging abstract thought or social change, neither does it discourage it. The necessary flexibility to ensure survival in the forest could not permit the development of such rigidity.

No *yiran* has ever said "don't" before the deed, nor come forward with "Ten Commandments"; its displeasure is apparent only *after* the event and very often communicated immediately—the sudden illness, the misfortune, the marooned canoe. What this calls for, moreover, is not a grappling with the conscience or a chain of puzzled "why's," but simple propitiation to square accounts again. When the Balante guerrilla had called upon the tribal magician for prebattle ceremonies, he was simply storing up good will against the unpredictability of *yirans*.

The taboos and rules for social behavior existing within the tribe are usually based upon long-forgotten but still very serviceable motives which are reinforced by tradition and the weight of public opinion. Within this framework, it can be seen that valuable time and energy is therefore freed for the more fundamental problems that every bush Guinean will be facing every day of his 35 years, the average life span of an African villager here. These are the finding of food, water, clothing, and shelter while using very simple

214

tools or no tools, and scratching it all from his very indifferent environment.

What the Portuguese administration had done was rob him of his ability to do so, either by causing unnecessary obstruction or by whittling down the very tiny rewards of his labor.

Not content with that, the administration then forced him into abandoning his fields for weeks at a time to labor at schemes which meant nothing to him and for which he was barely paid, beat him when he rebelled, then sent him home to think things over. It was all part of the Christianizing and civilizing process, and having thought things over, the African decided that the main threat to his survival was not the *yiran,* not the forest or the magician or the labor in the ricefields, but the Portuguese themselves. And against them there was no weapon except armed revolution.

"Our people were so tired," the witch doctor in the PAIGC cap had said.

The 48-year-old president of a local village committee in one of the liberated zones told me: "Everything that you see that has remained from the old administration was made by our own backs, our own hands, our own hoes. A guard stood over us with a whip and even our wives and children had to work on the roads. They kept their eyes closed to our misery. They never gave us any education. If they did take a child and send him to school he was kept only a short time. If the father couldn't pay—and most of us couldn't—the child was sent home.

"It was prohibited to hold public meetings. They would disperse us. If we made a canoe, we had to pay taxes on it. If we had a ceremony, we had to pay a dance tax.

"If we were injured during work, they never helped us. We don't like war—only a fool does. We wanted to settle peacefully but they wouldn't listen to us. They never helped us and they never changed. We died like animals. They told

215

us we were savages and they made us live that way. I prefer to fight to the death than to live like that again."

Then there was the judge on the village tribune, 31-year-old Guad Naman, who sat on a tree stump and poured out his grievances against the old order.

"We wanted our land to be free like other people's. The Portuguese maltreated us, and our situation here, our poverty, is the fault of their administration.

"They didn't pay us, and we had to pay taxes. In my own experience, the only thing they did for us was to beat us. We were put into the local jail for nothing, and our families didn't even know our whereabouts.

"If they did find you and brought you food, they were often not permitted in to see you. Because there was a shortage of guards, you could easily be neglected. They would deprive you of water one day, a spoon the next. If there was only one guard and he left the vicinity, you could stay two or three days begging for water. There was no place to relieve ourselves and we stayed on our own excreta.

"Because of these things we revolted. We are people, too, as they are. We worked so much but we never had anything. We were farmers but we never earned anything and we didn't even know where our products went. The Portuguese set the prices. When they took our products to sell, they would give us less than their worth, then give us a tobacco leaf and say 'that's enough for you.'

"We are happy now, because we are organized. We have another kind of life. If we were sick or hurt before, they never helped us. We have help now, and a school. Many of us have begun to read and write, even the elders. There is a great enthusiasm for learning and reading.

"Before, we lived our lives in obscurity, mentally and physically. Our women were badly treated and our animals given to the Portuguese chief of the post. Every Sunday we had to take two or three head of cattle to the administration center.

"If they paid us, they also deducted taxes at the same time and almost nothing was left. At that time, we were divided against ourselves, each believing the other was bad.

"The Portuguese caused this division. They would take some groups and promote them, even sending some to school. This caused jealousy among us, and division."

Without the PAIGC would the Balante have rebelled anyway, eventually? If they had, it would probably have been on a tribal basis, for the concept of nationalism, or even patriotism had never filtered into the Guinean interior. The history of Portuguese Guinea is filled with abortive resistance movements, doomed before they began because of the sharp ethnic divisions between the tribes: the Portuguese against the Feloups and Mandjaques (1878-80), against the Peuls and the Beafadas (1882), against the Oincas (1897), the campaign against the Mandingos of Geba (1907-08), against the Bissagos on four different occasions up until 1936.

These rebellions, which were always connected with Portuguese "pacification" attempts, had never been instigated in the name of national unity, nor was a common front organized of more than two tribes. It was the classic example of divide and rule and made doubly easy because of the ignorance of the inland tribes. For centuries the tactics had worked, engaging and subduing each group separately, then neatly dispatching the next set waiting across the river.

One of the main tasks confronting early PAIGC mobilizers had been the exposure of the tactic and the organization of unified efforts to combat it.

"I would be a liar if I told you that the Balante, for example, were inherently nationalistic," the director of the PAIGC's information office, José Araujo, had told me.

"We had to create the idea of a country and a people ourselves. In fact, we are still creating these feelings, and strengthening them all the time. One of the victories of the

217

PAIGC has been the very creation of this nationalistic spirit.

"It doesn't mean that before the revolution the Balante felt themselves to be Portuguese, or even Guinean. They felt only as Balantes, as did each tribe."

With some exceptions, mainly the loyalist Fula, the PAIGC had managed to promote the new concept among those whom they could reach during mobilization.

One of the earliest of these politicizers was a tall, soft-spoken cadre called Serafim Sanaa, who had originally gone into the bush with Nino and now walks an average of 40 miles a day in sandals, from village to village. He is the commissar of a key sector, cooks his meal of rice enroute, and is high on the Portuguese list of wanted men. Until now, he has managed to elude them.

"Our people never really accepted Portuguese domination," he told me. "There was always revolt, even before our movement was formed, and only through division had the Portuguese managed to remain.

"Because of mobilization and the war, a unity has been achieved. We told the people that they must forget their divisions and promote their owns lives instead. We explained the mechanics of their domination, how as farmers they were being used, and the possibilities that existed for freedom if they fought united. Gradually they came to understand that they had been divided for a purpose, that our riches were taken all those years to build Portugal.

"Our people had no evolution," he said. "They remained primitive and they were forced to stay so. If they built a decent house, for example, the Portuguese closed it or levied a heavy tax on it There were so many ways, subtle and open, to keep them down.

"After the decision of the party to take up arms, the people came to understand that the war was for them. They realized that they could have a life like other people in the world—a good house, for example, hospitals, schools, and decent clothing. They want to change their children's lives, make them better than their own."

What of the population's endurance, and how was morale maintained in the face of so much bombardment?

"I think that the qualities of endurance that you have seen were developed under the Portuguese, doing roadwork without pay and living so miserably on what little they could earn from their crops. This went on for generations, and there seemed no alternative to this.

"But it is inevitable that bombardment will affect their morale, will shake their confidence even temporarily. In these cases we explain over and over the difficulties that occur in their road. And when people realize that they are being bombed to break their morale, then this morale is reinforced. Their courage always depends upon their understanding of the suffering necessary to achieve their aims, a real comprehension of this, not simply a surface acknowledgment. Over and over we explain this, and the people accept it because they know that this war is being fought for them," he concluded.

The director of a village committee, Boubacar Djassi, who is on the spot when the bombers attack, told me: "The war has naturally changed our lives. We are about 150 families and because we must disperse into the bush because of attacks, this has naturally affected day-to-day stability. But we won't give up. Our village grows food for the combatants as well as for our own needs, and we also give salt, meat, and fish oil when we can. We are always discussing the war, and we have volunteers from our village to carry munitions and food into other regions.

"Three of our people have died during Portuguese attacks, one during a bombardment and the other two by cannon fire. But we go on."

Later I watched a village woman addressing a large circle of men sitting around her on the ground. She was a member of her local committee and stood in their midst

219

barefooted, an infant tied around her back. Her name was Kanjao Camara and she estimated her age as 33.

She spoke in a tribal dialect called Nalou which was translated into Balante, then Creole, then Portuguese, and finally into French. She was "responsible" for barter programs in her village, she told me, and also for social and cultural affairs. The social part entailed sorting out personal and marital problems and encouraging families to send their children to school although extra hands might be needed during the rice harvest.

"I joined the PAIGC during the early mobilization period," she told me, "because I was so tired of the Portuguese and my other life. Personally, I was not mistreated, but my father was. He was taken to a Portuguese post and beaten—his hands were flailed—because he had a dispute with a guard while working on the roads. He was never paid for this work and that was the cause of the trouble."

This was fertile ground for early mobilizers like 29-year-old Avelino Sousa Delgado, who was a sector commissar and temporary head of the militia. He had been recruited in Bolama in 1959 and was later trained at the party school in Conakry. There had been four years to prepare the villagers for the shooting war.

"It was really very hard for the mobilizers then," said Avelino, "especially from the physical point of view. The areas were thick with troops and we couldn't even use the footpaths. We always marched at night, and always *through* the forests, never on the trails. Most of us were barefooted and you can understand what it did to our feet. There was very little to eat, only what friendly villagers could give us, and we had no clothing. Nobody quit though."

In 1961 there had been tentative PAIGC sabotage operations against enemy installations, roads, and communications networks. A main object at this time, Vasco had told me, was "to test the militants, see who were more courageous, more active. In 1963 we began the all-out fight, at first with little groups of isolated guerrillas and always mobilizing at the same time.

"Then we organized little ambushes, taking every weapon we could away from the Portuguese. It wasn't easy —the enemy was everywhere and our men were always hidden in the jungles. It was very difficult to find food when their own stores were exhausted. Sometimes the troops arrived when our men were around the villages, and the people hid them."

At the same time, arms had begun to trickle in from abroad, but a major problem was to get them past Portuguese blockades. It was Pedro Ramos who organized the first major weapons convoys into the South, and later to the North where the PAIGC intended to open a second front. Already alerted by guerrilla activity in the South, and aware that weapons were being stockpiled there as zones were liberated, the Portuguese made every attempt to cut possible supply routes to the North, stepping up patrols and reconnaissance, guarding river crossings and infiltrating the villages with black agents. It was again up to Pedro to penetrate the barrier and get supplies to isolated guerrilla groups holed up there.

"We had no possibility of bringing in arms across the Senegalese border," said Pedro, "which left only two routes open to our Northern Front. One was through the South, which meant crossing certain regions still not freed, and the other through the East which was still under total enemy control. And it all had to be done on foot."

From a small nucleus of 30 volunteers, Pedro recalled, the carriers eventually swelled to 600 men willing to undertake the mission. Originating in the still occupied North, these human caravans infiltrated into the southern zones, collected the arms, then began the long march back through Portuguese lines.

Traveling only by night and under guerrilla escort, the carriers crept through the game-infested jungles and forded the rivers under the nose of the enemy, carefully skirting the villages to avoid ambushes and informers.

The journey took ten nights on foot and they did it every month for three years, carrying their rice ration in little cloth bags and hardly daring to light a cooking fire.

"Sometimes our food ran out before the end," recalled Pedro. "We just went hungry."

But the convoys were never caught and Pedro never lost a man. "We had an excellent guide," he says, "who was also in the security section."

Pedro, who still coordinates material and ammunition supplies to the fronts, said that a major preoccupation continues to be security for transport.

"All groups carrying supplies are given an armed escort, and it is the responsibility of each sector through which they pass to carry out reconnaissance beforehand. If we lost our supplies, there would be no possibility of fighting."

Some of the men, he said, could carry from 1,800 to 2,500 rounds of ammunition on their heads, depending upon the distances to be covered.

The arms, which usually originate in Russia, China, Eastern Europe, or Algeria, are given either by African countries, through the OAU, or unilaterally, along with financial help and food donations. Money and other material contributions, excluding arms, come from Sweden, certain private organizations in the West, and also from local committees formed there which support the aims of the black liberation movements.

"The Portuguese are far better equipped than we are," said Pedro. "She has the aid of all her allies in NATO. Except for this, we would have already won our independence.

"The arms that we do have are all right for the infantry," he said, "but the equipment of the enemy goes far beyond that, much more sophisticated than our own—G-3 automatic rifles, Mausers, and French helicopters, for example. We don't even have enough antiaircraft guns. But we know that we must fight with what supplies are available to us, and we accept that. We cannot give out the guns that the individual fighter might prefer, and they all know this."

Left to themselves, most guerrillas would choose the machine-pistol for bush warfare, that lethal little hybrid of submachine-gun and pistol which combines both power and lightness for close attack.

"I remember very clearly how it was back in 1962, when our villages were attacked and we didn't have enough arms to fight back," said Armando Vieira, now a commissar and also a coordinator in the South.

"There was a Portuguese captain who ordered his troops to massacre anybody suspected of supporting us. When his forces cordoned off a village, they entered and shot everyone they believed had fed or hid our men. The population was terrified and hesitant then, and it was up to us to give them courage to continue their support.

"After a massacre we would return to a village and spend a long time building up their morale. We told them that these things happened in all revolts, and no matter how many of us they killed, there would still be one left to continue. It was all or nothing. We told them that they could not remain quiet or stand aside during this war, for we were certain that we could win it. It was a difficult time, for the people were very intimidated and we could not protect them as well as we can now. Later, as the war progressed, they became more resolute.

"They suffered then, and they are still suffering, but they understand that this is a sacrifice of war and one day it will all be over. But until then they must hang on. Now it is not easy to attack these villages, except by air, for in each one a militia group has been formed for defense purposes, in addition to the guerrilla forces in the area.

"Village morale is good, but of course we always want it

better. To reinforce it, we never let up. We talk to them every day, visiting them personally to explain and encourage. We are very aware of their sacrifices and we tell them so. But we also stress that while some people go to the front as their contribution, others make sacrifices in other ways. These ideas are also gotten across by example, our own and that of others."

I had already noticed that among both the population and the guerrilla groups, self-pity was a luxury to be promptly discouraged. Problems could be discussed, and remedies applied whenever possible. But to permit an entire village to wallow in self-pity after the bombers struck, or a cadre to complain of hardship or the vintage make of his arms when there was no alternative except more of the same, would mean a serious impairment of revolutionary vitality built up with so much sacrifice.

With party help, schools and villages were rebuilt elsewhere and daily routine quickly restored. There were discussions and explanations and new confidence promoted. There was compassion but also firmness, and the population itself was shown the choice which lay before them: either continue, suffer, and fight back, or revert to their prerevolutionary status. In reality, there was no real choice.

As for the occasional cadre foundering in some temporary depression, or loneliness, or the sudden yearning for normal life—"we are not born revolutionaries, just ordinary people . . ."—there were quiet talks with a perceptive commissar, a new assignment in a fresh sector, a brief rest until equilibrium could be restored, and as a last resort a cadre could always leave the revolution voluntarily, with no stigma attached.

Most stayed, and the more reflective among them carried the pride of having overcome a bewildering and very personal *crise*.

Although bound together by camaraderie and common

224

cause, there is as much variation among militants in intellect and sensitivity as in any other group, and while human resources at all levels are exploited within the revolutionary framework, there are always differences in the depth of response, in the capacity to react, to feel—and of course to suffer.

Some of the men would always be alone or restless or introspective, while others would be buoyant and self-confident. There would be those who made light of hardship and some whom it would overcome. Beneath the common denominator of the revolution was a social grouping whose personal problems could be found anywhere—fear of death, personal disappointments, illness, sexual frustration, unrequited love, emotional insecurity, separations. For some they would be forgotten in the urgency of events; for others they would always be a torment.

There were dreams, too, vague, still fuzzy outlines of some modest well-being after the war—"a good house with a tile roof and two rooms . . . ," "the solace of a woman . . . ," "plenty to eat and some clothing . . . ," "my first child . . . ," "I will ask to study . . . ," "to see my mother again. . . ." They were always spoken with hope and awe, wistfully, for personal wants, like personal problems, were so out of context when the misery of the mass was so apparent.

These populations in the interior, these villagers who had stood still for so many centuries, were their expectations primitive also? Previously they had been conditioned not to expect, only to survive, and freedom would mean different things to different people, it seemed.

For the majority, who had never experienced the comparative freedom that affluence could give, who had never been exposed to the impact of the mass media or higher education—even to city streets or cinemas or restaurants—it would mean abundance within the village framework, and, above all, security: livestock, clothing, steady food supplies, schools, medical help, shoes.

Most of all, it would mean the freedom to develop, a process which had been arrested for 500 years, and the experience would undoubtedly be a heady one. Which direction this took would depend very much on the guidance of its leadership whose moral responsibilities would be far more burdensome than that of counterparts in the West, for example.

For an enlightened African leader knows that he is setting an entire handicapped nation on its course after a long age of darkness, a group with no education, no experience, and no means with which to make comparisons until it's too late.

What a good black leader sees, and what many whites fail to see in the African villager, is his potential. And if the white man did see it, even the best-intentioned setting out to civilize the native, it was often buried in the confusion of despair and frustration which followed years of individual effort with little apparent result. And they could forgive the African less because they, the well-meaning foreigners, had voluntarily sacrificed a great deal in the black man's name. The best that could be managed then, as an alternative to complete moral collapse, was paternalism. The next step was a very offensive superiority.

What a black leadership must possess to a very high degree is patience in dealing with its followers—with their mistakes, their contradictions, their thickheadedness, their suspicion, their slowness in grasping ideas to their own advantage.

A leadership knows that it is not even dealing with a developing nation at the onset, but a suspended one. Above all, it will find that its own vitality can be sustained only if it honestly loves them. At times, a black leadership will find this almost as difficult to do as the white man had. But not quite.

An African leader is far closer to his own villager than the foreigner could ever hope to be. Although his own background may not be identical, and the educational gap extremely wide, there will be shared experiences as a people, even the common one as a multitribal unit under a colonial power. He will know how much he can ask of his people at a given time, and will blame himself, not them, if he miscalculated.

If he sees a black villager responding to a new idea or situation with an expression of utter blankness, he will understand the ignorance and attempt to correct it. Or if the case is hopeless, he will turn to his brighter brother in the next hut.

And what he doesn't know about his people he makes great efforts to learn, for to rally them he must analyze them in depth. The black leader also has an additional incentive. What he learns about his own people he is also learning about himself.

There would also be the mistakes which even a healthy and collective leadership can make, but there would also be sufficient self-criticism to remedy them.

"And we made many mistakes in the beginning," the PAIGC leader Amilcar Cabral had told me. "The first major one was in thinking that independence could be won through fighting in the towns, through urban guerrilla warfare and demonstrations there. Because of our particular circumstances, this was a great tactical error and we had to stop it.

"Another mistake was in our analyses of the social situation. We thought that the Fula chiefs would join the liberation structure regardless of class conditions. Instead, they supported the Portuguese because they thought it in their interests to do so."

How well had other revolutions been studied beforehand, and to what extent had they influenced PAIGC tactics?

"We learned that it was important that we, the leadership, base our tactics upon the *realities* in our own country, our own conditions here, and on the realities of the enemy," said Cabral. "Of course we read everything that we could and we still learn much from the experience of others outside. But we cannot pretend to apply blindly the experience of others. We must create our own conditions. We even learn from our miserable people. Most cannot still read or write, but we listen."

In an analysis of the basis and aims of national liberation in Guinea, Cabral had already pointed out that "our experience shows us that in the general picture of our daily fight, no matter what kind of difficulties the enemy causes us, the fight against our own weaknesses is the most difficult fight of our people, at present as well as in the future.

"It is the expression of internal contradictions in the economic, social, and cultural (therefore historical) reality of each one of our countries.

"We are convinced that any national or social revolution that lacks as its fundamental basis the adequate knowledge of this reality runs great risks of being condemned to failure.

"We indeed know that the orientation (or development) of a phenomenon in movement, regardless of its external conditions, depends principally on its internal characteristics.

"We also know that, on a political level, no matter how beautiful and attractive the reality of the others may be, we can only really transform our own reality based on the concrete knowledge of it, and by our own efforts and sacrifices.

". . . fortunately, or unfortunately, national liberation and social revolution are not for export."

What kind of state did he envisage after the revolution?

"More or less what you have seen," Cabral said. "We are not for great things. We must work within the reality of the country, and make our people rule themselves step by step.

We think that the idea of local autonomy in some regions is a good principle because it teaches the sense of responsibility.

"We are ready for relations with other peoples and with all kinds of states, regardless of their orientation. But at the same time we must protect our people from any kind of exploitation. For example, we accept the principle of capitalism, and that it has to gain. But it doesn't have to exploit. What we would say is 'come and put to us your conditions.' "

Regarding the Portuguese government, Cabral felt that "they have lied too much and it is impossible for them to reverse the situation, whatever losses they have. If they free Guinea, they know that it is finished for them in Mozambique and Angola as well."

Materially they were still strong, he said, but not morally or psychologically. Yet arms were still coming in to them from their allies. "If we destroy 100 of their trucks this year, next year they will have another 100. Whatever we destroy their allies replace."

Earlier I had asked Araujo to define the political orientation of the PAIGC. "It is a nationalist party," he had said, "orientated to the progress of our country."

Arms and ammunition were accepted gratefully from wherever they came, "but because we accept arms it doesn't mean that our political orientation is exactly the same as the country donating them. Our platform is and will remain the same as it was before the war began," he had said.

"We had asked arms from all countries, but the East and certain others were the only ones who helped us, not because they thought that we were Communists but because they knew that our purpose was serious. When we asked help from the West, we were refused because of NATO and Portuguese membership in it.

"If the West would give us bazookas as good as they give

the Portuguese, we would accept them gladly—or the G-3 or the FAL. Our fighters like them. The Portuguese are now manufacturing them in Lisbon, but they are not doing a very good job of it. They pack up after a few shots and their own paratroops in Guinea refuse to use them. What they would really like would be to get our Russian-made AK-10, which the Portuguese call our G-4. It's the best of all."

19

COMMANDANT UMARU DJALLO'S MEN WERE TO ATTACK the Portuguese fort of Cufar on the Southern Front that Sunday night, and I was to go along on the operation.

"It will be a quick assault," Umaru said, "and we'll get out fast. The Portuguese will probably open fire immediately, and there is also the possibility of an ambush on our flanks unless we can box them up in the fort. If you can't run like hell, my men will have to carry you."

"I can run," I said stoutly, aware that he was eyeing my haggard face and unkempt uniform, the result of four days on the march to meet him and his commandos.

They were already bivouacked temporarily near a food production center where black prisoners from a nearby fort had been brought for questioning. They had been ambushed during a hunting expedition, when they wandered too far from the post and, although armed with Mausers, had surrendered immediately. Umaru told me that the Portuguese had often encircled villages adjacent to their camps with barbed wire on "strategic hamlet" lines, where they could maintain close control over the inhabitants and isolate them from PAIGC mobilization attempts.

The villagers then constituted a well of unpaid labor around the camps, being used for road repairs, trench digging, and other tasks. Once inside the hamlet, the families found escape difficult. Each camp normally had only one exit, always guarded, and only trusted civilians were permitted beyond without an armed escort. There were also African collaborators who had remained inside willingly, and were used to infiltrate PAIGC-controlled zones and villages.

It was always a problem for guerrillas to ascertain into which category captured Africans fell, for a black spy would always maintain that he had been an unwilling Portuguese hostage.

"Their black agents can often do us more damage than the soldiers," said Umaru, "for they can always claim to be passing through from some remote village and in the meantime learn information about our positions and our people."

Included in the captured hunting party were two children and an eighteen-year-old boy who had been separated from the others and now sat in a frightened row on a fallen log, obviously afraid of the worst.

"What will happen to them?" I asked Umaru, as we surveyed the pinched little faces sitting mute and waiting. "We'll feed them and send them back to their parents," he said. "They are from villages in the liberated zones. The older boy we will question again—you notice that he's wearing camouflage trousers which is part of the enemy bush uniform, and he was armed as well. If he's in the Portuguese army he'll be a prisoner of war."

What of the other three Africans who had been captured with them? They were adults, I had been told, and there was no sign of them.

"They haven't been shot, if that's what you want to ask,"

said Umaru. "If they turn out to be spies, there will be a trial, a fair one. If not, they will be sent to live in liberated villages. Once they learn what we are fighting for, they often join us. Remember, these people have been shut off for years."

The decision to abandon a fort after prolonged guerrilla attack apparently poses a problem for the Portuguese about what to do with the civilian population there. According to the PAIGC, they are either relocated or eliminated.

Vasco had told me that in February, 1969, after Portuguese troops had abandoned the Madina de Boé area in Eastern Portuguese Guinea, the guerrillas had found "hundreds of cadavers there. They were all African civilians and all had been shot. They had been living under Portuguese control when the fort was abandoned, and we believe that they were killed because the enemy would have found great difficulty in moving them. And if they had fallen under our control they might have informed us of Portuguese plans and emplacements."

"What was the fate of Portuguese troops captured by the PAIGC?" I asked Umaru. Considering the havoc already caused by them, did the guerrillas consider themselves justified in "totaling" their captured opponents, in taking revenge in the name of lost comrades and dead civilians? After all, the disappearance of enemy individuals could always be ascribed to wild animals or jungle mishaps, with no remains left about in evidence.

It seemed that the PAIGC did assume responsibility for them. The army, militia, and guerrilla units were under strict orders to take prisoners of war, and, once taken, to treat them according to Geneva Convention regulations.

"We respect these rules," Umaru told me, "but unfortunately the enemy does not. If one of our men fall into their hands he is sure that he will not survive. If by chance he does, he will be tortured or tied up and used as a guide.

"When we find enemy wounded, we give them the best possible treatment in our hospitals or first aid posts. We are sorry to say that they do not do the same for us. Rarely will they take one of our casualties for treatment. Generally, he is left mutilated and dying, or shot. We know, because we find them later."

This is one reason why PAIGC guerrillas make every effort to recover their own wounded.

"There is a very good spirit among us," Umaru said, "and people are great friends. They know that they will protect each other. If a friend falls, he knows that he will not be left behind, either dead or wounded. When I myself was wounded, my friends came back for me. And as we bury our own dead, we also bury those of the Portuguese."

As a commandant, how would he react if one of his men showed fear during a fight?

"All men don't have the same amount of courage, and we know this," he answered. "It is natural for people to sometimes feel fear. What is important is his morale, and that he stays and fights. Our men are given much political education, and they know exactly why they are fighting. This is a very important thing to know. We have been shown the way to liberate a country, and we know that we are fighting a just cause. If a man has confidence in his purpose, his fear will pass."

The PAIGC maintains a military court to try infractions of rules, and a combatant is punished according to the severity of the case. One of the greatest humiliations for a guerrilla is to be disarmed, and one of the highest crimes is running away during an engagement with the enemy. For this, a guerrilla could be sentenced to death by his own court. These cases, apparently, were very few.

Umaru, who has lost count of the number of ambushes he has led or participated in—"we mount two or three a day in this sector"—joined the revolution eleven years ago in

Bissau, where he grew up in the African quarter. He is now 29, and one of the few guerrillas I saw who wore a full beard.

He readily recalled the early days of the war, when the Portuguese used river boats to raid villages near the shore, until "the guerrilla danger stopped that."

Then the enemy tried other methods, he said, including the concentration of troops in a fort stronghold from where they infiltrated the surrounding area and pounced *en masse* on the huts.

"Guerrilla ambushes caused them heavy casualties, and that was also stopped.

"Now they use helicopters. First they send in six or seven jets to strafe the villages, and then the bombers. Finally they arrive by helicopter, usually twelve to sixteen of them, each carrying about fifteen men. Occasionally the aircraft come at night to look for lights. Then they bomb. . . . .

"With their helicopters, they attack supply depots, hospitals, schools, villages, and small guerrilla forces, their reconnaissance planes having already picked out likely targets and possible landing areas. Their attacks usually last an hour, and if they attack our men, they usually outnumber us.

"Our main difficulty now is their aircraft. Man for man, I think that we are better fighters. Although they are far better equipped, we have other advantages. They are not interested in sacrificing themselves for any cause. They are afraid of the snakes, the forests, and the climate, while we know the land.

"They realize that we are aware of their movements, for our men are always within a mile of their camp. Whatever they do, we know it, even their helicopter movements. That group of men you saw at the last village, they are part of a mobile unit which follows their helicopters from zone to zone. All of our units, in fact, are mobile. We have no troop concentrations as they have, and this is a great advantage for us. We can always know where they are, but their problem is to locate us.

"Generally, they are more active during the dry season than during the monsoons, while we can act at any time.

"The guerrillas are given special training in all types of ambushes," Umaru said. Every ambush has a certain aim, as has every attack against a fort. It does not consist merely in crouching behind a bush to shoot at any target which passes.

Its purpose may be for harassment, for capturing a post, for grabbing arms and ammunition, vehicles, or food. And the tactics often differed.

There were dawn or dusk offensives set up several hours before. "We can leave our bivouac at 5 P.M. and wait all night for them to leave with their trucks at first light. Or we can camp in closely and launch a quick raid, always knowing exactly where we shall go afterward. If there is a possibility of helicopter support for them, we must carry enough bazookas to use against them. Or if there is to be a close ambush, we know that they cannot bombard us because they will kill their own troops. We try to plan every detail. Otherwise they can damage us a lot through our own lack of preparation. Alternatively, we can turn one of their own offensives to our own advantage.

"I remember one confrontation back in 1967," Umaru continued, "when the Portuguese mounted a great attack in the Southern Sector. They were looking for some of our leaders, and the whole operation lasted six days.

"There was a great troop concentration, and we sent in small groups to harass them, to draw them out. We were well-camouflaged and we mined everything around our encampment as we withdrew. We also booby-trapped our ammunition boxes left deliberately behind and when they opened them, it was a holocaust. They had about 40 dead and what was left of their force was attacked as they fled. The mines that we used were the very ones that they had intended for us."

With Umaru on many of his missions is a nineteen-year-old reconnaissance man called Philippe Saco, who often acts as battery commander during concerted attacks. He is one of several reconnaissance men assigned to either the infantry or battery and when preparing a major attack will survey the area and the target on three separate occasions beforehand.

Armed with revolvers and binoculars, Saco and his assistants first reconnoiter the terrain, check target distance from positions offering the best cover, then calculate range and angle according to the firing capacity of whatever heavy arms will be used.

Maps are then drawn for the guidance of the commandant which show nearby rivers, villages, and other landmarks, as well as the exact position of ricefields in relation to the forest and to the fort. Also included are airfields, if any, and the suggested point of attack and its exact distance from the target. Besides the preparation of maps, there are also conferences with the group commandant beforehand.

One of the biggest dangers for the reconnaissance man is the investigation of mined areas. Extreme caution is needed, and there is always close cooperation with area security men whose surveillance groups keep the forts under continual observation, including their mine detail. Another problem arises when one fort must be passed to attack another, which then provokes fire from both directions and can block an effective guerrilla retreat. Portuguese firepower is always stronger than that of the PAIGC attackers, with key forts equipped with heavy cannons and long-range mortars.

Although their whereabouts can always be pinpointed in the dark due to gun flashes, the guerrillas operate under the same handicap and must change positions rapidly during attacks and be prepared to pull out immediately if enemy reinforcements appear.

Saco said that he has lost two of his best friends during attacks, one against a fort and the other on a minefield. "My morale dropped to its lowest level then," he said, "and I didn't know where to turn. Then Nino spoke to me and encouraged me, and made me understand that sometimes we may lose our friends. My confidence returned, and after several missions I became a battery commander."

Saco has just returned from a reconnaissance mission to Cufar, the fort which was to be our group's target the next evening. To reach it, we would cross two local rivers, the Rio Grande and the Rio de Cabulone, then through ricefields and woodland savanna for the approach to the fort. The attack would be timed to begin just after dusk, when the guerrillas would use the shadowy twilight to take their positions and open fire just after the quick African nightfall. Within seven minutes, the darkness would cover our retreat unless, of course, we fell into a delayed ambush.

Most of Umaru's men had already left the present zone for a bivouac about eight miles from the fort where we were to rendezvous the next noon. From there, the attack group would set out for the fort, and I was to be included in this column.

To insure that I would not be overcome with fatigue at the critical stage, I was to sleep at a local first aid post that night and continue the march to the bivouac in the morning. With me at the post would be Umaru, Barry, a security man called Carlos, and, I discovered on our arrival that evening, about 75 other guerrillas.

The post lay in thick forest, well-camouflaged but hot and airless. One of the more spacious huts contained beds for guerrilla and civilian casualties, and directly opposite was the cooking shack where Awah and Tambo perspired over the calabashes. Smoke and flames shot toward the

238

bamboo roof as the fires were poked up for guerrillas streaming in with tea kettles and buckets.

Among the stacks of rice sacks around the huts were rifles, submachine-guns, bazookas, and rucksacks, and the men were already searching through the piles for their mosquito nets.

In the background was the hum of *Radio Libertaçao* from Conakry, distorted and weakening on its frequency, then collecting itself to blare out the strange, timeless rhythms of the Casamanse region.

"*Radio Libertaçao* wishes you happy listening time . . . and now for the international news in Creole."

Later, it would come over in the local dialects and include the war news. Every village would be tuned in to the communal transistor. In our camp, Umaru's tall, broad giants with their gentle faces and bush knives hung over the radio for news of other battles. Tomorrow night it would be Cufar and they would leave their mascot, a spindly gray mongrel called "Lutte," safely behind. He always found them later, somehow, and liked to run along with the column on their marches, ears flattened and tongue lolling as he raced down the footpaths only a split second ahead of their enormous sandaled feet and swinging guns.

There were only eight beds in the entire post, and I was given the best near a window. The men had strung sheets around to serve as a mosquito barrier and to insure privacy; they had also marked off a kind of antechamber for me across which hung a ground sheet. Another fourteen guerrillas would double up in the remaining beds and several others, including Barry, would lash their hammocks to the columns supporting the hut. I was both amused and grateful for the efforts they had made to insure my privacy, for I had often slept alongside them during the treks, sharing the same ground sheets under the same trees, awakened by the same sentry on patrol, and dropping off to exhausted sleep again. None of us considered it unusual. But it seemed that

239

whenever privacy was possible, however makeshift, it would always be offered when a roof and four walls were available.

In all the time that I had spent with them, I had never been uneasy because of the proximity of so many men, whatever the circumstances, and a display of false modesty before them would have been an unforgivable insult to their honesty and forthrightness. However intimate our living and sleeping conditions, however close our companionship had become, they offered nothing except consideration and respect. This is not to say that they were not male, for they were more than that.

In them I sensed a startling and total sensuality of which they seemed entirely unaware, perhaps because it was such a normal and delightful part of their natures. It seemed inherent in the way they walked and reacted, in the warmth that their bodies threw off, in the "solace" that they spoke of when talking of the women they loved. It was expressed in the eroticism of their poetry, a warm, giving, and breathing eroticism in which the subject remained the subject and not the object in relation to themselves, whether that subject was a woman or the revolution or the jungle in which they lived. They were incapable of calculated violence for its own sake, or of crudeness, and because they lived so harmoniously with their own natures, I could trust them instinctively and in every way.

Almost two platoons would bed down for the night outside our hut and those who owned mosquito nets were already stretching them from low branches. One of the men had already commandeered a canvas deck chair which the men had hauled in from the border for me and which was dangerously near collapse.

The ludicrousness of this lone deck chair in the midst of jungle warfare, perched unsteadily at the side of a path or in a village clearing, sometimes at the edge of a shifting swamp, so that "madame's" throbbing muscles could be eased, never failed to cheer me.

There would be no time for breakfast next morning, and we ate generous portions of wild boar, tea, and sweet potatoes that night. Bath water had run short, however, and it meant washing in antiseptic solution and whatever water remained in a clay container. By now I had become quite adept at this, and had also worked out certain other ground rules for ladies regarding bush survival. Among them:

1. Carry only the most essential clothing and equipment in your rucksack. This means throwing out the extra towels, headscarves, cosmetics, and other refinements which are welcome but add so much weight. They can never be found anyway when needed.

2. Carry at least two changes of uniform and an extra shirt. This will enable clothing to be laundered and dried at the first opportunity. Don't stuff wet clothing into your pack because you will be very sorry.

3. Leather boots can be hot and uncomfortable in the African bush, although they were highly prized by the men. Canvas boots and tennis shoes are hard-wearing, lighter, and cooler.

4. Carry an ample supply of soap, toilet tissue, and cigarettes. (Nonsmokers always fare better in the bush: less wheezing, more staying power, and no *Weltschmerz* when supplies run out. It also eliminates the necessity for smoking banana leaves instead, or rolling cigarettes from airmail paper.)

5. Always carry eau de cologne (in plastic bottle), toothpaste, antiseptic, mosquito repellent, fungus cream, and calomine lotion.

6. Use water purifying tablets and don't forget to take your antimalaria pills.

7. Wear either a cap or a headscarf, never a pith helmet. Pith helmets made bald empirebuilders.

A scarf, I found, served many purposes and made a good emergency bandage or an arm sling.

8. Always carry two pairs of sunglasses or prescription glasses and keep them in hard cases. Replacements in the jungle are impossible. In Mozambique, I sat on one pair, and in Portuguese Guinea squashed another against the rim of a canoe while carrying them carelessly in my pocket. Without my replacements, I would have been as helpless as a mole.

9. When searching out a *retrete* at night, carry a flashlight and reconnoiter the area first for snakes or small animals hidden in the leaves. Don't linger and don't reach into any bushes. Stay within calling distance of other people. It's no good being too modest, because you can work yourself into hysterics and nobody's looking anyway. If you hear any snuffling or hissing in your immediate area, run.

10. Plastic bags are useful for carrying small articles, particularly for laundry and as a container for wet soap. Don't use a facecloth as there is never enough water available with which to remove the soap, and it will become a stiffened rag.

11. Carry a small plastic bowl to use as dipper and wash bowl, keeping the supply in the bucket always clean. When bathing in the bush, soap yourself all over first, then rinse with the clean water. Wear a pair of plastic sandals for this operation.

12. Carry a mosquito net and two sheets. Four would be ideal, but it means extra weight for the carrier hauling your pack for you. And he has no sheets at all on which to sleep. I did carry a lightweight, mini-pillow stuffed with feathers which weighed only a few ounces. It rolled up

242

neatly into my pack and I found that I could sleep anywhere with this support under my head.

13. If attacked by stinging ants, don't panic or leap about. Pinch them against your body as they bite and get out of their path promptly. They march in columns and swarm with incredible speed up any obstacle they meet, inflicting a vicious bite which is the torment of man and animal in the jungle, including lions. On one occasion, unknown to me, they had followed me into my hut and in an instant had swarmed into my open pack and onto the bedding. They stung like a hundred needles and were only diverted when Barry rushed in with armfuls of flaming straw and burnt both the floor of the hut and the earth surrounding it outside.

14. Carry glucose tablets for strength, and also remedies against headaches caused by heat and fatigue. During long hours without food or rest, I was given a thumbnail-sized chunk cut from the kola nut on which to chew and told to swallow the bitter juice but spit out the pulp. This is a mild stimulant little stronger than coffee, and it provided enough energy to keep me upright. The men sometimes used it after long hours without food, for it dulled hunger pangs. They used no drugs of any kind, however.

20

UMARU'S BIVOUAC NEAR THE FORT WAS LITTLE MORE THAN a cooking fire and a few groundsheets under a canvas tarpaulin. His men lounged against the trees alongside their weapons, dozing or talking until the signal to rise was given. There had been no sign of tension among them, and they had occasionally burst into laughter at some involved story someone was telling.

Situation humor was much appreciated here, and a favorite joke was about the guerrilla in the North who awoke one night to find a lion peering through his mosquito net. He opened fire immediately, but as a result spoiled a perfectly good net and was teased unmercifully about it afterward.

We left the bivouac at 4 P.M. for the 6 P.M. attack, at normal marching speed, and in a column of 30 equipped with cannons, bazookas, and automatic weapons. The cannons had been dismantled and the parts carried across the shoulders of the strongest. The ricefields were muddier than usual after a recent rain and we slopped and slithered across the top of the trenches in which the flooded crop was planted, the men frequently tapping the mud from their sandals as we trekked through the puddles.

There were three forts in the area, and we kept to the forest's edge whenever possible to avoid being sighted by aerial reconnaissance.

As we marched steadily on, I watched the casual, unworried faces of Umaru's men and wondered if the troops were waiting for us. I knew that dusk attacks against the forts were frequent and that they were better armed than we with heavy guns at each corner and a helicopter pad in the rear.

I wondered how I would react if we were ambushed. I knew how the guerrillas would react, for they were armed and I was not. And if I had been armed, would I have fired too? Or would I have stood there stupidly and looked on while the whole, violent nightmare unfolded before me, stunned by the awfulness as bullets whacked into living flesh and men screamed and died in the Guinean mud while I threw up on the sidelines or got caught in the crossfire.

We crossed two rivers, paddling over in stumpy little dugout canoes, waiting our turn and kneeling in the sloppy bottom and landing with a sharp bump against the opposite shore. It was lovely country now, and moss-hung trees leaned into the water in the late afternoon sunshine. I could smell the heat from the men and felt the comfort from their warm voices. The commander had stopped joking and the escort drew closer around me. Suddenly there was Saco before us, smiling questioningly in his leather jacket, and we followed him toward the fort, quietly now and more spread out. The guns went off "safety."

"For God's sake, can't they see us by now?" I thought. "What were they doing inside?"

Almost 6 o'clock and probably dinner time there, with a single glass of wine to each man if it had been included in the last helicopter shipment. Some of the guerrillas held branches above their heads which bobbed up and down as we advanced. The darkness was closing in rapidly.

245

I suddenly glimpsed the fort through the trees. It looked like a graceful, turreted chalet lonely in the rolling grassland. I thought of long, cool corridors and cities and seafood at one of the Portuguese fishing villages.

Our cannons opened up on the illusion with a tremendous crack and the shells tore into the darkness. And another and another, spitting fire which lit up the intense faces of the men crouched low around them.

They looked like tinny, Napoleonic cannons as they rocked back and forth with the recoil, and then the fort burst into flames. Twenty seconds later a machine-gun raked our hide and spewed up the dust around the row of rocking guns firing repeatedly like ships of the line.

The Portuguese gunner didn't take his finger from the trigger for a moment, just fired in a low, wide arc, back and forth, holding off a raid and not caring if his barrel turned white-hot. And then their mortars began and the shells came down in dead ground before us.

"No bai—no bai—let's go!" said one of the men, grabbing my arm. Our cannons were still firing and they wanted to get me out should the Portuguese attempt a flanking movement.

There was no other sound from the fort, no voices, no running feet, only the machine-gun firing low to the ground to cut off our legs if we advanced across the no man's land.

This was an harassment operation, however, not a raid, which would have been planned differently. But guerrilla intentions could not be known within the fort and the troops were bracing themselves for the worst.

And there would be no reinforcements either, for the two other forts in the far distance to our right were now in flames also. It had been a three-pronged attack and every fort in the area was pinned down, cut off, and virtually helpless although they outmanned and outgunned by far their guerrilla attackers.

And now we had to run, back into the inky blackness with no moon to light the way, and no flashlights to reveal us should air support be called in or we find ourselves encircled.

The terrain was difficult enough to negotiate during the day, but at night it was a thorn-strewn, ditch-scarred nightmare, flooded with muck and swampwater and so black I could barely see the running men beside me.

We reared and plunged over the embankments which flashed up in the darkness, upon us before we saw them. The men were swift as deerhounds, their long, hard legs devouring the ground before us while behind machine-gun bullets hailed into the darkness, searching for our retreating forms as we sped toward the river.

Our bazookas streaked back toward the fort and by now I was reeling with exhaustion.

"Pick her up," somebody yelled in Balante, and I was flung onto the shoulders of one of the giants who immediately buckled under the sudden extra weight and almost went down with me.

But he regained his balance and I was suddenly seven feet above the ground, weaving and bobbing over the pitch-black battlefield, and hanging on for my life while the unfortunate guerrilla beneath was desperately trying to free himself from the hammerlock I had around his neck.

"My glasses!" I hollered, in the midst of it all, for they had slid down from my nose and were hanging from one ear. I could barely see anyway, for the sweat was running into my eyes. If I loosed my grip from around the man below I would crash over backward at high speed. An unseen hand reached over and recovered my glasses and after another twenty yards I was transferred in midflight to the back of another guerrilla, then to yet another who ran bent double under the dead weight.

Then there were no backs left, for the rest of the men

were racing flat out with the cannons and other arms. I was set down between two men who grabbed each hand and raced me along with them, my feet barely in contact with the earth.

Within half an hour we were at least five miles away and in another two hours were loping into a village where we sat on tiny wooden stools while the sweat ran from our bodies and the hovering villagers built brush fires to keep the mosquitoes away. I thought that I would never rise again, but I had reckoned without the ritual bath hour, and suddenly we were fanning out into the forest again, plastic pails in hand.

That night, I had been confronted by revolutionary theory translated into revolutionary reality, and at the same time by the violent, almost mechanical reaction it provoked from those defending the status quo. The revelation shook me to my bones.

It is at this point that a man or woman is forced to make the very critical decision which divides the sympathetic supporter, the reformist, the articulate and staunch defender of human rights into the cool, slogging revolutionary who never looks back.

The decision is not only "do I sacrifice my own hide for the cause?" but "do I believe in that cause enough to see it through, whatever the upheaval and damage to my personal well-being, my comfort, and my identification with the mainstream of society?"

For a revolutionary is, in fact, alienated not spiritually but mentally from those unlike himself. What had separated me from these men was this knowledge, and the fact that they had made their choice and I had still to do so. It is always a question of degrees of rage, and an honest revolutionary picks up a gun only when he can no longer talk it out, when there is no breath of hope left to draw upon. For these men there had been no hope, and they had made their decision in the coldness of this reality, with no more doubts within themselves. "Nobody *likes* war, only a fool does."

248

We slept in snoring heaps around the village, rose within a few hours, and by early morning were several miles away. We walked steadily and kept to the jungle trails.

There had been no casualties among us. But what of the chaos inside the burning forts, I thought, among the troops who loathed assignments to the bush to defend a policy they barely understood.

"We pity them too," one of the men told me. "We often find their letters, and sometimes their photographs from home. But they are directed to kill our people every day, to destroy us if we let them."

". . . we are not born revolutionaries, just ordinary people. . . ."

Epilogue

IN MOZAMBIQUE, FOLLOWING THE ASSASSINATION OF Eduardo Mondlane, FRELIMO elected its commander of military forces, Samora Moises Machel, to replace him as the organization's president, with Marcelino Dos Santos as vice president.

Machel's wife, Josina, a front-line guerrilla whom he married three years ago and who sometimes accompanied him on marches through the Mozambican bush, died in April, 1971, after an illness. She was 25.

According to FRELIMO, in the past two years there has been a noticeable change in the attitude of certain churches and church organizations in the West toward the liberation movements, and urgently needed material aid has been promised by them to help alleviate civilian and refugee hardship.

Further, in June, 1970, leaders of the three main liberation movements in the Portuguese colonies, FRELIMO, PAIGC, and the MPLA of Angola, were received in special audience by Pope Paul VI in Rome, a widely publicized encounter which brought strong and immediate protest from the Portuguese government.

A year later, members of the White Fathers missionary order working in Mozambique announced their decision to leave the colony because the church in Portuguese African territory had become identified with Portuguese rule. The mission's General Council complained that church activities intended to promote "true social justice" were considered "subversive activities" by the Portuguese authorities. Following the announcement, the government declared the White Fathers to be prohibited residents and ordered them from the country. Their activities, it was claimed, had included attacks on Portuguese sovereignty, and one of the White Fathers was charged with inviting the inhabitants to rebel and to join FRELIMO.

An all-out Portuguese air and ground offensive against liberated zones in Mozambique during the spring and summer of 1970 cost the lives of 400 guerrillas and destroyed 25 FRELIMO bases, according to Portuguese army communiqués from Lourenço Marques and Beira. A main target was Cabo Delgado province.

During the operation, more than 35,000 troops and 15,000 tons of equipment were used against FRELIMO-held areas. Nearly a million propaganda leaflets were dropped and about 150 miles of roads were bulldozed through the jungles.

According to FRELIMO, the troops were expelled by November of the same year from all except two areas in the liberated zones following guerrilla counter-offensives. FRELIMO also reported that most of the guerrilla deaths claimed by the Portuguese army were, in fact, civilian bombing casualties.

Diolinda Simango, my companion during the trek into Cabo Delgado, now holds an important post in FRELIMO's administration. Her first child, born within a year of her marriage to Fernando Raoul, died in infancy.

In Portuguese Guinea, the guerrilla with the Afro hair-style, Pansao Na Isna, was killed in the course of a Portuguese airstrike against PAIGC guerrilla units about 15 miles from Bissau. He left a wife and son.

The PAIGC's regular army, which has operated primarily in the north, has stepped up attacks against Portuguese military installations in the country's main towns, including operations in Bissau and Bafata. During the summer of 1971, there were 109 attacks against military camps and forts throughout the country, and 35 ambushes of convoys and patrols. The PAIGC has so far avoided attacks against Portuguese civilians in the colony.